THE BEAST WITHIN

The classic image of the bloodthirsty werewolf
(From an eighteenth-century engraving, Mansell Collection)

THE
BEAST
WITHIN

Adam Douglas

CHAPMANS

Chapmans Publishers Ltd
141–143 Drury Lane
London WC2B 5TB

First published by Chapmans 1992

ISBN 1–85592–574–5

A CIP catalogue record of this book is
available from the British Library

Photoset in Monophoto Plantin by
Ace Filmsetting Ltd, Frome, Somerset
Printed and bound in Great Britain by
Butler and Tanner Ltd, Frome and London

Acknowledgments

This book began with the suggestion of my agent, Julian Alexander, that I write it, and I am further indebted to him for all his subsequent good offices. Bill Monter of Northwestern University, Illinois, then managed to give me in the course of a morning's conversation more pointers than could fit into a single book and alerted me to a number of sources I might otherwise have missed: chapter seven obviously owes something to his own published work, but chapter eleven in particular had its genesis in our conversation that morning. My thanks are also due to Steve Ackhurst and Alex Melman of RKA Films, particularly for their help in tracking down medical case-histories; to Simon Finch, for his generosity in allowing me use of his office and its equipment, and to Leandra Julien and Lucy Fryer, who had to put up with me whenever I was there; to Karen Thomson, for linguistic detective work; to Nick Kulukundis and Alastair Penny of Wandering Moonbeam, who saved me at that moment all authors dread – computer breakdown; and to Alegra Licudi for her continued support. I am fortunate to have had the editorial oversights of Mark Crean at Chapmans, and to live in a city so well-provided with libraries, particularly the London Library and the British Library, whose staff have been unfailingly helpful.

Contents

Illustrations

I

Barking Mad

Talk of the wolf and his tail appears.
Proverb

As the houselights dim, the cinema-goers take their seats, and a
sense of hushed expectancy spreads through the auditorium. The
film about to be shown could be any one of a number regularly
made on the subject since the earliest days of cinema – the plot
has been used often enough to have become almost set in stone.
The innocent hero of the film begins by breaking with his usual
routine, perhaps by wandering off the beaten track, visiting a
strange new country, or simply entering a dark forest. Suddenly,
in the first of several gasp-inducing moments of violent drama to
come, he is attacked by an unknown and terrible creature. The
audience watches intently as the hero recovers from the ferocity
of this attack and tries to carry on as normal, oblivious to the
implanted bacillus doing its destructive, invisible work within
him. Tension slowly builds all the while, the dreadful time
approaching as inevitably as the monthly reappearance of the full
moon in the night sky, the signal for that cataclysmic eruption
when the monstrous animal *alter ego* will burst forth in all its
snarling, hackle-raising fury. After this explosive high point the
film progresses more quickly, episodes of blood-boltered ferocity
alternating with scenes of bewilderment and pathos. Strange
magical remedies are discussed, but all is futile – at last the
terrible curse must be eradicated, at the sad cost of the life of the
hero. The final shot lingers on the hero's body, returned to
human shape, peaceful in death.

The audience files out of the cinema, sated. The film has
offended none of its collective sensibilities. The film is supposed

to be about lycanthropy – the transformation of a man into a wolf
– but the film-makers have not been so naïve as to give a
straightforward treatment of this peculiar metamorphosis. They
are too aware that a real wolf looks disarmingly like some of the
household pets on which many of their patrons lavish hours of
care and attention, and are perhaps also conscious of growing
public unease over the wolf's ecological plight. They know that
they must play up the monstrous angle, and so their furry
creations look only vaguely like real wolves as they snarl and
stumble (almost always on two legs rather than four) to their
inevitable end. They are also confident in the knowledge that
their audience is, by and large, a sophisticated one – a group of
people at least dimly aware of the subtle trickery of artful camera
work, wise to the potential uses of rubber, yak hair, and skilful
make-up, a group of willing accomplices to their own terrorizing.
And finally, for all their careful tiptoeing around public sensibilities, the film-makers get away with presenting this lurid ninety-
minute spectacle of blood, violence, and magic for the simple
reason that for not more than a few deliciously fleeting moments
of suspended disbelief does the audience really give credence to
the existence of these wild, hirsute creatures. For sane, rational
people living in the modern world, the werewolf is pure fiction.

For people whose sanity and rationality is in question, the
matter is not so clear-cut. In 1988 a group of psychiatrists
working for the regional prison service at Bordeaux, France,
reported the case of a man they designated only as X.[1] This man,
twenty-eight years of age, was imprisoned after an incident in
which a fifty-two-year-old man had been found dead in a car, his
face showing signs of violent assault. Two other people were
arrested on suspicion of involvement in his killing: a male
accomplice of X's (referred to in the psychiatrists' report as Y),
and a forty-four-year-old woman with whom X had been having
a relationship for the past three years. Although the stories of the
suspects conflicted to some degree, both the accomplice and the
girlfriend agreed that the murder had resulted from a drunken
meal all three had shared with the dead man, a meal which had
got disastrously out of hand. The woman had stolen the dead
man's wallet and demanded that he strip naked, threatening him
and taunting him with accusations of homosexuality. According
to both her and Y's version of events, X became fatally involved

at this point, bludgeoning the man to the floor in a wild rage. Afterwards, they both maintained that X had cleaned up all traces of blood and burnt several papers which would have been incriminating evidence.

When setting out to discover any possible cause for this alleged outburst of murderous violence, the prison doctors found themselves confronted with the archetypal 'hard man', a muscular prisoner with deep-set, staring eyes, his face and heavily tattooed forearms extensively criss-crossed with a network of old scars. His explanation for his behaviour was as dramatic as his appearance, for X announced to his startled interrogators that he was, and had been for many years, a werewolf.

'It is blood trouble,' X told the doctors:

> It is when I make myself bite like a rabid dog . . . as soon as I see blood I want to swallow it, to drink it . . . if I happen to cut myself, I drink my own blood . . . when I suffer an emotional shock, I feel myself undergoing a transformation, it's like my fingers are paralysed, I get a feeling like ants are crawling in the middle of my hand, I am no longer master of myself . . . I have the impression of becoming a wolf, I look at myself in the mirror, I see myself transforming, it's absolutely no longer my own face changing, the eyes stare out, wild-looking, the pupils dilate, I feel as if hairs are bristling out all over me, as if my teeth are growing longer, I feel myself in another skin, and afterwards I lose consciousness.[2]

X believed that he was reincarnated from some former existence, and that he had other strange powers in addition to his ability to undergo these wolfish transformations, powers which he attributed to having sexual relations with older women. According to him, he had satisfied his enormous cravings for blood by visiting the quayside abattoirs and drinking horses' blood while it was still warm, 'but it isn't animal blood I prefer, but human blood'.

Questioning of X's mistress suggested that this was not just a fantastical confession dreamt up on the spot to impress the prison psychiatrists. She told them that during their relationship X had often howled like a wolf at night and banged his head against the walls, and that he slept only lightly, like a wild animal. Throughout their relationship he had tormented her with his sadistic sexual desires, on many occasions biting her and becoming wildly excited at the sight of her blood. She had witnessed several of his transformation episodes, when he became extremely aggressive and violent, beating her and smashing up everything in the house. The doctors noticed also that X was receiving visits in prison from an old girlfriend. During these visits, she and X would exchange deep, bruising bites on the neck, becoming intensely excited while they did so.

Seeking the cause of these curious, apparently inhuman urges, the psychiatrists questioned X about his childhood. He told them that he was born in 1954, and that his father had killed his pregnant mother and two of his brothers. He had been in and out of many jobs, being a fireman, forger, medium, circus trapeze artist, and a member of the French Foreign Legion for ten years. He said that he had two daughters but unhappily both had been killed, the first by an incompetent doctor, the second squashed by a truck. He told the psychiatrists this tale without any significant variation several times, both verbally and in writing, and to different doctors at different times.

The only thing wrong with his account was that it was totally untrue. The doctors discovered that X had in fact been born in 1960, one of six children. While not as dramatic as having a murderer for a father, his early childhood had indeed been disturbed, his mother dying when he was only eighteen months old, and his father proving unable to raise him. Brought up from the age of five by his uncle and his late wife, X had become an aggressive and undisciplined child, forever running away from all forms of authority. He had suffered convulsions as a baby, was incontinent until the age of ten, and had been hospitalized many times, including a period at a psychiatric hospital. At the age of fourteen he entered the first of a number of homes for juvenile delinquents, and two years later was given a detailed psychiatric examination at the request of one of the many judges before whom he appeared. This examination revealed that X, although of average IQ, exhibited such instability of character that the psychiatrist could not foresee him ever holding down a lasting job. He suffered major anxiety and depressive episodes, he showed an inability to relate successfully either with members of his own family or with other children in the home (where he was nicknamed 'the house madman'), he had mutilated his own arms and chest on several occasions, and he led an intense fantasy life which spilled out in numerous romanticized stories.

His behaviour did not show much improvement on reaching adulthood. He fulfilled the juvenile court psychiatrist's prediction by proving unable to hold down a steady job, preferring to sponge off others or extort money from friends and lovers. He was married for a short time, but his wife became pregnant by someone he had known at the children's home, and they separated in 1983. In 1979 he had already been deemed unfit for national service, and when he later applied to join the Foreign Legion, he was turned down as unsuitable for entry into that legendary bolt-hole for misfits and desperadoes. He drank constantly, terrorized his neighbours, and was imprisoned a number of times on charges of theft, grievous bodily harm, fraudulent impersonation, and firearms violations.

The psychiatrists who examined him after the latest violent incident concentrated on the central question of whether X really believed his own story that he was a werewolf. They certainly had enough evidence that he had been in the habit of telling outrageous lies throughout his life: everyone – his immediate family, the authorities at the children's home, his frightened friends and neighbours – told them as much, and he himself had compounded that impression by giving them a completely fictitious autobiography while in custody. On the other hand, his former girlfriend's evidence suggested that his lycanthropic behaviour had been going on for some time, at least for the three years that she had shared his bed – evidence which implied that X's belief in his own story was strong enough to influence his behaviour quite profoundly. In seeking to understand their patient's condition, the psychiatrists revived the term *mythomanie*, coined by the French psychiatrist Dupré at the beginning of the century.[3] By mythomania, Dupré meant 'the pathological tendency, more or less voluntary and conscious, to lie and to create imaginary stories'. He distinguished this from other psychological conditions in which the patient might tell lies or untruths, such as delirium and dementia, where the behaviour would be out of the patient's conscious control, as well as from cases where lying or distortion of the truth occurs for entirely understandable reasons. Dupré characterized the most clearly definable form of mythomania as being vain, malign, and perverse. The prison doctors thought that X's pathological fabulation was most clearly marked by vanity, as it appeared to lack a perverse intention to harm others directly.

As the representative of the modern werewolf, X indicates many important features of current strategies to distinguish sanity from insanity and truth from fiction. Doctors like the French prison psychiatrists weigh up the value of stories like his, armed with the clear knowledge that werewolves cannot exist. Not only do the doctors not believe in them, they can hardly bring themselves to accept that their patients believe in them, even when those patients show symptoms of gross mental disturbance. Yet still they recognize some connection between the patient in their care and the hairy, lumbering star of the classic werewolf films, and they continue to write articles with 'lycanthropy' in their titles for medical journals in which serious psychological debate takes place. In doing so, they are following an ancient tradition.

The meaning of the word lycanthropy – derived from the Greek words for wolf, *lykos*, and man, *anthropos* – is habitually extended by doctors to cover all cases of the condition in which the patient believes he or she has been transformed into an animal, although the rarely used 'therianthropy' is the more accurate term for non-specific animal transformation. Yet even in its most restricted meaning, where the belief referred to is of transformation into a wolf, lycanthropy is one of the oldest diagnoses in psychiatric literature. As early as the fifth century AD the condition was being described by doctors as one which resulted from disturbance of the melancholic humour. One of the most influential accounts came from the seventh-century physician Paulus Aegineta, who practised in Alexandria. He described patients suffering from 'melancholic lycanthropia' as being characteristically pallid. They were deficient in both tears and saliva and so suffered dry eyes and excessive thirst. Their legs were ulcerated from travelling about on all fours, and they suffered compulsions to wander about at night, particularly into cemeteries, where they could be found howling until dawn.

Aegineta's diagnosis depended on the humoural theory rooted in the writings of two of his compatriots and predecessors, often regarded as the founding fathers of medicine: Hippocrates (whose famous Oath doctors still swear) and Galen, who lived during the first century BC and second century AD respectively. As the Periodic Table at that stage had only four recognized 'elements' – earth, air, fire, and water – it was reasoned that the human body was also made up of four elements: the bodily fluids, or 'humours'. These humours – melancholy (black bile), blood, choler (yellow bile), and phlegm – corresponded to the four elements and also, in some mysterious and largely unexplained way, to psychological states. This was an idea which was to remain important for an astonishing length of time, being the predominant theory in medical and psychiatric discourse for the next fifteen hundred or so years. The influence of its long reign is still felt today, in so far as 'melancholic', 'sanguine', 'choleric', and 'phlegmatic' are still recognizable descriptions of particular moods and characters. From the post-classical era right through to the Renaissance, diagnosis of a particular medical or psychiatric condition consisted of recognizing which of these four humours, or any combination of them, was being produced in excess, so that steps could be taken to remedy that imbalance. Paulus Aegineta's diagnosis placed the blame for lycanthropy squarely on an excess of melancholy or black bile, and most of the physicians who came across the syndrome after him agreed. Although the theory behind his medical practice now seems nonsensical and unscientific, his description of the syndrome itself is excellent evidence that, at an early date, people were exhibiting symptoms very similar to those of Monsieur X from Bordeaux.

Twentieth-century doctors have been much less willing to admit lycanthropy as a syndrome: that is, a particular, discrete concurrence of symptoms. Armed with what are felt to be more sophisticated explanations for abnormal behaviour, psychiatrists appear to have dispersed what lycanthropic patients they have under different diagnostic subheadings. Many authorities have noted a general decline in the numbers of patients presenting with animalistic symptoms of any kind, and in particular in the numbers of patients thinking themselves to be wolves. This is usually ascribed to the feeling that increasing industrialization has resulted in people living more and more apart from the animal world. In addition, the great decline in the wolf population, especially in North America and continental Europe, has inevitably meant that far fewer people have ever seen a wolf, let

alone felt drawn to identify with one. Towards the latter part of
the twentieth century a consensus seemed to have been reached
among western psychiatrists which regarded lycanthropy as an
outmoded or unnecessary diagnosis, the term being either omitted from psychiatric handbooks or simply described as extinct.[4]
Yet cases do still occur which Paulus Aegineta would certainly
have recognized as belonging in his category of 'melancholic
lycanthropia'.

In 1975, Doctors Surawicz and Banta reported two cases of
lycanthropy, the first of which, the case of Mr H, a twenty-year-
old Appalachian man, was apparently largely explicable through
the patient's history of long and chronic abuse of a variety of
drugs, including marijuana, amphetamines, psilocybin, and LSD.[5]
While serving in the US Army in Europe, Mr H had taken LSD
during some time he had spent alone in the woods. He hallucinated that he was turning into a werewolf, and saw fur bristling
out on his hands and felt it growing on his face. Once transformed, he was filled with an irresistible urge to chase, kill, and
eat wild rabbits. Back at his Army base after two days, Mr H
remained obsessed with the idea that he was a werewolf and that
he had been made privy to satanic secrets. The sign 'feeding time'
in the mess hall convinced him that the others knew he was a wolf.
His delusion proved resistant to various remedial programmes,
and he remained obsessed with ideas of diabolic possession,
particularly after seeing the film *The Exorcist*.

If Mr H's grip on reality had been damaged by persistent drug
abuse, so the second case of lycanthropy reported by Surawicz
and Banta had a similarly concrete cause. The behaviour of Mr
W, a thirty-seven-year-old farmer, had been seen to deteriorate
over a period of time, as he gradually let his facial hair – or fur,
as he preferred to call it – grow long. He took to sleeping in
cemeteries, howling at the moon, and occasionally lying down in
the road in the midst of traffic. He explained his bizarre behaviour
by saying that he was transformed into a wolf, but doctors who
examined him were more concerned with transformations of a
neurological kind taking place in his brain. They were able to
compare their results with tests Mr W had previously taken while
in the United States Navy, at which time he had shown a normal
and average IQ. Surawicz and Banta's tests showed his IQ to have
slipped to levels of moderate mental retardation, and brain scans

and a biopsy suggested that this was due to some slow-acting brain disease. His episodes of thinking himself a werewolf seemed to have occurred as a direct result of his brain deteriorating, and although these werewolf delusions were prevented with drugs, Mr W remained an outpatient with impaired function and little sign of spontaneous mental activity.

Two years after the reporting of the cases of Mr H and Mr W, another lycanthrope appeared in the medical literature: a forty-nine-year-old American woman who suffered lupine obsessions which culminated in the delusion of transformation into a wolf.[6] During the twenty years of her marriage, she had been troubled by urges towards bestiality, lesbianism, and adultery, as well as by an obsession with wolves which led her to think and dream about them constantly. Eventually she acted on her impulses, tearing off her clothes at a family gathering, and adopting the mating position of a female wolf in front of her mother. The next day, after sexual intercourse with her husband, she spent two hours growling, scratching, and gnawing at the bed. She told the doctors that she had been possessed by the devil during these episodes and become an animal. In hospital, under a treatment programme combining drugs and psychotherapy, her delusions persisted for a few weeks and she was able to describe them in some detail: 'I am a wolf of the night: I am a wolf woman of the day . . . I have claws, teeth, fangs, hair . . . and anguish is my prey at night . . . the gnashing and snarling of teeth . . . powerless is my cause. I am what I am and will always roam the earth long after death . . . I will continue to search for perfection and salvation.' Her reflection, gazing back at her from the mirror, seemed to her to show 'the head of a wolf in place of a face on my own body – just a long-nosed wolf with teeth, groaning, snarling, growling . . . with fangs and claws, calling out "I am the devil."' In her reflection she had seen a terrifying distinction between her eyes: 'one is frightened and the other is like the wolf – it is dark, deep, and full of evil, and full of revenge of the other eye. This creature of the dark wants to kill.' During these episodes, she was in a state of wild and tormented sexual arousal, and was observed by doctors and fellow-patients making unintelligible animalistic noises.

Her doctors concluded that their patient suffered from 'chronic pseudo-neurotic schizophrenia' and responded to the kind of treatment used in cases of acute schizophrenic psychosis. They emphasized the sexual nature of the case, and believed that the strong internal conflicts aroused by the woman's compulsive thoughts of illicit sexual activity were expressed in her werewolf delusions. Despite the different terminology used, and the doctors' post-Freudian awareness of suppressed sexual motivations, there is a clear line of descent from Aegineta's lycanthropes to this patient, if only in her obsessive talk of graveyards. Even after her final lycanthropic episode, which coincided with the full moon, she wrote down her determination to continue the search 'for [what] I lack . . . in my present marriage . . . my search for such a hairy creature. I will haunt the graveyards . . . for a tall, dark man that I intend to find.'

Other cases subsequently appeared in the medical literature under the heading 'lycanthropy', although no more werewolves were immediately reported. Typical was the case of a sixty-six-year-old widow visiting friends in Ireland, who had become aggressive towards some members of their family for no particular reason, and had behaved in an animalistic way.[7] During these episodes she would drop onto all fours and bark like a dog. (Her symptoms are properly described as 'kynanthropic', from Greek *kynos*, dog.) In hospital she was able to recall these occasions, and said that she had thought she was a dog at the time. She said that the devil had done this to her, and that she had been very frightened that if she were left alone, he would come down and take complete control over her. Her delusions and aggressive behaviour left her after treatment with anti-depressants and a course of electroconvulsive therapy.

Yet even this weight of evidence that lycanthropy still exists, at least in the form of animalistic behaviour accompanied by the patient's belief that he or she has somehow become an animal, is not found convincing by everyone. Some authorities place more emphasis on the unique, and very specific, causes for the behaviour in the individual psychology of each patient. Such lyco-sceptics argue that allegedly animalistic symptoms occur in many psychological disorders, and that lycanthropy cannot be regarded as a medical or psychological diagnosis. What is needed is a wider frame of reference which might suggest how commonly such symptoms occur in a recognizably distinct cluster. Such an overview was provided in the late 1980s by doctors working at

McLean Hospital in Massachusetts, using the medical records of some five thousand psychotic patients who had been treated at their 250-bed private hospital in suburban Boston.[8] The doctors at McLean Hospital decided to go back through their case histories accumulated over the previous twelve years, noting any cases where, although it had not been diagnosed as such, lycanthropy seemed to have occurred. As a governing principle, they decided that they would distinguish lycanthropes from those other patients who exhibited various animal behaviours (barking, howling, biting, scratching, crawling on all fours, defecating on the floor, and so on), but who never said that they did so because they were animals. Only those patients who exhibited animalistic behaviour *and* at some stage explicitly declared themselves to be an animal were to be included in their series. Using these diagnostic criteria, the McLean Hospital doctors unearthed twelve cases of lycanthropy from their records.

The animals involved in these twelve cases varied. Only two of the patients could be described as true lycanthropes in the pedantic sense of the word, imagining themselves to be transformed into wolves. The therianthropic crawling, growling, hooting, twitching, and barking behaviour of the others came from two patients who thought that they were dogs, two who thought themselves to be cats, and one who insisted that he was a Bengal tiger. Perhaps more surprisingly, other bestial *alter egos* included a bird, a gerbil, and a rabbit who hopped around the ward for a day. Two patients exhibited general behaviour sufficiently feral to be included in the survey, but did not specify which animal they believed themselves to be. Five-sixths of the patients involved were male, and the ages of the patients ranged within a comparatively narrow band between sixteen and thirty-seven, although these data may simply reflect the general make-up of the hospital population.

It cannot be said that the McLean Hospital survey demonstrates that lycanthropy as the psychiatrists understand it is very often a particularly strongly-held or intractable delusion. Confronted by doctors, the 'tiger' and 'rabbit' both admitted that their animalistic behaviour was under their voluntary control, while another patient only developed the delusion of being a wolf after smoking hashish during a manic episode. In all but one significant case, the lycanthropic episode lasted a short time,

quickly remitting following either confrontation or anti-
psychotic drug treatments – the hashish-smoking werewolf held
out longest at three weeks. This was certainly consistent with the
generally speedy remissions in the other cases that had come to
light since 1975, although Surawicz and Banta's Mr H might be
regarded as an exception in this respect.

Anybody who hoped that Aegineta's fifth-century diagnosis of
'melancholic lycanthropia' would turn out to have survived into
the twentieth century under another name, that it would prove to
be strictly identical with some modern medical diagnostic entity,
was destined to be disappointed by the McLean Hospital survey.
The McLean doctors laid out their results in a table which listed
summary details of their twelve cases, with a column devoted to
a description of the diagnosis based on that made at the time by
the case doctor. The doctors felt justified in updating the original
diagnosis because the universally accepted terms used by American psychiatrists had changed during the twelve years covered by
the survey. Diagnoses are customarily based on the American
Psychiatric Association handbook, known as DSM. This handbook has been updated several times, and the latest edition the
McLean doctors had available to them was the third, known as
DSM-III, published in 1980. This handbook, which lists the
symptoms which are generally recognized as indicating a particular diagnosis, is an impressive attempt by the psychiatric profes-
sion to impose something approaching scientific exactness on
clinical judgements which are generally felt, at least by the
layman, to be intuitive, subjective, and inexact. The results,
however, occasionally reveal embarrassing evidence of just how
quickly psychiatric fashions can change: DSM-II, for example,
the edition used in the original diagnosis of those McLean
Hospital patients admitted before 1980, includes 'homosexuality' as a psychiatric disorder. Nevertheless, DSM-III offered the
best available guideline for generally accepted standards of
clinical diagnoses, and the McLean doctors were obviously
bound to use it. They also had the detailed original case-notes to
work from in instances where they updated diagnoses previously
made according to the criteria of DSM-II.

At first glance, the table produced a flurry of excitement,
because eight of the twelve patients met DSM-III criteria for
'bipolar disorder' (probably better known by its older name of

'manic depression', a rather misleading cognomen for the condition in which sufferers may be either manic or depressed, or both
alternately, but never both at the same time), six of them
characterized as manic. But the doctors were quick to point out
that this did not prove that there is a specific association between
lycanthropy and bipolar disorder, chiefly because approximately
half of all the patients admitted to the McLean Hospital with
psychotic symptoms of any kind met the criteria for bipolar
disorder, and a finding of eight bipolar cases out of twelve
patients, therefore, could well be attributed to chance. Furthermore, in two bipolar cases the doctors felt that the episodes of
lycanthropy could not be explained purely by reference to that
disorder: one bipolar patient thought he was a wolf only after
smoking hashish, while the belief of another patient that he was
a rabbit was very short-lived and appeared to the doctors to be
related to a 'factitious disorder with psychological features', a
judgement which echoes that of the French doctors' finding of
mythomanie in the case of their Monsieur X. The McLean doctors
concluded that although lycanthropy was a syndrome which
seemed to be very much alive and well in the twentieth century,
it could not be regarded as a syndrome which was specific to any
particular disorder.

However, another tentative conclusion which might have been
drawn from the McLean data, that lycanthropy is always a short-
lived syndrome, was dramatically shattered by the eighth case
listed in their table. Some of the doctors involved in that paper
returned to the subject in 1990 to give a fuller case history of this
remarkable lycanthrope.[9] The McLean Hospital Case 8 was an
American male, born in 1964, who, despite eight years of
virtually non-stop psychotherapy as well as treatment with a huge
variety of psychotherapeutic drugs, continued to insist that he
was a tiger. He dressed in tiger-striped clothes, allowed his
fingernails to grow long, and cultivated long hair and bushy facial
hair, all of which gave him a distinctly feline look. As a child he
had been unsure what kind of cat he was, but as he grew older he
had reached the conclusion that he must be a tiger because of his
size, and he came to believe that his real parents must have been
tigers, or else that he had a tiger ancestor. He was painfully aware
of his physical dissimilarity to a tiger, and regarded his lack of a
tail, stripes, or fur as a physical deformity. He spent a good deal

of time visiting tigers in the zoo, petting them through the bars, collecting balls of their fur, and talking to them in cat language, which he believed he had been taught to speak at the age of eleven by Tiffany, the family cat.

As with several other modern lycanthropes, sexuality appeared to play a prominent role in Case 8's condition. From an early age he had been having close relationships with cats, hunting with them and sharing their kills of small animals, and eventually he began having sex with them on a serial monogamous basis. At the age of nineteen, he began the most intense relationship of all, with a tigress named Dolly who lived at the local zoo. Naturally he was unable to consummate this relationship, but during one of his four psychiatric hospitalizations he developed the fantasy that Dolly had managed to escape from the zoo and was visiting him in the early morning, slipping into his shower to have sex with him. He believed that she became pregnant, but that the cubs were stillborn and she stopped coming to the hospital. Dolly was eventually sold to a zoo in Asia, which caused him such intolerable grief that he attempted to hang himself.

Perhaps unsurprisingly, Case 8 had a deeply disturbed background and family history. Both his paternal grandfather and first cousin had committed suicide and two of his aunts had died in psychiatric hospitals, their conditions undiagnosed. Of his immediate family, he was closest to his two older sisters, both of whom suffered from very severe early-onset Crohn's disease (inflammation, thickening and ulceration of the intestine). He regarded his parents disdainfully as eccentric, inconsistent, and limited in intelligence. In his early infancy, his depressed mother had taken to her bed for long periods, allegedly because of her menopause. To keep him out of harm's way, his parents had often simply tied him to a tree alongside the family dog. He recollected that it was on these occasions he first began to behave like an animal. Later, when he developed his relationship with Tiffany, the feline who taught him 'cat language', he idealized her as a better parent than the emotionally unstable couple whose fights and threats of divorce upset him so much throughout his youth. When asked about the qualities of cats, it was noticeable that he mentioned that cats are excellent parents, unlike humans.

In many respects Case 8 was able to lead a normal life. Apart from his lycanthropic delusion, his thought processes and perception were reported to be usually logical. Although he suffered recurrences of major depression and some hallucinations during his psychotic episodes, at other times he was able to combine his human and feline activities quite successfully, something which he said was encouraged by Tiffany. He had been involved in a number of successful sexual relationships with women, although he claimed to prefer cats, and the doctors noted that his infatuation with Dolly had begun immediately after the breakup of his closest human sexual relationship. Drug treatments proved effective in controlling his major depressions, and he was able to return to his steady job as a research scientist, and to the apartment he shared with two friends and a cat. And yet his central belief that he was a cat proved entirely intractable to any treatment.

Obviously the psychological significance of his peculiar upbringing is crucial to an understanding of Case 8's lycanthropy. A case with some similar features was reported by the child psychologist Bruno Bettelheim, in which a child suffering from poor parenting grew to identify with the family dog.[10] In that case the mother had apparently shown more affection for her dogs than for her daughter, saying that the thought of living with her daughter 'made her so sick that she couldn't sleep or eat'. She had beaten the child severely and locked her in cupboards, and, whenever she could, had sent the child off to foster parents. Ironically, her most heartfelt complaint about her own childhood was that her mother treated her 'like a trained dog'. Around the age of two, the girl began to act like a dog. She crawled around on all fours, shared the dog's food, and chewed up furniture and rugs. Taken into care at the age of four because of parental neglect, she identified only with the dog at the specialized foster home in which she was placed. She ate dog biscuits, bit and scratched anybody who interfered with her, and carried objects around in her mouth, just like a puppy. However, the important difference between hers and Case 8's history is, once again, the remarkable endurance of Case 8's delusion. Taken from her mother and given appropriate psychotherapy, Bettelheim's dog-girl soon abandoned her kynanthropic behaviour – indeed for a while she became deeply agitated whenever she saw a dog. What her prompt recovery of human faculties suggests is that, given extreme circumstances, anyone may temporarily behave like an animal, but that there may be some extra factor which pushes people like Case 8 one step further into long-term delusion.

Most contemporary psychiatrists – adherents of the so-called medical model of mental illness – argue that this is true in all cases, that while the particular nature of a psychosis may be explained by the patient's individual circumstances, not all people who suffer similar deprivation go on to develop mental illness. A possible medical explanation for Case 8's persistent lycanthropy was indicated by an electroencephalograph reading which suggested that he was suffering from a form of epilepsy. He had already reported visual distortions and episodes of *déjà vu* which had occurred from the age of seventeen onwards, and, taken with the EEG reading, this accorded with a diagnosis of temporal lobe epilepsy. The McLean Hospital doctors pointed to a study which estimated an incidence of persistent psychosis in over 10 per cent of cases of temporal lobe epilepsy.[11] The same source cited a number of studies which pointed to the existence of a particular psychosis among such patients, a psychosis characterized by a high incidence of delusional states which would otherwise be regarded as rare. Such patients will appear otherwise normal, but will be preoccupied with old delusional ideas. The McLean Hospital doctors pointed out the similarities between this psychosis and the history of their Case 8.

This intriguing modern medical evidence, when taken as a whole, shows clearly that lycanthropy is a syndrome, albeit rare, which turns up on a regular basis. In western psychiatric hospitals it is usually found to be short-lived, but in combination with certain other catalysts may persist for some considerable time, and can sometimes even resist all the best efforts of modern psychiatrists, using their twin weapons of psychotherapy and drugs, to wipe it out. It is reasonable to assume that in less technological societies, where psychology and pharmacology are not employed to the same ends, a proportionally greater number of lycanthropes will be able to persist in their delusional state (although this begs the question whether the modern patients would have imagined themselves to be werewolves if they had not a pre-existing cultural figure to emulate).

As a group of symptoms, it is obvious that lycanthropy cannot be linked with any one particular diagnostic category of mental illness, and a definitive inquiry into its causes looks like a hopeless task. However, a number of areas of possible inquiry are suggested by the collected case histories. One noticeable feature, both of the French case of Monsieur X and of the American Case 8, is the evidence of distressing emotional deprivation in childhood, in the latter case particularly associated with the idea that someone treated like an animal may eventually begin to behave like one. Bettelheim's dog-girl seems to back up this idea, and there is a great deal of historical evidence which can be put forward in favour of this thesis, although, of course, many people who are treated badly in childhood do not subsequently develop such bizarre delusions. They may be tied up like an animal as a baby, without behaving like one in later life.

Perhaps a more fruitful initial line of inquiry is suggested by the relationship between the lycanthropic episodes and the patients' expressions of their own sexuality. The wolf-woman tearing off her clothes and crouching down before her mother offers the most startling evidence of this relationship. In her case, it is clear that the adoption of the werewolf *alter ego* supplied her with an outlet for the expression of 'bestial' urges which both she and her immediate social circle would have much preferred to keep submerged. Even after the lycanthropic delusion had faded away, she was able to retain the important idea that the delusion had revealed a hidden truth, that she was searching for some kind of sexual fulfilment she had yet to find in her married life. Case 8, too, expressed his sexuality through his lycanthropic episodes – indeed, of all modern lycanthropes, he is the only one who is reported actually to have committed bestiality in the old-fashioned or theological sense, by engaging in sexual activity with an animal. Even here, though, the coincidence between the end of one of his human sexual relationships and the beginning of his infatuation with the zoo tigress suggests that his relationships with animals were, in some sense of which he himself was unaware, a replacement or substitute for relationships with humans. In the same way that he turned to and idealized the cat Tiffany as a parent after the failure of his disastrous early upbringing, so he idealized the tigress Dolly after the failure of one of his adult attempts at normal human sexual relations. Monsieur X's bestial urges, on the other hand, his sadistic sexual practices and blood-fetishism, are more of a piece with his self-image as a hard man, seeking to intimidate even the prison doctors with his deep, staring eyes, an observation reinforced by the French doctor who mentioned vanity as the abiding characteristic of his mythomania.

Such psychosexual analyses can only tell part of the story. Evidence of organic disease affecting the brains of these lycanthropes would provide a much more specific aetiology for the syndrome, and there is a tantalizing glimpse of such evidence in at least two of these cases. Case 8's temporal lobe epilepsy was seen by his doctors as a factor possibly explaining the persistence of his delusion, while poor Mr W was described by the neurosurgeon who performed a biopsy on him as having a 'walnut' brain, the outer layer, or cerebellum, showing signs of distortion and degeneracy. His werewolf delusions seem only to have occurred during the period when his brain was undergoing this slow deterioration. Apart from Case 8, two other McLean patients showed neurological abnormalities, but these were only slight and were felt to be unremarkable by the doctors. Apart from disease, the other agent which might produce changes in the brain sufficient to account for lycanthropy would be a drug of some kind. Mr H's werewolfism was accounted for by his doctors as resulting from chronic abuse of a wide variety of drugs, together with a particular incident of LSD use, and one of the McLean lycanthropes developed his werewolf delusions after smoking hashish while in a manic state.

Two distinct werewolves stalk the dark forests of the modern psyche: the cinematic and the psychiatric. On a superficial level, the differences between them are readily apparent. One dwells in a purely imaginary world where internal change is expressed through external metamorphosis, where the cycle of the moon brings forth yellow eyes and snarling fangs, where a single bite is fatal, where the sad but effective remedy of the silver bullet will stop the beast; the few examples of the other have been co-opted to a purely factual world of science and medicine, where learned papers give sophisticated analyses of psychological trauma and neurological damage. The cinematic werewolf lives on as a vivid image of what Plato called the beast within us, man's individual capacity for slaughter and rapine, although it is an image that usually belongs only to the past, a Hollywood Gothic of shambling monsters and panicky villagers, a world at once melodramatic, vaguely laughable, and safely distanced from our everyday lives. The psychiatric werewolf lives on in sadder isolation, surrounded by well-meaning doctors who carefully probe the workings of his mind in the hope of uncovering clues to this and greater mysteries. Subjected to a blizzard of questions about his childhood, targeted by a hopeful fusillade of pharmaceutical silver bullets (over an eight-year period Case 8 alone was prescribed an unstated number of tricyclic antidepressants, trazodone, isocarboxazid, lithium carbonate, carbamazepine, valproate, and haloperidol), occasionally even subjected to the dubious last resort of electroconvulsive therapy, the psychiatric werewolf, like his cousin on the silver screen, is kept at a discreet distance from respectable society. When his delusions and deceptions are catalogued even by the most sympathetic, non-judgmental observer, he is always in danger of arousing incomprehension and ridicule only slightly tinged with pity, of being casually dismissed with the colloquialism 'barking mad'.

2

Animal Magic

The life of the wolf is the death of the lamb.
JOHN CLARKE,
Paremiologia Anglo-Latina

The history of the werewolf is one with roots buried deep in the past. We are surrounded by many such fragments of forgotten history, the detritus of those who have been here before us. Our modern myths, folklore, and religious ideas all contain within them such fragments, but their original or earlier significance is often obscure for us. Many ancient symbols, once richly significant, survive into the modern world at the price of becoming well-nigh incomprehensible. Among such symbols the werewolf looms large; after all, the idea that a human being can be transformed into an animal strikes the modern rationalist as peculiar, not to say downright ludicrous. As the psychiatric literature makes clear, such a figure was being discussed and treated as early as the fifth century AD, but its history is older even than that. The mental leap required to understand more about the origins of this puzzling avatar must take us back into the earliest known beliefs of human societies, in an attempt to uncover the universal significance of this mythical creature. Universal it must be, as it is well-known that the werewolf, which is predominantly a figure found in European folklore, is by no means the only such half-man, half-beast known around the world. The 'were' element in the English name is popularly supposed to derive from the German *wer*, cognate with Latin *vir*, simply meaning 'man' – the word means 'man-wolf'. (This is a contentious matter, although practically all other Western European names for the creature – Norman-French *loup-garou*, Italian *lupo-manaro*, and the rest – are constructed in a comparable way.[1])

However, many different kinds of man-animals, or were-animals, are recorded. In South America, for example, the animal involved is usually the jaguar. An ancient tradition of were-bears survives in the northern parts of Europe and Asia, while in China and other easterly parts of Asia the were-tiger is a staple of myth and folklore. From Japan come reports of widespread delusions of possession by the spirit of a fox. Evidence of belief in the werewolf legend is found throughout the whole range of the wolf's former habitat: from the northern tundra of Europe and Asia down to the shores of the Mediterranean, as far east as India and China, and throughout North America in the west. In all these cases, the common denominator is that the animal involved is the largest predator indigenous to that particular region. This makes sense when one considers the violent, aggressive aspect of the were-animal, yet anthropological evidence suggests that this is by no means the only way of looking at these curious beings.

The present-day Banyang, for example, who live in an afforested area of West Cameroon, have a rich and complicated belief in a variety of were-animals, which they call *babu*. Although the Banyang occasionally report seeing actual physical transformations of humans into animals, transformations little different from those depicted in modern werewolf films, most hold a much more spiritual notion of what a were-animal is. Among the Banyang, someone is said to 'own' a were-animal. The property is envisaged as a spirit-double of that person, capable of being sent out at night while the owner lies asleep. Opinions differ as to how the were-animal is to be acquired in the first place: usually it is said to be passed on from parent to child; others state that were-animals can be purchased, or that special herbal medicines must be prepared before the were-animal can be assimilated. Unlike the werewolf, especially as portrayed in the western cinema, the were-animals of the Banyang are not regarded as uniformly evil. Different were-animals are understood to have different potentials for good or evil. Nevertheless, the owner of a were-animal may find himself in difficulties even when his were-animal is not consciously used by him for malign or selfish purposes. This is most often true of the were-animal which is the closest parallel to the wolf found among the Banyang: the leopard. Like the wolf, the real leopard is a killer whose depredations are feared particularly by the domestic herdsman. Among the Banyang, as elsewhere in Africa, the leopard is a noble symbol of leadership and political authority, but its less exalted role as slaughterer of goats and other domestic livestock (and occasionally, it is believed, people) endows its were-animal counterpart with an ambivalent moral colouring. The hapless owner of a were-leopard will sometimes find himself being blamed for actual damage caused to livestock by real leopards. This must be a tempting accusation for someone with a grudge against one of his neighbours to make, and it would not be surprising if it were commonly levelled, but apparently the temptation is usually resisted by the Banyang. The owner of a were-leopard is more often regarded as suffering from various ailments which have originally been injuries caused to the were-leopard. A severe cough or breathlessness, for example, in the human is seen as caused by the relentless running of the were-leopard.[2]

Banyang cosmology expresses a view of the world which is largely alien to us, a world in which spirits can roam free of bodies, and where damage inflicted on one being is, by the process known as sympathetic magic, transferred to another. Crucially it is a world in which animals play an exalted role. The modern westerner tends to divide the animal kingdom into a simple hierarchy of household pets, edible foodstuffs, and vermin – and strokes, eats, or tries to poison them accordingly. The Banyang conception is infinitely richer, bringing through the concept of *babu* a wide variety of animals into intimate involvement with the spiritual life of the people. As such it offers a clue into the origins of the apparently impossible idea that a man may turn into an animal. An understanding of the werewolf legend relies on an understanding of its origins in human prehistory.

At the earliest stage, animals were superior to humans in every respect. Poor, bare, forked man stood in awe of the dramatic variety of nature: the eagle wheeling high in the sky above him, the elephant crashing over the plains, the remorseless fury of all the varied predators who competed with man for the flesh of every herbivore – all were infinitely greater in their physical capacities. Choose just one method of locomotion – running, for example – and man failed every test. A horse or bison could run further, a wildcat or cheetah quicker over short distances, a monkey could scamper through the flimsy top branches of trees, a lizard over shifting sands. When men and women looked around themselves at the vast spaces of the earth, they saw only creatures outdoing them. They perceived the universe as divided into three worlds of air, land, and water, and two of these three were decisively beyond human mastery. Only on land could man survive, and to do so he had to steal the skins of other animals to warm his hairless body, and submit himself to the co-operative discipline of the pack in order to pull down even the smallest food animal. The first decisive step out of this apparently insignificant ecological niche, taken perhaps 600,000 years ago, was an intensification in the use of tools.[3] Even then man was utterly dependant on the animals among whom he lived. Archaeological evidence suggests that his first tools were probably the lower jaws of large antelopes cut in half to make saws and knives. Gazelle horns with part of the skull attached served as rudimentary spades. The palates of large apes (or sometimes those of other humans) could be used to scrape away at the earth for roots and grubs. Even weapons – that distinctively human solution to lack of fangs or claws – were created by the inelegant but effective conversion of leg bones of gazelles into hefty clubs.[4]

Mankind's lot improved quickly (it took only some two or three hundred millennia), and the addition of fire-hardened stick and chipped stone, and later iron, to the armoury was decisive. But even as successful hunters, using the precious evolutionary gift of their formidable brains to outwit their prey, either simply by quick thinking or – and this was another radical departure – by talking over their strategy in advance, men were no different from the rest of the animal kingdom. Caught away from his fellows, delving into the dark recesses of an unexplored cave, a lone human hunter might come across a wildcat or, more terrifying, an angry bear. Then all his cranial capacity and linguistic panache, all his smart Palaeolithic technology, would be of little practical use as he scrambled frantically for safety. And once back with his tribal cohorts out on the plains, watching the herds of bison or antelope sweep past, hoping with the others to pick out some straggler or dawdler, he marvelled at how many there were, how that dusty mass seemed to rumble on forever, and how the few kills humans did manage to inflict never diminished the whole.

On those occasions, through the dust and thudding hooves, he might also catch a glimpse of another alert, intelligent, pack-hunting animal at work on the edge of the herd. He would have seen packs of wolves at work before, envying them their warm fur coats and stamina, and the ease with which the pack could pull down even the largest of victims. Man pondered how to harness this awesome power in his own interests, for hunting had become one of his most important activities, engaged in far more regularly than the brief forays after meat sporadically undertaken by his close cousin, the chimpanzee, and providing vital proteins and nutrients to feed him and his offspring in their prolonged infant-hood. Any lessons to be learnt from the wolf would be of great value to the killer-ape. Much later, man was to find a partial solution to the problem of co-opting the wolf's power to his own, a solution elegant in its simplicity: he set to work taming the wolf. Some 12,000 years ago man began the breeding programme that was to result, within what is biologically a very short space of time, in the divergence of the genes of the common canid ancestor into the hundreds of breeds of dog which nowadays adorn (usually pointlessly) man's easy life. The first successful experiments, exploiting and protracting the wolf cub's playful and trusting character, resulted in a wolf-dog which accompanied man on the hunt, tracking prey for hours along the secret routes of scent and sound that are beyond the range of man's simian senses. The wolf was tricked into adopting the human pack as its own, and its innate urge to work within such a group gave man the ideal opportunity to study techniques of stalking, circling, ambush, and chasing more efficient than his own. A singular metamor-phosis had been achieved.

But, by the time of the origins of the domesticated dog, modern man had been hunting on his own for some 40,000 years or so, and in that time he had made particular use of the skills of the wolf in a more indirect way. From earliest times man had sought to appropriate one predatory characteristic which was essentially alien to his ape nature: the wolf's ferocity in the kill. Walter Burkert, in his celebrated book *Homo Necans*[5] ('slaughtering man', in telling contrast to the usual species title of *Homo sapiens*), emphasizes the importance of hunting to the early human psy-che, laying particular stress on the changes this wrought in man's social organization. Killing is not easy work, either practically or emotionally. Most humans, especially those with no special training to inure themselves against an innate revulsion to the act, recoil in shock from violence or bloodshed. The typical individual response to the sight of flowing blood is the triggering of what modern doctors call the vasovagal syncope, an internal reflex which produces a relaxation and widening of the blood vessels: blood rushes away from the head down into the enlarged vessels of the body, starving the brain of oxygen and resulting ultimately in loss of consciousness. This is certainly not a modern phenomenon, brought about by the softening influence of civilization. All societies have been aware that the violent behaviour required for the continuance of civilization – the violence both of the butcher and of the soldier – is at odds with an instinctive, albeit idealistic, human desire for peace and tranquillity. The ancient Greeks speak in their myths of a golden age, before the first bloody act of killing, in which men and women lived as peaceful vegetarians, and this kind of story – idealizing the pre-social period, and accounting for the origin of human society in a disruptive act of bloodshed – can be traced in a wide variety of narratives: for example in the legend of Cain's murder of Abel, immediately succeeding their parents' vegetarian life in Paradise,[6] or of Romulus killing his brother Remus and founding Rome. Although human-killing-human has usually been regarded as the ultimate act of violence, human-killing-animal has never been far behind, especially in those early societies in which the relative status of humans and animals was less asymmetrically distorted than today.

Humans suffered from an inconveniently squeamish predisposition, and in order to achieve the kind of intense aggression needed to overcome it on a regular basis, Walter Burkert argues, a male hunting sub-group emerged within prehistoric human society, a group tied together by bonds forged in the hunt, which by the use of conspiratorial rituals and communal fellowship could generate the aggressive drives necessary to bring success on the killing plains. Such male hunting cliques naturally sought to assimilate the qualities of those animals they envied for their prowess in the kill. They preserved their separateness within the larger social grouping by the use of secrecy, fearsome initiation rites, and the fellow-feeling engendered in the danger of the chase, urging each other on to greater slaughter. Here lies the origin of tribal societies like the leopard men of Africa, who dressed in leopard skins and took upon themselves that animal's strength and aggression. Such 'leopard societies' were feared by the European colonial powers in Africa well into the twentieth century, and enjoyed awe-inspiring reputations for ferocity, and particular notoriety for demanding cannibalism of their members. That their society is not a recent invention is shown by a wall painting from Çatal Hüyük in Anatolia, done about 6000 BC, which shows a group of hunters girdled with leopard skins swarming in the kill around stag and boar. An observer in the North American plains as late as the 1830s would have seen a re-enactment of this same primal scene, as Sioux hunters dressed in the pelts of white wolves tracked down buffalo. The Nazis recognized the value of the group spirit engendered by these hunting societies: in the 1920s a secret right-wing terrorist group in Germany called 'Operation Werwolf' prosecuted political murders, and apparently indulged in some rather peculiar initiation rites, including group nudism. Goebbels revived the organization in the last days of the Second World War as an underground resistance movement, and Himmler gave a peptalk urging them to harass Allied lines of communication 'like werewolves'.[7] Modern-day hunters in their blood-red coats, whose prey has degenerated to the inoffensive and, as Wilde memorably pointed out, inedible fox, still enjoy small rituals of group blood-initiation and an agreeable sense of themselves as a social elite different only in scale from those of the prehistoric wolf-brotherhoods.

The prehistoric hunt was clearly the focus for a great deal of ritual activity, traditionally characterized as magical, undertaken to ensure success in the chase. While the brotherhoods of hunters dressed in the pelts of predators to assimilate their feral power, the shamans were donning animal skins and horns for complementary reasons. Such a shaman, or medicine-man, seems to be illustrated in the famous figure known as the 'Sorcerer of Trois Frères', a late Palaeolithic wall painting discovered within a system of caves deep below the Pyrenees. The 'Sorcerer' is a curious figure, hovering indeterminately on the brink between animal and human form. He is seen sideways in a dancing posture, raised slightly on his human feet, but leaning forward as if he may at any moment drop onto his bear-like forepaws and assume four-footed gait. Large stag's antlers protrude above his bearded face, from the middle of which two owlish eyes stare towards the onlooker. At his hindquarters, a bushy wolf's tail swings back, revealing a phallus in the high position of some feline species, perhaps a lion. Joseph Campbell[8] points out that the awkward position of the painting, on the wall of a cave which can only be reached by crawling on the belly through a connecting passage some forty or fifty yards long, suggests that it had some mystical and religious significance, but it almost certainly also illustrates Palaeolithic hunting practices of imitating the quarry. Such practices were observed among the Blackfoot Indians of Montana during the nineteenth century, where a medicine-man disguised in a buffalo head and pelt would attract the attention of a number of members of the buffalo herd and lead them into a trap set at the edge of a cliff. With such a scene in mind, it becomes possible to imagine a group of prehistoric hunters at work, the horned and pelted shaman at the front enticing the animals towards some ambush, while the wolf-warriors work as a team around the back of the herd, harrying the animals into an ever tighter mass before finally falling on them with their burnt-stick 'claws' and flint 'teeth'.

The complex emotions aroused by the slaughtering of animals for food lingered long after the killing had subsided, a guilty feeling persisting among the hunters that they were exploiting the animals, whom they recognized as at least their equals, if not in many cases their superiors. This guilt was accompanied by a simple selfish fear that hunting might eventually wipe out their prey species. An example of how this fear might come to be assuaged through magical ritual was stumbled across by the celebrated anthropologist Leo Frobenius, travelling in the Belgian Congo in the early years of the twentieth century. Frobenius happened to meet some indigenous huntsmen of the forest who accompanied his expedition for a week or so. As food was running short, Frobenius casually asked the three men one afternoon if they would kill an antelope, knowing that they were skilled hunters and the task would be easy for them. They, however, looked at him in amazement. Eventually one volunteered the reply that they could certainly bring him back an antelope, but it would have to be done tomorrow, as no preparations had been made: they would begin at dawn the next day. Frobenius's professional curiosity was aroused by this, and the next morning he secretly followed the men to the nearby hill they had chosen as the site for their preparations. He saw that the hunters had a woman with them who contributed to the muttered imprecations they made, while with his finger one of the men scratched something in a clear patch of sand smoothed out for the purpose. After that they waited. Eventually the sun came up over the horizon, and as its rays hit the clearing in the sand, one of the men raised his bow and shot an arrow into the ground. At the same time the woman raised her hands towards the sun and gave loud, unintelligible cries. The men then rushed off into the forest with their weapons.

Frobenius waited until the woman had set off back to the camp before stepping out from his hiding place to examine the site. Scratched in the earth in the middle of the cleared patch of ground was a picture, some four feet long, of an antelope: the arrow had pierced its neck. He dashed back to the camp for his camera, but the native woman realized what he was up to and pleaded with him not to go back to the hill. The huntsmen eventually returned with a fine specimen, shot through the neck with an arrow. They left the animal with Frobenius, and set off back to their hill with a few tufts of the antelope's hair and a gourd full of its blood. Frobenius's expedition continued on its way, and it was a full two days before the hunters caught up with them again. Frobenius was desperate to find out more about their ritual, and in the end he winkled out from the oldest of the three the information he wanted: they had gone back to smear their drawing of the antelope with the blood and hair, remove the arrow, and then rub out the picture. The hunter would only say that if this were not done the 'blood' of the antelope would be destroyed.[9]

The Congolese ritual witnessed by Frobenius, a fair indication of the cautious preparation with which prehistoric peoples approached the practice of hunting, operated on the same basic principle of sympathetic magic as the Banyang use to explain a cough in the man who owns a were-leopard. The possibility of sympathetic magic essentially rests on the notion that the cosmos is a whole, and that likenesses and correspondences may be detected within it by which magic can be worked. In the Congolese ritual, the drawing stood for the real animal, and received the wound in the same way as the real animal would in due course. This connection between the shooting of the image – the drawing of which was accompanied by magical incantations to ensure that the parallel was effective – and the shooting of the real quarry gives some clue as to the purpose of the dramatic cave art of the Palaeolithic period, in which the powerfully rendered buffaloes and stags bristling with the arrows of the hunters were probably depicted thus both to ensure their death in the hunt and para-doxically to ensure their continued survival as a species. Another practice which seems to be enacted on the same principle is the widely attested ancient custom of gathering together the bones of slaughtered animals and replacing them inside their skins, thus symbolically making the animal whole again. There are some problems in assuming that this particular practice dates back as far as the Palaeolithic era, chiefly arising from the difficulty of detecting whether or not humans were involved in gathering together the jumbles of broken animal bones which are the main contemporary evidence for such magical reconstructions, but the frequency with which the motif appears in later mythology makes the assumption likely. With such rites, the hunter expressed something akin to respect for his prey, pretending that a killing had not happened, and reassembling the victim's bones almost as an act of apology for his presumption in killing him for food.

Evidence for one specific type of animal reconstruction which has a close, almost symbiotic, relation to the werewolf myth has been traced throughout a huge continuum, across the whole northern circumpolar region, through Finland, northern Russia and Siberia, Alaska, and the north-west American coast, and as far south as the northern islands of Japan. This particular type of animal reconstruction at least can certainly be traced back as far as the early Palaeolithic period. In 1923, in a cave near Montespan, Haute-Garonne, south-west France, a rough clay statue of a beast dating from this era was discovered. Although obviously intended to represent a bear, it was carelessly modelled, with none of the concern for detail exhibited by other clay animal statues of this era, and lacking a head. Nevertheless, this last defect was clearly not accidental, as the neck had been smoothed off cleanly, and a hole had been drilled down into it, apparently to support a shaft. Between the clay forepaws the archaeologists found the skull of a bear. From this they deduced that the statue was intended to support the head and pelt of a freshly killed bear.[10]

Such a ritual involving the reconstruction of a slaughtered bear
has been witnessed among the modern Ainu, the people who
occupy the northern islands of Japan. The Ainus have always
been the subject of anthropological curiosity as they exhibit a
number of physical features, including abundant body hair and
Caucasoid eyes, which set them decisively apart from the other
Japanese. Some explanation for this difference is offered in the
theory that they migrated to their present position from Siberia
or some other northern part of Asia. Every so often the Ainus will
catch a black bear cub in the mountains, and bring it back to the
village alive. This is an occasion for great rejoicing, as the Ainus
regard the black bear as a god come to visit the world of men. At
the village, the bear cub is suckled by one of the women, and plays
with the children until it grows too big and fierce to be allowed
to continue to live among its human playmates. Then it is
confined to a secure wooden cage, where it is fed on fish and
millet porridge, and treated as an honoured guest. After about
two years, a festival is held called *iyomande*, meaning 'sending
away'. The whole village turns out to celebrate the bear's
departure, and prayer-sticks, called *inao* ('message-bearers'), are
prepared. One of the men approaches close to the cage, and asks
the bear-god to carry messages back to the other gods telling them
how kind the villagers have been to him. The bear is then released
from the cage and led around by a rope. Small blunt arrows are
fired at him, arousing him to fury; then he is quickly grabbed by
his limbs and spreadeagled, an arrow is fired into his heart, and
two heavy poles are squeezed together across his neck. Once he
is dead, the bear's head and hide are removed together and set up
in a place of honour in a house, with the prayer-sticks and other
offerings arranged about it. A feast is prepared of the bear's flesh,
while some of the men drink the blood for strength and daub their
clothes with it. The concept is maintained that the bear has taken
the prayers and the small gifts of food back to his parents, the gods
dwelling in the mountains, and in conveying these presents,
along with messages of how well he has been treated among the
Ainu, has ensured the gods' continued favour for the village.[11]

The earliest human altars of any kind yet found, dating from
not later than 75,000 BC, show persuasive signs of having been
used for exactly this type of bear-cult, and the motif has spread
across a huge part of the northern hemisphere, related legends

and folk-art being found even in places like Queen Charlotte Island and Iceland which have never supported bear populations. The ancient bear-cult is one of the earliest known manifestations of the use of ritually slaughtered animals as spiritual messengers, envoys from this world to the next. The practice springs from the prehistoric hunter's empathy with his prey: the dead beast stands proxy for the man, and the rite reaffirms the idea – consoling to both hunter and hunted – that killing is not killing, that life and death are not opposing states but only two complementary aspects of the eternal. The animal chosen for participation in this important rite is usually not the everyday food animal (although the flesh of the 'god' is eaten as an integral part of the ceremony), but often a predator like man, thus making the identification between man and the sacrificial victim even closer. Headless clay animal-figures similar to those found in the French Palaeolithic cave have been found in the twentieth century on the Gold Coast, West Africa, where they are used to support the head and pelt of leopards, and in the French Sudan, where they are used to reconstitute the bodies of man-eating lions or leopards. The Palaeolithic cave-bears whose remains are found at the earliest bear-cult sites were apparently fairly harmless beasts, vegetarians whose deep hibernation in the glacial period must have made them easy to kill for food. Nevertheless later descendants of the cave-bear were not so mild-tempered, and human identification with, and admiration for, the immensely strong, occasionally bipedal animal led to its assuming in the northern lands the important role of ritual messenger to the land of the dead. Most of the human graves so far discovered from this very early period also contain the remains of animals, apparently ritually buried alongside the human corpse, and it is probable that these were included for much the same reason, as guides to the other world.

Palaeolithic societies must have realized immediately that this hypothetical other world, the land of the dead, could not be inhabited by corporeal beings. They had consumed the actual flesh of the bear, after all, and they knew that the innards of their bear reconstructions, however lifelike they might appear in the flickering half-light of the cave, were only roughly hewn clay. Likewise they witnessed all around them the physical decomposition undergone by all dead bodies, including their own. Some essence of the bear, its spirit, must have gone forth from it at the moment of death, they reasoned; and a similar spirit must therefore inhabit all living creatures, including humans. It has been said that the idea of an incorporeal spirit, or soul, was forcibly suggested to humans by the vapour rising from a pool of spilt blood, or by the clouds of mist breathed from the mouth in cold weather (which may be why many cultures have regarded the lungs as the seat of consciousness, or have visualized the soul as a wisp of vapour).[12] Whether or not this idea first came about from exactly these external stimuli, the notion expressed in the Ainus' bear ritual and others like it – that the spirit world can be reached by an animal messenger – was a hopeful one: it implied that human affairs could be altered for the better by intervention in that other world. In this, the animal messengers clearly lacked one important attribute: they were unable to return and communicate in human language the intentions or desires of the spirit world. For this a human messenger was needed, and the functionaries who took on this crucial role were the shamans.

Although our knowledge of shamanism has to be extrapolated from recent anthropological evidence largely gathered among the indigenous peoples of the Arctic Circle and northern Asia, where shamanism has survived into the present century, it is clear that similar practices were among the earliest essayed by mankind. The shaman assumes for him or herself the vital role of travelling to the spirit world to negotiate on behalf of the whole community in such important matters as the success of crops and livestock and their freedom from disease. To do this he must release his own spirit from its corporeal bondage. This is the rationale behind the shamanistic trances, induced by repetition of intensely rhythmical actions like dancing and drumming and/or the ingestion of ecstasy-inducing drugs, from which the shaman emerges with messages from the other world, sometimes also producing a small physical token of the immensely arduous journey with which to amaze his audience. In his voyage to the other world, the shaman naturally seeks to co-opt the spiritual power of the animals, either riding on them to his spirit destination or transforming himself into one of them for the journey, and this aspect too is probably implicit in the illustration of the 'Sorcerer of Trois Frères'. The shaman's spiritual authority is given physical expression by his assumption of animal attributes which enable him to communicate with the land of the dead.

Although a shaman might have been the only member of society able to control his spirit well enough to travel in animal shape to the land of the dead, lesser mortals were also regarded as having a spirit of their own, as in Banyang society, and the spirit was normally envisaged as an animal, particularly in hunting societies. Much recent anthropological attention has focused on initiation rites in this type of society, those particular staging-posts in a person's life which mark his or her progress through the social order. In hunting societies of the Palaeolithic era, the most important initiation rite was that marking the passage from boyhood to manhood, at which time the young boy would be circumcised or forced to suffer some other physical mutilation, be put through a period of physical and mental deprivation, and eventually learn of the spirit-animal which would be his sign or totem thenceforth. If he was joining a band of hunter-brothers, he might be welcomed into the Wolf clan: such societies have many hierarchical grades, often named after different animals, as for example the Little Birds, Pigeons, Dogs, Raven Bearers, and Bulls of the North American Blackfoot tribe in the nine-teenth century.

At this early stage, the tendency of man's thinking with regard to animals was still to elevate them to mythic status. In the many and varied accounts of how the earth came to be like it is, animals often played leading roles. Many cultures tell stories of a golden age when animals ruled the earth, and in creation stories, for example of how the sky was first lifted up, it is often an animal or bird that performs the crucial act. Sometimes, especially in those societies where hunting was less important, the animals chosen seem comically unsuited to the grand roles assigned to them in the universal drama: the Andamanese islanders, who inhabit an isolated archipelago in the Bay of Bengal, tell tales of Sir Monitor Lizard and Lady Civet Cat. Sir Monitor Lizard was the first man, and he was out in the jungle hunting pig when he became entangled in a tree by his genitals. Lady Civet Cat freed him from this embarrassing position and the two were married and became the progenitors of the Andamanese.[13] However lowly a tribal ancestor a monitor lizard might appear, the Andamanese were limited in their possible choices by the animal life they saw around them. Their archipelago supported a fairly meagre selec-tion of native fauna from which to choose: a species of pig, a few

kinds of bat and rat, a tree shrew, and of course the civet cat and
monitor lizard of the myth. The versatile monitor lizard, able to
swim in water, walk on land, and climb trees, was to the islanders
the 'master of the three worlds', and so eminently suitable for
elevation to the role of Adam in their version of Genesis.
Traditional peoples living in grander natural surroundings, with
a wider selection of animals to choose from than the comparatively deprived Andamanese, naturally picked out other animals
as their ancestors, particularly those which to them exuded
nobility, strength, and grace: all the qualities they sought to
inculcate in their own tribal societies.

It did not seem in any way odd to prehistoric peoples that their
ancestor should have been an animal. The categories of human
and animal which are so rigid today were infinitely more malleable in early societies. The transformation or mutation of animals
either to form new animals or to become human was a popular
theme. One of the Andamanese myths, for example, tells how the
ancestor of man was a kingfisher. In this version, as in others of
their stories, the creator of the earth was a curious figure named
Biliku, a feminine personification of the north-east monsoon.
The ancestors decided to steal fire from Biliku, and sent the
kingfisher while she was asleep. As the kingfisher was making off
with her fire, Biliku awoke and threw a pearl shell after the thief,
cutting off his wings and tail. He fell into the sea, but managed
to swim ashore and pass fire on to the other animals. Thereafter,
the kingfisher became a man, and Biliku raged off somewhere
into the sky, where she has lived ever since. Such tales, familiar
from Kipling's naming of them as 'Just So' stories, were used to
explain the origins not only of mankind but of all animals, so that
the story of how man came to walk upright on two legs was told
with a similar intent to one about how the leopard got his spots.
Much the same kind of primitive tale is embedded in a story as
late as Genesis, the grand drama of Adam and Eve's temptation
serving incidentally as a traditional narrative to explain why the
snake has no legs.

Prehistoric man's elevation of animals to leading roles in the
universal drama was such a pervasive theme that there is scarcely
a religious system that does not bear a trace of it. In many of these,
the shamanistic conception of animals as spirit-messengers is
clearly preserved. The ancient association between birds and

such spirit-messengers is particularly common, probably because so many cosmologies envisaged the other world as being
situated in the sky or at the top of a mountain, and so a bird was
a particularly appropriate carrier of messages to those regions.
Another interesting set of wall paintings from Çatal Hüyük in
Anatolia depicts huge vultures and a number of headless human
corpses. Some scholars think that the birds shown may not be real
vultures, but priests dressed up as vultures, although the events
depicted are otherwise fairly clear: the vultures or were-vultures
are picking the flesh from the bones of dead humans. In archaeological excavations of nearby houses, skeletons were found
buried under the floors, their flesh having been removed before
burial, and it is supposed that this excarnation had been carried
out as the wall paintings suggest. As a method of getting rid of
corpses, excarnation has a number of advantages, particularly in
regions where the ground is too hard or unstable for burial, or
where firewood for cremation is at a premium. Attracting scavenging birds to undertake the task is a good deal less gruesome
than employing other humans, although a special caste of
vulture-priests may have fulfilled this function, perhaps acting in
tandem with the birds by cutting the sinews so that the flesh could
be removed more speedily by them. Once the flesh was removed,
the body, now only a skeleton, was regarded as stable, unable to
undergo any further deterioration, and so could be safely stored
in close proximity to its family. From this funerary practice,
which appears to have been fairly widespread among a number
of cultures, it is a short step for the practitioners to imagine that,
in consuming the human flesh, the scavenging birds are carrying
away the essence of the human – the soul, in fact – to the spirit
world.[14]

The image of a bird-like creature as spirit-messenger occurs in
many religions – one thinks of the winged angels and cherubim
of medieval Christian imagery – but their particular association
with death and funerary ritual lent a horrific aspect to many
personifications of bird-like spirits. In Sumerian demonology, for
example, there existed a terrible being called Ardat Lili, or Lilitu,
a winged and taloned female creature who flew through the night,
accompanied by owls and lions, attempting to seduce sleeping
men and suck their blood: the Graeco-Roman Lamia was her
close cousin. In Greek myth, the Harpies were hideous half-

women, half-birds: in the *Argonautica* they scream down from the
sky at poor blind Phineas, snatching away the scraps of food left
out for him, and leaving in their wake a revolting stench. Such
mythical figures of horror represent the connecting link between
ancient funerary practices involving carrion-feeding birds and
later fears of the night-flying witch.

Like the vulture, the wolf is a scavenger, although on an
occasional basis, and as such has an inevitable association with
death. Indeed, some authorities, who see the conception of the
noble wolf-brotherhood of hunters as too idealistic, argue that
man's earliest identification with the wolf may have arisen
because both were often reduced to mere scavenging, and that
the wolf usually proved rather better at it than man. One of the
most purely theriomorphic religions of the ancient world was that
of the Egyptians, who worshipped gods in animal shape almost
exclusively in the pre-dynastic period before about 3000 BC. Even
as late as classical times, the Egyptian gods retained their animal
heads or other animal characteristics as reminders of their
ancestry. The Egyptian god of death was Anubis, whose head was
that of a jackal, the wolf's fellow canid. Other mythological
associations between wolves and death are not difficult to find.
Charon, the ferryman of Greek mythology who rowed the shades
of the dead across the river Styx, is depicted in an Etruscan source
with wolf's ears, for example, while Soranus, the Sabine god of
death, was served by priests called *hirpi*, or wolves.[15] Such an
association was probably maintained through to the classical age
and beyond because wolves (and, in Egypt, jackals) were always
liable to scavenge near human settlements, particularly in burial
grounds, a factor which probably has a great deal to do with
Paulus Aegineta's classic description of the graveyard-haunting
'melancholic lycanthropes'. Yet further still behind this concept
of the wolf may lie ancient excarnation rites in which wolves were
used in the same role as were the Çatal Hüyük vultures.

There was one additional strain to early man's thinking about
the wolf, however, in which the animal appears in a more
appealing light. Perhaps because by imitating the wolf's hunting
or scavenging strategies man had first learnt how to obtain a good
supply of meat, the wolf is in some traditions associated with
plenitude of food. This idea is expressed in an Amerindian totem
story told by a member of a Wolf clan, in north-west Canada, in

the town of Towq. The town totem-pole there is topped with a wolf's head, and the following story was told to explain why the wolf came to be the totem for the town.[16] The people of Towq had formerly lived on the sea coast in front of the present town of Prince Rupert. Their hero was a shaman-figure named Kamlugyides, who had gained his spiritual authority after an encounter with inhabitants of a ghost-village across the sound, coming away with a ghost-mask as a sign of his victory. Some time after this, the people of Kamlugyides' village were starving. In the midst of this famine, they were further terrified by the howling of a wolf nearby. Kamlugyides bravely set out into the woods in the direction of the howls. There he found a large wolf pacing up and down in evident distress. Kamlugyides called out to the wolf, asking what its trouble was. The wolf came nearer, and Kamlugyides looked down its throat and saw that a deer-bone had become lodged in its gullet. He reached in and removed the bone, whereupon the wolf showed its gratitude by licking his hands and feet, before racing off into the woods with the rest of its pack. A few days later, the villagers heard a wolf howling again, but this time it seemed to be calling for Kamlugyides. He set out for the woods again, and met the same wolf that he had helped before. The wolf was overjoyed to see him, and led him to a deer carcass lying in the forest. Kamlugyides took the carcass and was able to feed his villagers. Each day the same thing happened, and his villagers were able to feed themselves amid the famine that was afflicting the whole district. Kamlugyides eventually planned a great feast at which he would don his ghost-mask and assume the crest of the Prince of the Wolves, and he enlisted the wolf's help in gathering together a great profusion of game with which to feed his guests. Ultimately a dispute arose over the ownership of the ghost-mask, and Kamlugyides set out with his people and settled on the upper Nass river under the Towq group of the Wolf clan.

Already the picture of possible origins of the werewolf legend is more complex than the simple image of the wolfman given in the cinema or the delusory states of modern psychiatric patients might suggest. The theory of prehistoric wolf-brotherhoods, in which young hunters donned wolf-skins and assumed feral attributes in order to succeed in the kill, offers an elegant suggestion as to how the practice of imitating the wolf might first have originated. But it is also clear that Palaeolithic man lived in much closer proximity to the animal world than does modern man, and that animals had important spiritual functions in early societies, being particularly associated with the need to communicate with the other world. The wolf had a special association with death in its unpleasant guise as a scavenger and devourer of human corpses, yet, as the Canadian wolf-totem story shows, it was also recognized as having some connection with the winning of fertility and plenitude of game. Both these sides of the wolf – the horrific and the benign – were to be fully represented in the later development of the werewolf legend.

There is one quintessentially Hollywood werewolf motif which seems unarguably to have its origins in this prehistoric period – the idea that a man will become a werewolf at the time of the full moon. No werewolf movie would be complete without a night-time shot of clouds scudding across the face of that ominous silver disc, the legendary signal that the startling transformation is about to take place. Such a connection can already be seen in the prehistoric hunting era, for the moon is one of the most ancient symbols associated with the hunt in all cultures. At first sight the reason for this is not immediately obvious, unless one believes that man's fervour for the hunt had to be built up by group rituals, and could not be maintained at the same level indefinitely. Early societies collected food by gathering as well as by hunting, as a few societies still do, subsisting usually on a vast array of roots, berries, nuts, grubs, and wild grains. Because of the relatively poor level of nutrition provided by this *mélange* of foodstuffs, especially in the less fertile environments during the glacial periods, gathering activity had be undertaken continuously on a low-level daily basis. Hunting, on the other hand, which provided an essential source of protein, was an episodic activity, the phases of the moon serving as a signal to the blood-brothers of the animal societies that they should begin working themselves into a frenzy for the chase, a signal doubly emphasized at the full moon by the plaintive howling of the wolves the hunters had chosen to imitate. This ancient signal is still commemorated in the dubbing of a particular full moon the 'hunter's moon'. If nothing else, the lunar cycle would have been regarded as a convenient natural clock, as it was the only recognizable unit of time known to prehistoric man that was longer than a day and shorter than the long solar year. (The useful but entirely artificial seven-day week would have to wait to be established until about the second century AD.)[17]

Chris Knight, in his book *Blood Relations*, has put forward the fascinating theory that this episodic pattern of hunting may have an inextricable link with female menstruation, which is well-known to occur at the same frequency as the lunar cycle, every twenty-nine-and-a-half days.[18] It has long been regarded as puzzling that human females, unlike female apes or indeed any other mammal, should bleed so profusely and so often, and that their periods synchronize when they live in close proximity. Knight argues that the coincidence with the moon's cycle came about during the hunting era, and sees menstruation as early women's way of ensuring that all their men set out together on the arduous quest for food. The flow of bright blood occurring simultaneously throughout the social group acted as a temporary sexual repellant, diverting men's attention from indolent home life to the bloody business ahead. The promise of sex after a period of enforced abstinence and dangerous hunting would be all that was necessary to ensure that the men returned home with enough of the spoils to feed the women and children. Powerful taboos against sex during menstruation reinforced the message.

If Knight's theory is substantially correct, this would explain the association of the moon, made in so many cultures, with a female deity concerned with hunting. In later Graeco-Roman culture, this figure was Artemis (Diana in Latin), whose epithet in the *Iliad* is 'mistress of the animals'. One of the best-known stories about her in Greek myth concerns animal transformation: a young man named Actaeon out hunting caught sight of the goddess bathing, was changed by her into a stag, and was immediately torn to pieces by his own hounds. A close parallel to this story is known in the Akkadian *Epic of Gilgamesh*, dated around the early second millennium BC, in which the goddess Ishtar has a faithful shepherd who offers up sacrifices to her, but whom she turns into a wolf: like Actaeon, his own dogs then devour him.[19] This is the earliest known literary representation of the transformation of a man into a wolf.

In addition to her role as the fearsome, secretive goddess of the hunt, Artemis was the personification of the moon, called Phoebe and Selene (Luna in Latin), seen by later poets as having three aspects, Selene in the sky, Artemis on the earth, and Hecate in the underworld and in darkness. Hecate was customarily depicted with three animal heads (often wolves' heads, as in this incarnation she was a goddess of death), representing the goddess's triple dominion over underworld, earth, and air. There are tantalizing hints that in her most ancient guise Artemis had been a bear-goddess, thereby offering further evidence of links between the Palaeolithic bear-cults and later werewolf beliefs.[20] Although earlier 'mistresses of the animals' cannot be so well-known for lack of literary evidence, it seems clear that Artemis represents the survival of an ancient twinning of the activity of hunting with the phases of the moon. So, too, the equally primordial connection between the moon and lunacy: for the animal-skinned hunter preparing for the service of the mistress of the animals would have driven himself towards what seemed to calmer observers to be a form of insanity. It is in this complex of ideas – the prehistoric association of a killing fury arising from a human deliberately taking on the attributes of a wild animal, and the full moon acting as the signal for the timing of these occurrences – that the werewolf legend has its ultimate basis.

3

The Bloodline Begins

The *delirium of metamorphosis* or transformation into some form of animal
. . . is met with much more rarely today
than in past centuries.

L. BIANCHI,
A Text Book of Psychiatry

Although the four-thousand-year-old *Epic of Gilgamesh* had given
a brief sketch of a man turned into a wolf, the earliest substantial
description of a werewolf which is recognizable as the ancestor of
all later versions comes in a Roman horror story slipped into a
larger comic work by Petronius. Very little is known for certain
about the author, who lived in the first century AD, but the real life
of his era oozes out of his racy, often obscene comedy, the first
piece of writing generally referred to as a 'novel', which is
sometimes known by the title of *Satyricon* (the Italian director
Fellini filmed a version under that name), or, more usually, after
the best-known and longest section, *Trimalchio's Banquet*. The
star of the piece is the larger-than-life figure of Trimalchio
himself, a former slave who has managed to accrue enough
wealth to lay on the lavishly ostentatious banquet that gives this
section its name. He is rude, crude, and irresistible, and when he
orders one of his fellow freedmen, a man named Niceros, to step
up and tell the assembled guests a story, Niceros is only too
willing to comply. He warns Trimalchio that his story will be pure
fun, and that some of the cleverer guests may laugh at it, but as
he himself doesn't mind being laughed at, he will proceed.

Niceros says that the story he is about to relate happened to him
while he was still a slave. He was taking advantage of his master's
absence from the house on business to visit his mistress, Melissa,

and felt in need of company on the night-time walk. 'I persuaded a guest in our house to come with me as far as the fifth milestone: he was a soldier, as brave as Hell,' he tells them. So Niceros and the soldier trot off into the night, the full moon shining clearly down on them. In those days in southern Italy, tombstones lined the sides of the roads, and Niceros and his soldier friend stop to rest among these for a while. Niceros spends the time idly counting graves and thinking happily about his mistress, while the soldier goes off to read the inscriptions. But when Niceros looks up, he sees the soldier stripping off his clothes and putting them down by the roadside. 'My heart was in my mouth,' Niceros tells the banqueters, 'but I stood there like a dead man.' Then comes the astonishing transformation: the soldier urinates in a circle around his clothes and suddenly turns into a wolf. 'Please do not think I am joking; I would not lie about this for all the money in the world,' Niceros assures his audience. The wolf begins to howl, and runs away into the woods, leaving a bewildered Niceros to examine the clothes he has left behind – which have all turned into stone. Terrified, Niceros continues on his way, fearfully slashing out at shadows with his sword until he reaches Melissa's house and goes in trembling and weak. But Melissa has news for him: 'If you had come earlier you might at least have helped us,' she tells him. 'A wolf got into the house and worried all our sheep, and let their blood like a butcher. But he did not make fools of us, even though he escaped, for our slave stabbed him in the neck with a spear.' Unable to sleep that night, Niceros rushes back to his master's house at dawn, pausing only to see that the clothes have been removed from the roadside, in their place nothing but a pool of blood. At home, he finds the soldier lying in bed 'like an ox', with a doctor looking after his neck. 'I realized then that he was a werewolf [the Latin word is *versipellem*, literally 'turn-skin'],' Niceros says, 'and I could not sit down to a meal with him afterwards, not if you had killed me first. Other people may think what they like about this; but may all your guardian spirits punish me if I am lying.'

Here, in this one story written some two thousand years ago, Petronius has told in essence all other werewolf stories, grouping together for the first time the major elements which recur throughout later versions. The first characteristic of a werewolf is that, in the great tradition stretching from here to Hollywood, the bizarre transformation from man to wolf takes place in moonlight. Of course the prehistoric association between the full moon and lycanthropy is the primal source of this motif, but in this particular story the detail has another, purely practical function, because the evidence of Niceros' eyes is all-important for the telling of it. He claims actually to have seen the transformation from man to wolf take place in a graveyard at dead of night. If the moon hadn't been shining ('like high noon', Niceros says), he would never have been able to see anything, and Trimalchio's guests would not have had their story. Another notable feature of Petronius' story is that the werewolf must remove his human clothes before the transformation can take place, as if discarding those things that make him distinctively human before he can become an animal. Thirdly, the werewolf uses magic to effect the transformation: in this case, the soldier urinates in a 'magic circle' around his clothes. Once the spell has worked, he must return to the same spot and retrieve his clothes before reassuming human guise. The fact that his clothes have been turned to stone makes it impossible for anyone else to move or interfere with them while he is away enjoying himself in lupine form. The magical charm works both to make the transformation from man to wolf possible, and to facilitate the return to human form. Lastly, and this is perhaps the most persistent motif in later werewolf stories, Petronius has introduced the idea of the sympathetic wound – that is, the notion that a wound inflicted on the werewolf shows up even when he has returned to human form. Once again, this is an idea with origins in the ancient world-view of sympathetic magic, but on the simplest level it is essential to the telling of the story: if it were not for the wound, Niceros would not have been able to confirm the evidence of his eyes the previous night. He, or others, might have been tempted to dismiss his account of the soldier's transformation as a simple hallucination. The sympathetic wound is the narrator's proof that this strange episode really happened.

What little is known about Petronius suggests that he was a sophisticated man, decadent and cynical some would say, a worldly satirist who obviously understood to perfection the sometimes sordid workings of the southern Italian world of freedmen and parvenu businessmen he chose to write about, but who lived himself in the highly cultured, amoral court of the emperor Nero. In either of these milieux, he is a long way removed from obscure and primitive ideas of totemism and shape-shifting. One possible source for Petronius' story is treated in the works of a Greek writer, slightly later than Petronius, named Pausanias. He was a man principally interested in Greek art, and he set out to travel through Greece in the second century AD with a view to seeing all that then remained of classical Greek art and architecture. But Pausanias' trip became more than just an antiquarian traipse, the equivalent of a modern tour around the museums of Europe. Everywhere he went he was confronted with the natural beauty of Greece and the still-vital remnants of its great civilization. In the towns and rural communities he visited, he noticed the survival of ancient religious ideas, cults and rituals that were unusual or bizarre even to a man who had seen the wonders of Rome, the pyramids of Egypt, and the holy city of Jerusalem.

Perhaps the most alarming ritual Pausanias described took place at the peak of Mount Lykaion, an awesome spot rising out of the central highland region of Arcadia in the Peloponnesus, a height from which a man could survey the entire southern peninsula of Greece. The feeling of isolation on that mountain top must have been impressive in Pausanias' day, reinforced as it was by the fact that the whole land-locked region of Arcadia was cut off from the rest of Greece. Without any coastline of its own, travel or commerce between Arcadia and the rest of the country was arduous and infrequent. The poets later transformed Arcadia into a pastoral near-Eden, but the real place was inhospitably hard, a wild morass of limestone ridges and troughs intersected with cross-ridges to form inaccessible valleys, ringed around with forests and mountains rising up to the north and west. Myths and legends flourished here: Lake Stymphalos, almost entirely sur-rounded by dizzily steep cliffs, and the river Styx, crashing down a sheer drop of 600 feet into a dark, fearsome valley to become the mythical river of death flowing through the underworld, were among the region's natural wonders which cried out for super-natural explanations. In those days thick forests of oak clung to the less vertiginous slopes, although with such irregular rainfall, neither olives nor any other profitable crop except a few vines could be dependably grown. Where the forests gave way to upland pastures in the south and east, it was possible to scratch out a living breeding mules, but the cautious herdsman always kept an eye on the encircling forest for any sign of his natural enemy, the ever-present local predator – the wolf.

Here, Pausanias states, the annual sacrifice to the Greek sky god in his local incarnation as Lykaian Zeus took place. On that mountain top high above the Arcadian plateau, as the sun rose up in the east, the priest of the Lykaian cult entered the *tenemos*, the sacred precinct of the god, made his ritual obeisances over the circular earth-and-ash altar, prepared his sacrificial knife, and raised up before the worshippers the body of the sacrificial victim. And here Pausanias falters. He refuses to divulge the exact details of the ritual, an unusual display of squeamishness for him. Is this a dark hint that the victim was not the usual pig, sheep, or goat, but a human being? Pausanias is more forthcoming about other details: he says that the Arcadians believed that every year at this barbaric ceremony some unfortunate worshipper was transformed into a wolf. In this condition he was forced to wander for nine years, but if he managed to avoid eating human flesh during that time, he was able to regain his human shape. If, on the other hand, he had tasted it – and being a werewolf he might find that hard to avoid – he was doomed to remain a wild beast forever. There was even a sports story associated with the ritual: Pausanias was told of an Arcadian boxer called Damarchus who had won an Olympic victory around 400 BC after having changed into a wolf and then back again nine years later. According to Pausanias, this ritual originated from a myth. The myth had it that a legendary king of Arcadia, King Lykaon, had sacrificed a baby to Zeus and was instantly changed into a wolf for his crime.

Pausanias took all this with a pinch or two of salt. He was an educated and widely travelled man, although not unduly sceptical. Throughout his account of his travels, he exhibits a consistent belief in the existence of the gods and heroes, but he is often willing to criticize the myths and rituals relating to them. In this instance, perhaps surprisingly, he makes it clear that he believes the story of Lykaon's original vile sacrifice, but that he does not believe that anyone ever turns into a wolf during the Lykaian ritual, nor that the Arcadian team at the Olympics ever had an unnaturally hirsute boxer in its ranks. But if Pausanias' attitude to these myths was down-to-earth, that of the ordinary contemporary Greek in fact, it appears to have been significantly different from that of the Arcadians. The geographical specificity of Pausanias' version is important, for Arcadia was in every respect an isolated place. Shielded by its arid mountains and impenetrable valleys, this highland region had escaped the invasion of the Dorian peoples that all other parts of Greece had experienced a little over a thousand years before. Arcadians had retained their own dialect, their own superstitions and religious beliefs, and had in most senses fallen behind the rest of the Greek world. The other Greeks thought them 'older than the moon', and found it easy to believe of their mountain fastness that it was the abode of witches.

As with most Greek myths, there is more than one version of the Lykaon story. Apollodorus (who is reckoned the best of the ancient Greek mythographers, but who like Pausanias wrote in the second century AD) has left another account: that Lykaon had fifty unpleasant sons and Zeus visited them in disguise to see if they were as vicious as he had heard. They killed a boy and mixed his innards with the sacrificial meats offered to the stranger. Zeus overturned the table in disgust (at the place known as Trapezos, or 'Table') and blasted Lykaon and his sons with a thunderbolt. After this, he further punished their sins by sending the world-wide deluge that only Deucalion and his wife survived, bobbing on top of the flood waters in their ark.

The versions of the Lykaon story given by Pausanias and Apollodorus are often treated as virtually interchangeable, but although in many ways the two stories are obviously related – they both feature the figure of Lykaon and the killing of a child – it is clear that there are important differences. Pausanias was a traveller and a geographer, writing about the physical sights and rituals he encountered, not a professional mythographer like Apollodorus. In his account of the Lykaian sacrifice Pausanias is recording a strictly local ritual and its accompanying myth, whereas the version Apollodorus tells is much more like other heroic myths. Apollodorus includes the traditional figure of Zeus dispensing thunderbolts, the customary identification of an unusual geographical feature in Greece with the mythical action, and the detail that the ultimate consequence of Lykaon's misdeeds is the well-known deluge of Deucalion. But Apollodorus' apparently confident assimilation of the Lykaon story into the pattern of Greek Olympian religion is misleading. The most noticeable feature of his telling of the tale is that it immediately brings to mind the much better known myth of Tantalus and Pelops.

The story runs that Tantalus invited the gods to dinner and cooked his own son Pelops to see if their immortal palates would spot the difference. Demeter, still mourning the fate of Persephone, absentmindedly picked at a shoulder, but the other gods immediately saw through the gruesome deception. Pelops was brought back to life and given an ivory shoulder to replace the one Demeter had chewed, while Tantalus was horribly punished by being placed in Tartarus, the region below even Hades, fated eternally to stretch for food and drink kept just out of his reach (hence the English word 'tantalize'). This Tantalus myth is both much more widely known and more fully integrated with other Olympian myths than either version of the Lykaon story. One suspects that because the Lykaon story shared one essential detail with it, the sacrilegious offering of a child's flesh to the gods, Apollodorus has used the pattern of the better known Tantalus myth to make the specific, local Arcadian story more accessible to a wider Greek audience.

Another intriguing element in Apollodorus' version is his attachment of the Deucalion myth to this story. Such 'deluge myths' are widespread in many ancient cultures, but it is most probable that the origin of the deluge myth we have in the Deucalion story lies in southern Mesopotamia. The ancient Mesopotamians built their cities along the banks of the river Euphrates. In this precarious position they were liable each spring to catastrophic flooding, and to account for these disasters, the Mesopotamians told stories of their angry gods punishing mankind's sins. This Asiatic myth spread gradually outwards over the succeeding generations, perhaps best known today in its Hebrew guise as the story of Noah and his ark. The myth reached Greece, but the Greek writers tell so many versions of the story that it is clear that they were uneasy about assimilating it into their mythology. This is understandable when one considers that a country of low rainfall and good drainage like Greece could hardly appreciate the terrible power of destructive floods. In Egypt, a country in which a flood has almost exactly the reverse meaning, where the annual flooding of the Nile Delta brings not destruction but renewed fertility, the myth never took hold at all.

But the Greeks persevered with it, various writers chipping away to make it fit into their particular cosmogony.

Apollodorus may have seen reason to connect the deluge with Arcadia because, to add to all their other troubles, the Arcadians had a little local difficulty with flooding. Although their annual rainfall was very low, the only drainage in the eastern upland plateau of Arcadia was a curious system of underground channels running down through the limestone rocks to spread the precious water onto the rich coastal plains miles below. If these channels became blocked and it should happen to rain heavily, as it very occasionally did, a whole highland valley could be inundated. Although this was not such a disaster for the poor subsistence agriculturalists of Arcadia as having whole cities washed away had been for the Mesopotamians, it may have been enough for Apollodorus to have given the story a tentative home in Arcadia. It is possible, of course, that he heard a version of the *Epic of Gilgamesh*, and made that further connection between Mesopotamia and Arcadia.

But Apollodorus' version is too rich in mythological resonance, too literary, to allow many firm conclusions to be drawn from it. The fact that Pausanias visited the actual place in which this myth was set makes his account more convincing evidence of what the Arcadians themselves believed. What is more, in addition to the myth, Pausanias gives details, murky admittedly, of the rites that accompanied it. This combination of myth and ritual usually produces the equivalent of a feeding frenzy among the big fish of the anthropological and mythological worlds, because one school believes passionately that myths are invented by primitive peoples to explain their strange rituals, while another believes just as passionately that rituals arise out of existing myths. Such arguments are irrelevant here, because the coexistence of the Lykaon myth and ritual – whichever came first – simply reinforces the idea that what Pausanias discovered proves that the Arcadians firmly believed it possible for men to be turned into wolves.

This might not seem surprising, considering how prevalent in traditional cultures the blurring of distinctions between animal and human could be. But scholars protest that this was in general less true of the Greeks at the height of their classical civilization. Even the widespread mythic idea of transformation into an animal is somewhat unusual in Greek belief. In general, it is noticeable that the Greek gods are all like men: the Greek religion is anthropomorphic to a remarkable degree. The classical Greeks imagined a time, not when men and animals talked together, but when men and gods dined together. And just as other cultures recognized that this Golden Age was in the past and kept men and animals in rigorously separate categories, so the Greeks kept men and gods apart: although heroes might have a god or goddess for a parent, no mortal (with the notable exception of Heracles) ever became a god. But the theriomorphic past, when Greek religious thought was perhaps more like the Palaeolithic cosmologies, is often hinted at. The Greek poets, for example, customarily referred to Athena and Hera as 'owl-faced' and 'cow-faced' respectively, a clue that these two goddesses were once worshipped in animal form. Instances of immortal shape-shifting can be found elsewhere among the Greek myths – Io turns into a cow, Zeus into a bull, and so on – although these animalistic elements of Greek religion sometimes seem remnants only of older beliefs.

However, considerably heavier hints of theriomorphic beliefs are to be found in myths and rituals associated with Arcadia. Here it was, for example, that the gods Poseidon and Demeter were worshipped in horse-headed form, although of course a similar figure in obverse form – the *hippokentauros* or centaur – was well-known to all Greeks. The more significant story of Zeus' childhood was known in a variety of versions, most of them set on Crete, where his mother, Rhea, was generally said to have gone to escape the attentions of Kronos, who wanted to murder their new-born son. According to one version, two female bears raised the infant-god, hiding him in a cave on Mount Ida, and in gratitude Zeus transformed them into stars in the heavens, the constellations of Ursa Major and Ursa Minor. The Arcadians, however, believed that Zeus had been born, not in Crete, but in a region of Arcadia called Creteia, and one of his nurses had been not a bear, but the daughter of Lykaon. This version seems to have arisen out of confusion with the story of Lykaon's daughter Kallisto, who was Zeus' mistress and was herself, according to another account, turned into the constellation of the Great Bear. Kallisto was also conflated with the goddess Artemis, who at the sanctuary of Brauron in Attica was served in her cult by little girls in saffron-coloured dresses who were known as 'bears'. In fact the

Arcadians regarded themselves as bear-people, arguing that their name was derived from *arktos* or *arkos*, a variant Greek term for bear. All this demonstrates either how unsystematic the Arcadian mythography was, or how confused modern scholars are in their attempts to unravel it. Nevertheless, it is a suggestive confusion, hinting at the continuing interdependence of bear- and wolf-cults, and implying an ancient substratum of belief that tended to be disregarded or misinterpreted by the more sophisticated classical Greeks.

For these supposedly obsolete ideas to have survived in Arcadia may mean that they, and the Lykaon myth in particular, supplied some specific need of these fierce mountain people. The Lykaon myth's most obvious purpose is to express a taboo against the eating of human flesh, although ironically Pausanias suggests that human sacrifice was demanded by the barbaric Lykaian Zeus. The whole ceremony was surrounded by terrible taboos, the idea that one of the participants was doomed to become a wolf being only the most horrific. The very area of the sacrifice, the *tenemos*, was ringed around with fearful caveats: it was said that anyone who entered it lost their shadow and would die within the year. Naturally the reputation of such a place has fascinated archaeologists, and in 1902 an expedition set out to excavate the earth-and-ash altar on the peak Pausanias describes. The archaeologists dug down through bones and ash to a depth of four and a half feet before hitting bedrock. However the fruits of their digging cast two major doubts on Pausanias' evidence. First, coins and pottery found mixed in with the ash and bones suggested that the site had been used from about 600 BC only into the fourth century BC, stopping well before Pausanias' time. Pausanias seems therefore to have been passing on local tales of some antiquity, rather than his own or a contemporary Arcadian's firsthand observation. Much more damning, however, was that although bone fragments of several species of cow, pig, and smaller animals could be distinguished among the ashes of the altar, no human bones were found.

W. Arens, in his book *The Man-Eating Myth*, has pointed out how often the existence of cannibalism turns out to rely on hearsay evidence: anthropologists find that is the neighbouring tribe that is accused of practising such disgusting rites, never the tribe they are themselves investigating. Interestingly, much the same can be said for evidence of lycanthropy in the classical world. Herodotus, for example, writing in the fifth century BC, recorded that the Scythians believed that their neighbours, the Neuri, turned into wolves once a year, and that nothing could shake them from what Herodotus thought of as a ridiculous belief. With this in mind, it might be possible to write off the evidence of Arcadian cannibalism and wolf-rituals as simply arising from cultural slanders made by the other Greeks who regarded Arcadia as backward and isolated. Nevertheless, although the archaeological evidence rules out the possibility of Pausanias having seen human sacrifice on Mount Lykaion, it need not necessarily mean that his Arcadian informants were deliberately misinforming him. It is quite possible that any observer of the Lykaian ceremony could have come away believing that he had witnessed human sacrifice. Human sacrifice was extremely rare, if indeed it was ever practised, among the Greeks, but many myths tell of the gods demanding a human sacrifice in which an animal is substituted at the last minute. In many sacrificial rituals the animal was treated with such respect that it was imbued with human characteristics. The Lykaian ritual may have deliberately mimicked human sacrifice, with an animal being substituted for the human victim at the last moment in such a way that both the worshippers and perhaps the awesome Lykaian Zeus himself were deliberately deceived.

Such deception would be nothing unusual in Greek sacrificial ritual, for in a sense the whole practice of sacrifice was founded on a lie. The Greeks were enthusiastic participants in sacrifice. It was by far the most significant element of their religious life. They slaughtered vast numbers of animals as offerings to the gods. Bulls, cows, goats, pigs, sheep, even dogs, all would be garlanded and led in procession, often perfumed and lauded, before their blood was spilt and their warm corpses flayed and hacked apart by the sacrificial altar. The idea behind it was, as usual, based on the Greeks' conception of their gods as men: the Greeks were sharing their food with the immortals as an act of worship, restoring for a moment the shared pleasures of the Golden Age. But the division of spoils between man and god in this later, mundane age was unequal, for the Greek priest was, in addition to his sacerdotal duties, a simple human butcher. When the sacrificial victim had been drained of blood, its skin and fat

stripped off, its limbs unjointed, the priest made sure it was men
who got the protein-rich meat and the gods who got the rest. He
would smear lumps of the excess fat around the bones of the
animal, stuff them back inside its skin, and burn this grisly
offering in the sacrificial fire. The Greeks were mortal and needed
to eat, after all, and the richly scented smoke drifting up from
their sacrificial fires offered the immortals something they could
enjoy in their turn. But this understandable substitution caused
the Greeks to suffer a sneaking fear that they were cheating the
gods and might be called to account for it. One of their myths tells
of the punishment that Prometheus endured after fooling Zeus
into thinking he had sacrificed an entire animal by wrapping up
the bones and fat in the animal skin to make it look whole again,
a process that exactly mimics that of the priests during their
sacrificial rituals, and clearly echoes the prehistoric practice of
animal reconstruction.

In addition to this guilt at the deception inherent in sacrifice,
the Greeks also felt some concern at the fate of the animal. The
brutality they exhibited in so casually hacking to death thousands
of animals in public ceremonies had first been engendered during
their days as hunter-gatherers. The Greeks had by Pausanias'
time abandoned the hunting lifestyle for probably as many as five
thousand years, and had long since settled down to agriculture,
but their aggressive urges apparently remained and found an
outlet at the sacrificial altar. Yet they shared the ambivalent
feelings of prehistoric hunters towards their prey. These mixed
emotions were expressed in the tendency to praise and humanize
the sacrificial victim, almost as if they felt obliged to apologize to
the beast for slitting its throat. And if the Greeks in general felt
guilty at animal sacrifice, much greater guilt would be engendered in a backward area like Arcadia where the chill spectre of
human sacrifice and cannibalism added to these uneasy fears.
The sacrifice of human flesh, and the eating of it, were to the
Arcadians then, as they are today, among the most powerful of
taboos.

Walter Burkert suggests that the sacrifices offered on Mount
Lykaion were originally part of the rituals of a wolf-brotherhood
among the hunting ancestors of the Arcadians, and may once
have been a terrifying initiation ceremony designed to impress
upon the young men joining the 'wolf-pack' the importance of

their calling. The initiands may even have been expected to live in the wild like a wolf for part of their training: the Spartans, a little further south on the Peloponnesus, incorporated similar exercises into their long military education. According to his theory, the motif of human sacrifice and cannibalism would have arisen out of a very specific use of taboo to ensure the forming of bonds of group feeling among the wolf-brothers.

Yet the fact that the punishment for breaking such a taboo should be transformation into a wolf can also be explained in simple terms, without recourse to ancient ideas, the most obvious being that the forests of Arcadia were notoriously ridden with wolves. Such a legend will obviously thrive where there is actual physical danger to humans and domestic livestock from a large number of wolves in the immediate locality. Wolves are feared most where they are plentiful, where they are believed to have strength of numbers enough to overcome their natural fear and attack humans and eat their flesh. It follows then that the violator of a taboo against the eating of human flesh should be turned into the most feared devourer of human flesh in the vicinity. Another factor may have reinforced the choice of the wolf as the accursed *alter ego*, something as simple and trivial as a pun: the names of Mount Lykaion and King Lykaon happen to have the same first syllable as the Greek word for 'wolf', *lykos*. This explanation certainly occurred to the Greeks. One later writer, perhaps thinking this too banal, offers the theory that the legendary King Lykaon originated as an old god to whom human sacrifice was made, with a non-Hellenic name similar to *lykos*.

There is another Arcadian version of the werewolf legend which the Greeks are recorded as believing. Pliny tells the story after a Greek writer called Euanthes. In this version of the story, the members of the family of Antaeus drew lots to choose a young man of the family to undergo the ordeal, and led him to the edge of a lake in Arcadia. He took off his clothes and hung them on a tree, then swam across the lake. He became a wolf but eight years later, provided he had not tasted human flesh, he could swim back across the lake and resume human shape. This is a werewolf story much closer to Petronius' telling of it: the werewolf-to-be must remove his clothing before the transformation can take place, and the magical agent of transformation is again a liquid, although the limpid waters of a mountain lake have a poetic charm that a soldier's stream of waste matter cannot match. As with Petronius' soldier, Euanthes' werewolf is able to return to the place where his clothes were originally discarded and resume human shape. The setting of the story in Arcadia leads some writers to assume that it must be identical with the Lykaon myth, but this is not justified by Pliny's text. Although Pliny mentions both the Lykaian sacrifice and the Olympic werewolf boxer Damarchus (the name corrupted to Demaenetus), it is clear that he has not taken these details from Euanthes' account but from distinct sources. That Euanthes' story is a separate narrative re-emphasizes that the Arcadians, in particular among ancient Greeks, held strong werewolf beliefs.

Although Greek religious thought had a great influence over the Romans, hence Petronius, it is tempting to surmise that, as a creative writer, Petronius himself was personally more stimulated by Greek literature. There he would find the idea of human metamorphosis into an animal given memorable expression in the earliest Greek literature extant, in Book 10 of Homer's *Odyssey*, the great epic written probably during the middle and latter part of the eighth century BC, which tells of the adventures of Odysseus on his return from the Trojan War, a poem with a surprising number of traces of werewolf beliefs. For example, Odysseus' grandfather is Autolykos (whose name means 'Himself-like-a-wolf'), and it is significant that it should be the wolfish grandfather who initiates the youthful Odysseus in the ancient secrets of hunting boar. It is during this hunt that Odysseus receives the wound that will eventually reveal his identity on his return to Ithaca. Autolykos was not associated with werewolf-ridden Arcadia, but with the geographically similar Mount Parnassus, on the north side of the Gulf of Corinth. There, the native Delphians were unambiguously said to worship the wolf. They believed themselves to have originated in Lykoreia, a place whose name means 'wolf-mountain', and Mount Parnassus was one of the leading candidates in various versions of the Deucalion myth for the site of the landing of the ark. Prominent members of Delphic society traced their ancestry right back to Deucalion.[1]

A more overt description of animal transformation from Homer concerns the beautiful Circe, on whose island Odysseus and his men land their ship. Odysseus sends out a search party to reconnoitre, and they come across Circe's house of polished stones. The house is surrounded by wolves and lions, tamed by Circe's sorcery, who greet Odysseus' men like large affectionate dogs, standing on their hind legs and wagging their tails. Circe invites the terrified men inside, and feeds them a mixture of cheese and barley, clear honey, and Pramnian wine, laced with drugs to make them forget their native land. The drink has a transforming effect on them. 'They had the head, the voice, and bristles, and the shape of a pig, but their minds were the same as before.' Once they have drunk the brew, Circe strikes them with her wand and drives them into her pig pens, where she feeds them acorns and chestnuts until Odysseus himself comes to the house to rescue them (and, as is the hero's right, beds the beautiful sorceress).

Although it is not very clear why Circe turns the men into swine, there are a number of details here which recur in later werewolf stories. Odysseus is protected against her magic by an occult herb called *moly*, black at the root and with a flower like milk, which is revealed to him by the god Hermes (who in some traditions is said to be the father of Autolykos, hence Odysseus' great-grandfather). 'It is difficult for mortal men to pick it up, but to the gods everything is possible,' Odysseus explains. Circe's second appearance in the *Odyssey* features animal sacrifice and necromancy: in Book 11, following her instructions, Odysseus digs a trench and fills it with a liquid offering to the dead, a mixture of honey, milk, wine, and water, mingled with the blood of two freshly-slaughtered black sheep (Homer really knew how to write a recipe). This attracts the shades of the dead like flies to a carcass, and by drinking the bloody mixture, they regain for a short time the ability to communicate with the living.

Although the whole subject of magic, and in particular animal transformation, is a proper subject for the austere grandeur of the Homeric epic, in the later phases of classical civilization magic became set on a path towards the prosaic and mundane. This was not from any lack of interest in magic on the Greeks' part. They were constantly adapting all sorts of obscure religions and cults to their own myth systems, although very often these foreign imports became mangled in the process. It has recently been fashionable to see in Circe, for instance, a goddess of a former religion or a priestess of a Mother Earth cult, who by the time she features in Greek mythology has become evil and dangerous (although not too evil and dangerous for Odysseus to accept her offer of a bed). It is clear that she also has many attributes of an ancient 'mistress of the animals': her house is guarded by them, and like the Mesopotamian Ishtar and the Greek Artemis she has the power of transforming men into animals. Another such misunderstanding is the source of the very word *magic*, which is derived from *magoi*, a Median tribe or caste of priests in ancient Persia. But however ancient and elevated its origins, the study and practice of magic had become a much more down-to-earth, everyday affair by the later Greek era, and it was in this environment that the werewolf legend was passed down the generations.

One place in the post-Homeric Greek world such quotidian magic was practised was the cosmopolitan city of Alexandria, new capital of Ptolemaic Egypt. The sources for this are a number of contemporary manuscripts, usually papyri, detailing magical spells and operations, together with the corroborating evidence of Theocritus, a Greek poet who lived in Alexandria at some time during the first quarter of the third century BC. During his stay he had the opportunity to observe at first hand the middle-class Greeks who had settled there, and he produced a few realistic poems about daily life in the great city, including his second *idyll*, a dramatic monologue given the title *Pharmakeutria*, a word which is usually taken to mean 'witch' or 'sorceress', derived from *pharmakon*, a versatile word meaning 'drug', 'poison', 'remedy', 'medicine', or 'spell'. The sorceress in the poem is a young girl called Simaetha, who prepares a magic formula to win back the love of her athlete boyfriend. These are actual magical practices in Theocritus' poem, corroborated by many of the operations he describes appearing also in the contemporary papyri. During Simaetha's recitation she addresses various spells and incantations to the full moon in the sky and to Hecate in the underworld, the ancient lunar hunting deity having become the guiding spirit for sorceresses such as her by the classical era.

Although Theocritus does not mention lycanthropy in the poem, his *idyll*, full of realistic magical details, was used by the Roman poet Virgil as the basis for his eighth *eclogue*. Writing two hundred years after Theocritus, Virgil stays close to the original story line, merely leaving out the details of those magical operations which were presumably foreign to him and adding a happy ending – the magic works and the lover returns. But his most significant addition is the introduction of a werewolf: 'Moeris himself gave me these herbs and poisons gathered near the Black Sea, where they grow in abundance,' Simaetha sings. 'I have often seen Moeris turn into a wolf by their power and hide in the forest, and often seen him conjure up souls from the depths of their tombs and move crops that have been planted to other fields.'

This would appear to be a very significant moment in the history of the werewolf: the first appearance in literature of a lycanthrope who has transformed himself voluntarily. Until this poem, written some thirty years before the beginning of the Christian era, most of the available literary evidence is that werewolves and other were-animals are forcibly transformed against their will, usually as a punishment for some moral transgression or by the arbitrary whim of a god. The shamanic theme in which men transform themselves into animals voluntarily through magical ritual had not then been depicted in literary terms. The werewolf in this poem, like both the soldier in Petronius' later story and the prehistoric wolf-brothers, has the power to transform himself at will. Petronius does not tell us his soldier's magical qualifications, but we know from Virgil's poem that Moeris is a warlock who has knowledge of rare herbs from far-off places. Virgil evidently recognizes this kind of sorcery as Greek in origin: the Black Sea, where Moeris gathers his magical herbs, was one of the traditional homes of Greek witches, another being Thessaly, such locations representing for the Greeks the extremities of the known world. Virgil's Moeris is quite a sorcerer. He has necromantic powers – he can conjure up souls from their tombs; he has telekinetic powers – he can move crops from field to field; and he has the power of lycanthropic transformation. And yet he is not as terrifying a werewolf as he might be. In his feral disguise he merely hides in the woods, rather than slaughtering and eating domestic animals or people, and in his role as provider of the rare herbs that bring back Simaetha's lover, he is clearly, within the particular world of the poem, a sympathetic character. Nevertheless, it is this portrayal of a werewolf – a magician who takes on the shape of a wolf for his own magical, and by extension wicked, ends – that the prosecutors of the later European witch-craze would prefer to stress.

It is clear that Virgil has incorporated strong Greek influences in this poem, especially magical beliefs and practices, just as he had drawn on the example of Homer in writing his epic *Æneid*. That poem sets out to create a myth of national origin for the Roman people, something which the new regime of the emperor Augustus clearly desired. An older myth of national origin shows another possible influence on Virgil's introduction of the werewolf, the story of Rome's foundation by Romulus and Remus, the twins suckled by a she-wolf. Augustus himself took a strong personal interest in this myth, and even toyed with the idea of adopting Romulus as his imperial name before rejecting it for its fratricidal implications. On the western side of the Palatine hill at Rome was the cave of Lupercus, the legendary site of the she-wolf's rescue of the infants, which Augustus had restored as part of a programme of raising this myth to the status of a national cult. The festival associated with Lupercus still flourished and needed no encouragement from the new emperor.

The rites of Lupercalia were supposed to commemorate a rather curious episode in the life of Rome's founders. The two heroes and their followers, stripped naked, were competing with each other in mock-battle, while priests prepared a sacrifice of goats to the god Faunus. Shepherds warned Romulus and Remus that brigands were making off with their cattle, and they set off in pursuit, not bothering to take their weapons. Remus returned the victor, and shared out the sacrificial meats with his followers, the Fabii. Romulus returned shortly afterwards, saw the bare bones of the goats, and laughed ruefully at the defeat of his Quinctilii and their consequent hunger. The festival of Lupercalia involved the sacrifice of goats and a dog, after which well-born young men divided into *luperci Quinctiales* and *luperci Fabiani* ran through crowds of onlookers dressed only in loincloths cut from the hides of the sacrificed animals, lashing out with thongs, called *februa*, or Juno's cloak, beating out a charmed circle to keep away wolves and other fearsome things. The festival was a complex affair, combining elements of an initiation rite – the young *luperci* were 'blooded' at the outset and were supposed to laugh as their faces were smeared – as well as a fertility rite, for a blow from one of the thongs was said to prevent sterility in women. If such a festival seems unsophisticated for the Romans, there was nothing unexalted about it. As well as the high-born participants, the ceremony was attended by the Vestal Virgins, who presented the first ears of the corn from the previous harvest. The most celeb-rated *luperci* was no less a figure than Mark Antony, who made his fateful offer of the imperial crown to Julius Caesar in his role as master of the *luperci Quinctiales*. The festival continued until AD 494, when it was converted by the pope into the Christian feast known as Candlemas. That Augustus should take advantage of this festival as part of his programme for consolidating his imperial power underlines its significance to the Roman imagination.

As for the real origins of these beliefs, explanations similar to those for the Lykaon myth have been proposed. A combination of imported myth, etymological coincidence, and totemistic significance can be said to explain all. The myth-as-pun theory begins with the name Lupercalia itself, which seems to be derived from the Latin word for wolf, *lupus*, but becomes much more intricate when dealing with the famous wild fig tree (*Ficus ruminalis*) where the twins were first exposed. This tree was sacred to a goddess Rumina (*ruma* means 'breast', which may have suggested the suckling theme) and the resemblance be-tween the name Romulus and the word *ruminalis* could account for the connection between the tree and the city's founder being made by local historians. The figure of the nurturing wolf is one of widespread antiquity in many cultures, but in this specific instance may well be an importation originating in Greece. A Cretan legend has it that Miletus, son of Apollo and a daughter of Minos, having been exposed by his mother, was suckled by she-wolves and later brought up by shepherds. Miletus subse-quently fled to Asia Minor and founded the city called after him. The Etruscans knew this myth, and it probably found its way to Rome via that route. Cynical Romans were not above suggesting other explanations of the legend. Livy, who was the official historian of the Augustan regime much as Virgil and Horace were its official poets, quotes one streetwise explanation, that the twins had actually been suckled by a whore (*lupa*, or 'she-wolf'). The wolf was for the Romans a symbol both of fierceness and, as the Lupercalian rites demonstrate, of fertility (or lechery, to take Livy's point of view). Its aspect as a symbol of fertility was invoked in the Roman marriage custom whereby the bride anointed her husband's doorpost with wolf's fat.[2]

In addition to such officially sanctioned beliefs, there is evi-dence that magical rites of all kinds were practised in Augustan

Rome. Often this took the form of ritualized cursing, by which one's dislike of someone could be formalized and made magically effective by various spells and incantations, although the many surviving recitations designed to alleviate pain and illness show the beneficial side of such magic. This unofficial magical activity so worried Augustus that he set out to run a political campaign to crush all forms of witchcraft. Harsh, repressive laws were hurriedly passed: one young man who dared to try out the prescribed spell for stomach disorders at a public baths, touching the marble tiles and then his chest while reciting the seven Greek vowels, was arrested, tortured, and executed.[3] Through Maecenas, Augustus enlisted his two greatest poets, Virgil and Horace, as propagandists for his anti-witchcraft crusade. It must be said that Virgil's *eclogue* hardly seems adequate to the task: Simaetha strikes the reader as a pleasant young witch. A much better performance in this respect is given by Horace, who wrote two poems featuring the loathsome hag Canidia which deploy the twin weapons of fear and ridicule against her. In one, Horace describes in gruesome detail the witches, led by Canidia, burying alive and then killing a boy so that they can grind up his liver for a love potion; in the other, he describes a wooden statue of Priapus watching Canidia and her friends digging for human bones at night and scaring them away with a gigantic fart.

Petronius' story did not then represent some fluke survival from prehistory. Another writer who worked with similar material, but a little later than Petronius, was Apuleius, the author of *Metamorphosis*, or, as it is often known, *The Golden Ass*. Apuleius was a Platonist and travelling lecturer of the second century AD, who took a keen personal interest in magic and occult science. He himself had been accused of witchcraft after having married a rich and attractive widow a few years his senior. Her relatives brought charges of occult practice against him, presumably because they wanted to avoid her fortune going to a foreigner (Apuleius was born in North Africa). His defence of himself at the subsequent trial has survived, and shows him to have been perfectly serious in his belief in the antiquity and distinguished precedents of the *magus*. But his most famous work is the novel *Metamorphosis*, in which the hero Lucius travels to Thessaly to study witchcraft. This work gives a very different idea of the dignity of the magician who seeks to transform himself into an animal.

Having arrived in Thessaly, Lucius befriends a girl called Photis, who works as a maid for a famous local witch called Pamphile. One night Photis tells Lucius that Pamphile is going to transform herself into a bird in order to fly to her lover, and she and Lucius hide themselves behind the bedroom door in order to witness this dramatic event. As they watch, Pamphile first strips herself completely, then rubs herself all over with a special ointment. All the time she is doing this, she mutters obscurities at her lamp and shakes her limbs vigorously. As they watch, her outlines begin to quiver, feathers and wings sprout, her nose becomes crooked and horny, and her nails take on the shape of talons. Pamphile has turned into an owl (reminiscent as she does so both of the Sumerian she-demon Ardat Lili, with her taloned hands, and 'owl-faced' Athena).

When Pamphile has flown off into the night, Lucius begs Photis to allow him to take some of the special ointment, and he greedily rubs his body with it, flapping his arms when he is covered with the stuff. But Photis has given him the wrong ointment and no feathers or wings appear anywhere on Lucius' body. 'Instead my hair turned to bristles and my tender skin into hide; my fingers and toes seemed to shrink and contract into hooves, and from the end of my spine a long tail began to sprout. My face became enormous, my mouth enlarged, my nostrils dilated, my lips pendulous, my ears oversized and hairy. The only good thing about this wretched transformation was that my genitals increased in size enormously; it had been getting difficult for me to satisfy Photis.' Lucius realizes that he has been transformed into a donkey.

At one level, this story shares many features with earlier were-animal tales. Like the soldier in Petronius' story and the young member of the Antaeus family in Euanthes' version, Pamphile has to take off her clothes before the transformation can be effected. She herself has no difficulty in changing her shape, in the venerable tradition of female demons or their servants which stretches from Ardat Lili to the medieval concept of the witch, a change which is undergone at night-time, although here the moon or moonlight is not specifically mentioned. She uses a form of magical charm to effect the transformation – an ointment this time – which has a similar role to the urine in Petronius' story. But the most striking difference between this story and earlier werewolf legends is that this is frankly comic. Lucius is gloriously laughable in his new guise, and the comic effect of his transformation was picked up and used by many later writers, notably Shakespeare in his portrayal of Bottom in *A Midsummer Night's Dream*. In one sense, the reader's sympathies are with the person who has been transformed against his wishes, but such sympathy is considerably mitigated by the fact that Lucius was consciously seeking his transformation, and was simply expecting to be turned into something more dignified than an ass. This is a were-animal story written not much more than a century after Petronius by a man with an acknowledged serious interest in the occult, yet it arouses little more than unrestrained laughter.

Petronius had a rich lode of sources to mine for his werewolf story, although of course he may not have been consciously influenced by all of them. He would certainly have known the episode of Circe transforming Odysseus' men into swine, and he may possibly have known Euanthes' werewolf legend, as well probably as Virgil's reworking of Theocritus' poem. But whether or not he knew all these sources directly, his first-century Roman world was steeped in the traditions of magic, shape-shifting, and animal transformation that provided an appreciative audience for his quintessential version of the werewolf legend. The point of entry for werewolf beliefs in the Mediterranean world was Greek, to judge from the ancient ritual of Lykaion and its accompanying myth which Pausanias was told of in Arcadia, a myth circumscribed by fearsome taboos against the sacrifice and eating of human flesh. Nevertheless, this primitive idea of animal transformation, as something terrifying and uncontrollable, only to be solved by the intervention of gods or heroes, was modified throughout the classical age of antiquity until by Apuleius' day it was a subject fit for comic treatment. But the modern reader is left to question Petronius' position in all this. How serious is he? Does he expect the reader to laugh or shiver at Niceros' tale?

There are several indications in the novel that Petronius was taking the subject as lightly as Apuleius after him, particularly Niceros' opening announcement that his story will be pure fun and that some of the cleverer guests will probably laugh at it. Niceros' repeated assertions of his truthfulness might also make one suspicious of the author's intentions. Petronius is showing his sophisticated Roman audience the kind of superstitious stories ex-slaves tell each other to wile away the evening, and their very status as provincial *nouveaux riches* practically guarantees that their stories should be laughable and unbelievable. Trimalchio, king among these freedmen, is certainly pleased with such a 'horror story', as he calls it, and immediately launches into one of his own, featuring witches, changelings, and mysterious deaths caused by sorcery. 'Ah! yes,' he says at the end of this grim tale, 'I would beg you to believe there are wise women and night-riders who can turn the whole world upside down.' After this comes the narrator's admission that by now the lamps were swimming before his eyes and the room was changing shape. Is this a gentle hint that these are stories best told late on in the evening, when senses are dulled by food and wine? But Petronius cannot be pinned down so easily. It is a feature of his literary realism that his intentions remain inscrutable. He presents a vivid imitation of the sights and sounds of southern Italian freedmen at raucous play, and makes no comment on their actions whatever, not even through the mouthpiece of his novel's narrator. He profits as a novelist by this, in that he can tell a werewolf story which at once satisfies both the sense of terror of the credulous and the sense of humour of the sophisticated. Later ages were to prove tragically incapable of maintaining such a delightful balancing act.

4

The Seeds of Superstition

The herded wolves, bold only to pursue;
The obscene ravens, clamourous o'er the dead.

SHELLEY,
Adonais

The Old Norse *Völsungasaga* describes the heroic actions of members of the Völsung family, tracing their ancestry back ultimately to Odin, the mythical lord of hosts and giver of victory. The first of these heroes to receive extended treatment in the saga is Sigmund, eldest son of Völsung. Sigmund's natural son, Sinfjötli, who was conceived by Sigmund's incestuous union with his own twin-sister Signy, joins him in the forest, and together they roam around, searching out men to kill:

> Now once on a certain occasion Sigmund and Sinfjötli ranged farther than ever into the woods to get riches for themselves; they found a hut and two men with heavy gold rings asleep inside the hut. They had been bewitched, because there were wolf-skins hanging over them, and only on every tenth half-day could they come out of those skins; they were both the sons of kings. Sigmund and Sinfjötli put on those wolf-skins, and could not come out of them to resume their human shapes and natures, until the time described before. Now they uttered wolf-howls, yet they could distinguish each other's voices. They betook themselves into the forest, each of them going his own way. They had agreed between themselves, however, that they would attack though there were seven against them, but no more, for then he who was being attacked should utter his wolf-howl.[1]

Sinfjötli, however, has from his earliest youth shown himself marked out to walk in the footsteps of his heroic father-uncle, and he now shows his mettle by taking on eleven men alone and defeating them all, although the effort exhausts him. His arrogance in attacking so many without howling for assistance enrages Sigmund. He springs at the young upstart and slashes his windpipe open with his wolfish fangs, then carries the young werewolf to a hut in the woods and watches over his body. One day he sees two weasels passing by the hut: one bites the other in the windpipe, then fetches a certain leaf which heals the wound. Sigmund goes out and sees a raven flying towards him, bearing just such a leaf. Sigmund places the leaf on Sinfjötli's wound, and the young werewolf jumps up, fully restored. The two heroes return to their wolf's-lair, and await the time when they can put off their wolf-skins. Then they burn the skins, 'so that they could never again bring bad luck to anyone'. 'In their bewitched shapes they had done many a heroic deed in King Siggeir's realm', the author adds, tantalizingly evoking other werewolf stories too myriad to be contained within this particular saga.

A few scholars have spotted in this lycanthropic episode vestiges of an ancient warrior-initiation rite.[2] As with Autolykos and Odysseus learning to hunt boar on Mount Parnassus, the relationship portrayed here is that between the older father-figure, more experienced in killing techniques, and the younger hero who will one day equal, if not surpass, his teacher. The point is made explicitly in the *Völsungasaga* that this time spent in the forest is to be Sinfjötli's apprenticeship in the ways of the hero, for he is the third of Signy's sons to be sent to Sigmund for such training. Earlier in the saga, Signy tested each child before sending them to Sigmund by sewing a seam through the sleeve of its kirtle into the child's flesh. The first two children cried out when she did this, but Sinfjötli bore it in silence, even when she ripped the kirtle off his arm, taking the flesh with it. The other two sons were sent to Sigmund anyway, but failed the very first test of bravery he gave them, and the wolf-warrior slaughtered them on the spot. Sinfjötli is clearly superior to his feeble half-brothers (his unique engendering in an act of incest makes him doubly a Völsung, hence doubly heroic) but he fails one part of his training: he breaks the rule Sigmund has established that he may take on only seven men before calling for assistance. Obviously his misdemeanour in tackling eleven men single-handed shows the stuff of the true hero, but he is severely punished nevertheless. This is the occasion for the climax of his training, the most severe trial imaginable for any would-be wolf initiate – for Sinfjötli must pass through the barrier between life and death. The magic that brings him back through this fearsome barrier is purely shaman-istic: Sigmund gains his skills as a medicine-man by imitating the behaviour of animals, and the animal bringing him the particular leaf he needs is that familiar spiritual messenger, a bird. Nor is it by any means far-fetched to see in the image of the single leaf in the raven's beak an echo of the small items triumphantly pro-duced by shamans as tokens of their journey to the land of the dead. Here, of course, the bird is explicitly an instrument of divine favour: the raven is Odin's bird, and this is one of several occasions in the saga when Odin intervenes in the action to determine the fate of his Völsung descendants. Once Sinfjötli has returned from the dead, the period of his training is over: Sigmund acknowledges that Sinfjötli has been well-tested, and the wolf-skins are destroyed. Together they set off to enter and destroy the castle of their enemy, King Siggeir, and restore the fortunes of the Völsung family.

It is apparent from certain aspects of the narrative that at least some of the werewolf details are obscure to the author, even though the entire early part of the saga is shot through with the theme. The saga as it now exists was probably put together by a Christian author towards the latter part of the thirteenth century, although it certainly uses material dating well before that time: there is, for example, a reference to Sigmund's heroic exploits in the Scandinavian epic *Beowulf*, which is reckoned to have been composed in Old English some time around the second quarter of the eighth century, and which likewise makes use of earlier non-Christian elements. In the *Völsungasaga* the werewolf theme is apparent from the first few words of the narrative, for the origins of the Völsung family are pinpointed in an act of violent bloodshed just as horrific as Cain's murder of Abel or Romulus's murder of Remus. The family founder, Sigi, one of the sons of Odin, sets out on a hunt with another man's thrall (servant). The thrall's bag at the end of the day is bigger than Sigi's, and Sigi kills him out of jealousy and buries his body in a snowdrift. The thrall's master asks Sigi what has happened to his servant, and

Sigi answers that he lost sight of him in the woods and hasn't seen him since. (This answer so closely mirrors Cain's offhand disclaimer after his murder of Abel that some biblical colouring might be suspected here, but the essential pattern of the story is so ubiquitous that its origin in the saga's non-Christian source is unarguable.[3]) The thrall's body is eventually discovered, and Sigi is made an outlaw for his crime, or as the author has it, 'they proclaimed him a wolf in the holy places': the Old Norse word for wolf, *vargr*, being also the legal term for outlaw. Thus, like Lykaon, Sigi has been turned into a wolf as punishment for his terrible crime, and his descendants, Sigmund and Sinfjötli, assume the shape of wolves for a fixed period.[4] Yet despite Sigi's dreadful crime, he lives on to become a powerful warrior-king and founder of the Völsung dynasty, just as Lykaon was one of Arcadia's first kings and Cain and Romulus were the founders of cities, thus re-enacting the enduring story in which society cannot begin without an act of primordial violence.

That the Völsungs are a wolf-clan is made clearer by their claim of descent from Odin, for the wolf was Odin's particular animal. The wolf, like the raven, is an eater of carrion, a feaster on the slain in battle, and thus an appropriate emblem and messenger for the Norse god of war. Odin was also the god of death, and in one episode in this saga appears as the ferryman, like wolf-eared Charon. Sigmund himself was marked out from his brothers through the agency of a wolf. Before his impregnation of his twin-sister Signy, he and his nine brothers had been captured by the wicked King Siggeir. The brothers were imprisoned in a huge set of stocks set out in the forest, and left alone for the night. Each midnight for nine nights an old she-wolf came and ate one of the brothers, until Sigmund was the only one left. Fearing for his life, Signy sent a trusted servant to him, bringing honey with which Sigmund smeared his face. That tenth midnight the she-wolf came again, but this time she smelled the honey and began licking Sigmund's face. Sigmund took his opportunity and quickly grabbed her tongue between his teeth. She pulled away fiercely, but Sigmund held on and tore her tongue out by the roots, which killed her. 'It is still the saying of some', the author adds, 'that this she-wolf was in fact the mother of King Siggeir, who had changed herself into this shape through trolldom and witchery.' While this last statement openly reveals the lycanthropic beliefs expressed in the story, it is also possible to detect behind this episode the ancient pattern of an initiation rite, in which a band of ten initiands are put out in the forest and pitted in combat against a fearsome supernatural opponent. Only Sigmund passes this test, just as, later in the saga, only Sinfjötli among Signy's sons succeeds in the tests set for him by Sigmund and proves his worth as a member of the Völsung wolf-brotherhood.

The survival of the *Völsungasaga* in this thirteenth-century version preserved for the medieval world the cultural ethos of a people whom mainstream history had passed by. As the *Odyssey* for the classical Greeks, so this saga and others like it mingled the mythology, adventure stories, and historical events of the Germanic nations in the Heroic Age. Exactly how far the *Völsungasaga* represents actual historical detail is a subject for debate, although it is incontestable that a later part of the narrative gives a mythologized version of the exploits of Attila the Hun (Atli in the saga), the most famous of the leaders of the Hunnish nation, whose historical victories over the Burgundians, represented in the saga by the family of the Gjukings, were reversed by his defeat at the hands of a Gothic-Roman army at the Battle of the Catalaunian Fields, probably near Châlons, in 451. Less convincing cases have been made for the historical originals of Sigmund and Sinfjötli, but there is really no need to find any, for these two belong to the earliest part of the epic, the section with roots stretching down deep into prehistory. This first passage, from Sigi's crime to Sigmund's death, forms a distinct sub-saga of its own, in which this particular Germanic people envisaged the origins of society, very much as the Arcadians had done through their Lykaon myth, as stemming from an initial act of violence that allowed man's beast-like nature to burst forth from within. This explosion of aggression, given visual form in the image of Sigmund and Sinfjötli turned into wolves, had to be channelled towards socially useful ends through the strict discipline of their wolf-brotherhood. By its transmission through the medium of the *Völsungasaga*, the werewolf emerged from the mists of prehistory into the light of civilized western Europe, arriving there little changed from its similar emergence in Arcadian Greece. But the survival of such culturally marginal ideas in Christianized medieval Europe was always liable to be denigrated by the authorities as mere 'superstition'.

The survival of the werewolf legend in the north was in part due to the cultural patterns in medieval Europe after the decline of the Roman empire. The two great waves of empire-building, first of Roman imperial expansionism and then of Christian evangelism, eventually produced a western Europe which could, by the early part of the second millennium AD, be divided into two main parts, north and south, most easily distinguishable by language. Those parts which had fallen under the dominance of Rome spoke the vernacular derivatives of Latin, the Romance languages; while an imaginary line, running from Boulogne on the Channel coast, eastwards across the Meuse above Maastricht, down through the Ardennes and across the Moselle, thence up into the Vosges and across into what is now Switzerland, marked the southward extent of the Germanic languages on the continent, the tide-mark where successive waves of unconquered northern barbarians had lapped against the eroding shore of the Roman Empire. The situation was more complicated in the islands of Britain and Ireland after the Normans' reclamation of the southern part of Britain for the Romance-speaking world in 1066: the re-emergence of the imported Germanic dialect which had become the native tongue there would have to wait a few centuries. The Romano-Germanic division was to be one of lasting significance, noticeably reflected, for example, in the differing attitudes taken either side of this line to the great religious questions of the Reformation, and, bar the return of England to the Germanic fold and some minor readjustments at the northern border of France, still maintained today among the language groups of modern Europe.

At the beginning of the second Christian millennium, the southern Romance-language area was dominant in relation to the Germanic north, at least to judge from those parameters of economic wealth, learning, and artistic sophistication by which the status of our predecessors has usually been reckoned, and the triumph over barbaric superstition soon seemed complete. From the lowlands of Scotland down to Sicily, a broadly uniform culture prevailed across medieval western Europe, a culture which was the inheritor of the faded remnants of Roman imperial greatness, newly mantled in the moral authority of Christianity. The Church triumphed in the Germanic world, too, of course – even in Sweden, most steadfast redoubt of the old heathen gods, a Christian bishop managed to get himself installed at Uppsala by 1164 – but intervening Roman influence had never been felt there, and the resulting cultural milieu was quite distinct. Latinate western Christendom gave the outward impression of having nothing to do with long-lost indigenous barbarism, with its hunting myths, sacrifices, and stories of animal transformation: the werewolf seemed dead within that mainstream culture. But at the fringes, in the far west at least, there survived reasonably pure remnants of a culture far older than Christianity, predating even the first northward surges of the Roman Empire, where such primitive ideas might linger on. In particular, Ireland, the highlands of Scotland, Wales, Cornwall, and Brittany sheltered peoples who were the last survivors of the once-widespread Celtic civilization.

The Celts were perhaps the nearest thing to a pan-European people the continent has ever known. The earliest archaeological evidence for Celtic culture in Europe dates from about the fifth century BC, and at their fullest expansion Celts could be found all over western Europe, from Britain and Scandinavia in the north, down through the Iberian peninsula and into north Africa, right across the Mediterranean, through northern Italy, Sicily, and parts of Greece, north-east to the Carpathians and beyond, and even, from the early third century BC, as far east as the Galatian settlements in Asia Minor. The Celtic world was bounded by the classical world to the south, and by the lands of Teutons, Slavs, and Finno-Ugrian peoples in the north-east. Theirs was literally a prehistoric culture, for it was not until the arrival of the conquering Romans, in 121 BC in Southern France, 58 BC in the remainder of Gaul, and AD 43 in Britain, that any account of their society was written which incorporated their own version of history. Where the Roman Empire did not reach, at the so-called Celtic fringe of the British Isles, the orally transmitted Celtic culture survived intact (albeit with some regional distinctiveness) until the arrival of literate Christian monks in the fifth century AD. Written evidence in either classical or Christian versions is obviously late, and necessarily biased to the point of view of the conqueror, and so much of Celtic culture remains obscure, particularly their religious ideas. Nevertheless, a surprising amount of the Celtic world-view survived its conquest by the Romans from the south and, later, the Teutons and Slavs in the east, and that world-view was to have an influence out of all proportion to the Celtic peoples' meagre political and nationalistic achievements.

While it is an over-simplification to represent the Celts as more backward than their conquerors, there is a distinction to be made, reflected in the contrast between the human environment of the Mediterranean, based on the brick-and-mortar-built villages or towns set in a landscape already largely cleared of impenetrable woodland, and the more haphazardly-planned settlements of the Celts, spread throughout plains, mountains, and the vast areas of uncleared forest which still obtained over much of northern and western Europe. The Celts had a distinct society of their own, and that society exhibited a number of features to suggest that it retained elements of the Palaeolithic hunting societies that had largely disappeared further south. In the British Isles, at least, there are signs that the early Iron Age Celtic economy centred around pastoralism, with wealth and status tied up in large flocks and herds, rather than the intensive cereal-growing allied to animal husbandry that prevailed elsewhere. Classical writers noted that some Celtic tribes, notably the Germani, practised nomadic pastoralism, a way of life significantly closer to prehistoric hunter-gathering than that of the settled agriculturalists of the south. This relative closeness to the hunting way of life is reflected in the Celtic attitude to animals, as expressed by the physical forms taken by their deities: Cernunnos with his stag-antlers, for example, Epona who is usually depicted with her horse, and the mythical boar Baco. But difficulties arise for the unwary as soon as an attempt is made to infer religious beliefs directly from visual representations of these gods. Probably the most famous artefact of Celtic culture is the Gundestrup cauldron, a first- or second-century BC ceremonial vessel thrown as a votive offering into a Danish lake, its sides covered in richly-ornamental scenes whose meanings are, however, largely obscure. The most famous image from the cauldron is usually taken to be that of the Celtic horned-god Cernunnos, but even this is far from being universally accepted. Some have argued that the cauldron itself was made not in northern Gaul but in Thrace,[5] the most easterly mainland extension of what is now Greece, and that the stag-antlered figure shown in his yoga-like posture is an Asiatic shaman. Others do not find it astonishing, or needing

elaborate explanation of imported outside influence, to discover
a shaman-figure at the heart of Celtic religion.

In many ways the Romans were not disposed to crush Celtic
culture in its entirety, and this is especially demonstrated by their
willingness to reconcile local Celtic deities into the Roman
pantheon. Where parallels existed, the Romans often allowed
local Celtic gods to take on some of the attributes of Roman gods,
and *vice versa*. In some cases, soldiers from the furthest reaches
of the Roman Empire imported their own religious figures, so
that, for example, a shrine built to the native Celtic circular
pattern near the Roman fort of Housesteads on Hadrian's Wall
is dedicated appropriately enough to the Roman god of war, but
in his Germanic guise as Mars Thincsus, attended by two
Germanic goddesses, the Alaisiagae: inscriptions found nearby
are those of German units of the Roman Army.[6] Thus the Celts
supplied the indigenous architectural style, the Romans undertook the military and economic conquest, and the Germans
imported their gods, recasting them in a way comprehensible to
the Romans and, in its triadic form, also characteristic of Celtic
imagery.

As a result of such syncretism, it is sometimes difficult to assess
in which tradition certain religious figures originated. One of the
most widely spread of these is the group of female beings
generally known as *Matronae*, 'the mothers', in whose honour
inscriptions are recorded from Roman times in Germany, Hol-
land, and Britain. Such female figures, which are usually thought
of as Celtic in origin, are sometimes shown singly or in pairs, but
most commonly in threes, sometimes seated on chairs or stools,
holding baskets of fruit, or horns-of-plenty, sometimes even
infants. Occasionally they are accompanied by hooded figures,
the *Genii Cucullati*. Carved stones in their honour were erected
from about the first century AD. Most are in the Rhineland, but
a few were erected as far afield as Hadrian's Wall, and the
accompanying inscriptions allotting them such names as the
Gabiae, meaning 'richly giving', emphasize that these are goddesses with the power of bestowing plenty. In later pagan
England, according to the Venerable Bede, the night correspond-
ing to Christmas Eve was known as *Modraniht*, 'the night of the
mothers', and this was almost certainly their particular festival. In
a single instance, an inscription found in the area between

Novara and Vercelli, north-east Italy (near the larger settlement whose name, Milan, is derived from the Celtic *Mediolanum*), these richly giving *Matronae* are associated with Diana, the ancient lunar goddess of plenitude in the hunt.

These and similar connections in religious ideas between the Celtic, Germanic, and Roman cultures are really not so surprising, for they reveal glimpses of a common heritage stretching back to the second millennium BC, at which relatively recent point the peoples of the classical world had begun to emerge from barbarism. Having survived thus far, it would be truly astonishing if these ancient ideas died out overnight. And indeed they did not. As late as the eleventh century Bishop Burchard of Worms condemned the superstition of some local women who had been reported to leave extra place-settings at the table for three women known as the Parcae, another incarnation of the *Matronae*, and there is overwhelming evidence that popular belief in similar fertility figures continued well into the medieval era despite the church's disapproval.[7] Such ancient religious figures, which the Romans had found little difficulty in assimilating into their own iconography, survived in demotic culture into the Christian Middle Ages, at the price of denunciation as pagan superstitions.

The Roman overwhelming of Celtic culture had one other significant effect on later attitudes to surviving pagan beliefs, for there was a particular element in Celtic religious practice which the Romans were in no way prepared to countenance – human sacrifice. However, a large element of doubt must remain as to whether the Celts really practised such terrible rites, or whether the Roman writers invented details of them as part of the inevitable propaganda war waged by imperial conquerors against the vanquished throughout history. Many of the contemporary writers on the Celts and their practices seem to have used a single common source: the *Histories* of the Stoic philosopher Posidonius, written at the end of the second century BC, in which he described the state of the Celtic peoples of southern Gaul prior to their conquest by the Romans in 121 BC. Posidonius' book has not survived, but his friend Strabo also wrote about the Celts and acknowledged Posidonius' direct influence. Strabo used the past tense when describing human sacrifices among the Celts, which he stated had since been suppressed by the Romans. The usual Celtic ways of bringing about the victim's death, he reported, were shooting by arrows, stabbing in the back, or the burning alive of human and animal victims together in a gigantic hollow statue made of wickerwork. This last extraordinary method of sacrifice, which is also mentioned by Caesar, another follower of Posidonius in ethnographical matters, has naturally inflamed the imagination of many (including the makers of a better-than-average horror film, *The Wicker Man*, set on a remote Hebridean island), but there is no archaeological evidence for it, nor any parallel in other cultures. Furthermore, if Strabo is right in stating that the Celts used bows and arrows for their sacrifices, they do not seem to have used them for anything else: bows and arrows are not mentioned in early vernacular texts, and the Irish names for them are loan-words from Norse and Latin respectively.

Nevertheless, the classical writers were virtually unanimous in attributing human sacrifice to the Celts. Apart from those who were clearly influenced by Posidonius, writers from the third century BC onwards repeatedly made references to human sacrifice among the Gauls and Celts. Cicero, Dionysius of Halicarnassus, and Pomponius Mela each mentioned the theme, and Tacitus, part of whose method was to contrast the vigour and health of barbarian civilization with the effeteness of Rome, and who might therefore be expected to put the best face possible on barbarian customs, wrote that the British Druids 'deemed it indeed a duty to cover their altars with the blood of captives and to consult their deities through human entrails'. Archaeologists too have inferred some evidence for ritual killings from the material excavated from several curious well-like structures which have been found scattered throughout Gaul and in parts of Germany and Britain. These shafts, some dating back as far as the middle of the second millennium BC, are filled with deposits of hundreds of objects such as pieces of pottery, animal and human bones, carved wooden figures, and, in one case, the stem of a cypress tree, all presumably thrown down as votive offerings to the deities of the underworld. At the foot of one such shaft, at Holzhausen, Bavaria, some 25 feet below ground level, archaeologists have discovered an upright wooden post surrounded by organic material possibly produced by the breakdown of flesh and blood. This last discovery brings to the mind's eye the horrific picture of some poor victim, bound to the stake, screaming his last as the Celtic priests shovel earth down on top of him, but of course where such minimal traces of human remains are discovered in the votive shafts, there is no hard evidence to show that the bodies were still alive when they were deposited there.

This basic objection is equally valid for another potentially gruesome aspect of Celtic religion, the cult of the severed head. A number of small Celtic stone-built sanctuaries exhibit the unusual decorative motif of human skulls set in niches cut into stone pillars, and accusations that Celtic chieftains were head-hunters, slicing the heads from the bodies of those they had slain in battle to keep as trophies, were common among the classical writers. This concept should not have been as alien to the classical peoples as it was later to be to western Christians. The belief that the head is peculiarly sacred as the site of the soul is widely attested. In the Palaeolithic bear-cult, it was the head and pelt only of the bear that was kept. The reason that the corpses in the Çatal Hüyük wall paintings are headless may well be that it was not felt proper to subject the head to the indignities of excarnation. In Homer the dead are often referred to as heads, whether or not the whole body is involved: 'But now I go to reach the slayer of that dear head,' says Achilles announcing his quest to avenge Patrocles; and having mortally wounded Patrocles' killer, he tells him, 'there is none that shall keep the dogs away from thy head'.[8] The preservation of human heads, in the belief that this will ensure the soul's immortality, is common in a number of societies. In the town of Hallstatt, Austria (it is significant that this is the type site for an early Celtic culture), a quaint burial custom was observed right up until the 1960s: when a local person died and had been buried long enough for all flesh to have fallen away from the skeleton, the body was dug up, and the cleaned skull and long bones neatly stacked with others in the town ossuary. Each of the hundreds of skulls on display is painted in pleasant colours, mostly greens or reds, with trailing vines and crosses, and the name and date of the person written across the forehead. The custom has recently fallen into disuse, but the ossuary is still kept open as a tourist attraction. There can be little doubt that this is a survival of ancient tradition, by which the preservation and display of the skull ensured that person's immortality. The sight of something similar among the Celts may well have caused misunderstanding among Romans with their own living heads full of wild stories of barbaric human sacrifice.

Naturally it hardly matters whether or not the Celts actually practised human sacrifice or head-hunting, only that they were believed to have done so. The early Church fathers like Tertullian, Augustine, and Lactantius were certainly keen to repeat the charges of those classical writers who had followed Posidonius, as they emphasized the pagan barbarism from which men could only be redeemed through the teachings of the Gospel. When interest in the ancient religious beliefs of Europe was revived a good deal later, in the sixteenth and seventeenth centuries, those charges had stuck, and writers made much of Celtic human sacrifice and the cult of the severed head. The illustrated title-page to Elias Schedius's *De Dis Germanis* of 1648, for instance, depicts a knife-wielding Druid before a grove of decapitated corpses, and a woman next to him beating on a drum with two human thigh bones, a graphic example of how antiquarianism could descend to lurid horror when the classical and post-classical Christian propagandists were too readily believed.

Unlike the Mediterranean world, both classical and Christian, where religious ceremonial was largely conducted in the stone-built temples, churches, and cathedrals of ecclesiastical architecture, the Celts had practised their rituals, which were firmly believed to have involved human sacrifice, amid the organically sculpted cathedrals of forest and mountain. Most of their sanctuaries were simple clearings in the woodlands, containing by way of human architecture at most perhaps a timber-built shrine. These forest sanctuaries were out-of-the-way places where Druidical rites could be held in secrecy, away from the prying eyes of would-be suppressors. In the first century AD Tacitus described the annual sacrifices of the forebears of the Germanic Alamanni which took place in a sacred wood: seven centuries later Abbot Pirmin found it necessary to speak out against local propitiatory rites of prayer and magic still carried out by the Alamanni in the same forest clearing. The dark uncharted forests of northern Europe were the Celts' natural element, and the Greek and Roman writers constantly registered fear and awe at this hidden world. Western Christendom inherited this horror of the forest, and allowed it to colour its own theological ideas: Hell was imagined as 'surrounded by very thick woods', as an eleventh-century poem puts it, and Dante's vision of the Inferno included *la dolorosa selva*. Wild, hairy men and women were said to live on in the forests in the company of all manner of supernatural creatures, where they occasionally feasted on some child unlucky or foolish enough to stray from the path. As the Arcadian highlands stood as the last refuge for dimly remembered ancient practices in classical Greece, so the uncleared forests of Europe harboured ideas of similar antiquity in medieval Christendom: from both emerged hirsute figures of terror to haunt the imagination.

The *Völsungasaga* is far from being the only evidence that the non-Christian peoples who succeeded the Celts in continental Europe held a variety of beliefs related to werewolves and other were-animals. One of the most notable expressions of these, met with in both German and Scandinavian tradition, is the figure of the *berserker*, the warrior who fights with exceptional courage and vigour. One description of these warriors comes from Snorri Sturluson (1179–1241), the great Icelandic preserver of Scandinavian myth. His *Ynglinga Saga*, a history of Sweden from the earliest times, describes followers of Odin 'who went without their mail-coats and were mad as hounds or wolves, bit their shields, and were as strong as bears or bulls. They slew men, but neither fire nor iron had effect upon them. This is called *berserkgangr* [going berserk].' The derivation of the word *berserk* used here is usually held to arise from *ber* (bear) and *serkr* (shirt), the implication being that these warriors wore bear-skins as shirts instead of chain-mail, thereby assuming the animal's ferocity in battle, an idea familiar from the prehistoric wolf-brotherhoods.

The image of the fearless bear-warrior is given more concrete expression in *Hrólfs Saga Kraka*, the story of an early king of Denmark. One of the king's champions is Bodvar Biarki, whose father Biorn had been transformed into a bear by a witch. Biorn was able to resume human shape during the night, and during these times as a human he was visited in his cave by a woman named Bera, who bore him three sons: the first was half man and half elk, the second had dog's feet, yet the third, Bodvar Biarki, seemed outwardly normal. The child thus born could hardly be said to be short of bear ancestry: his father's name means Bear, his mother's She-bear, and Biarki itself simply means Little Bear; the Bodvar part of his name seems to be an honorific related to a Norse poetic word for battle, which is appropriate as it is during the great battle in which old King Hrólf is finally vanquished that

Biarki at last shows his true lycanthropic nature. Hrólf's army is hopelessly outnumbered, but in the midst of battle a great bear suddenly appears in front of the troops, lashing out with his razor-sharp forepaws at all the king's opponents, seemingly impervious to the weapons wielded against him. The tide of the battle appears to be turning in Hrólf's favour, but meanwhile Biarki's best friend has been looking for him, and he finds the valiant champion sitting alone in his tent, quite motionless. Upset by this dereliction of duty, the friend berates the silent warrior, until at last Biarki rises up and leaves the tent, saying as he does so that he will now be able to do less for the king than if he had been left undisturbed. Sure enough, when he reaches the battle ground, the marvellous fighting bear has disappeared, and although he and all his fellow-warriors fight bravely, the battle is inevitably lost.

This story and Snorri's brief reference give views of the *berserk* from opposite poles. Snorri's account is the dry, factual version of the historian: he is telling his audience about particularly brave human warriors, and although he compares them to animals – hounds, wolves, bears, and bulls all get a mention – he gives little hint that he believes them to have been lycanthropically trans-formed. The old, so-called 'lying saga' of *Hrólfs Saga Kraka*, on the other hand, reveals some of the legendary material behind the historical description by its fantastical story of the warrior fight-ing in bear shape while his human body remains elsewhere in a trance.

An old theory had it that the word *berserk* does not have any real connection with bears, and that it derives from *berr* (bare, naked), and as supporting evidence it was pointed out that Snorri does not mention bear-skins, only the fact that the berserks fought without mail-coats. There are two arguments to be brought against this theory: first, that Snorri himself, a Christian writing in the thirteenth century, may have failed to understand the traditional idea, or more likely, wished to play down the mythical element behind the naming of these soldiers whom he knew to have been important constituents of historical armies in pre-Christian Scandinavia; but secondly, and more importantly, is the fact that the berserks are known to have contained within their ranks a subdivision whose equally animalistic origin matches their own, the *úlfheðnar*, or 'wolf-coats'. Another Icelandic tale,

Vatnsdœla Saga, makes clear that a wolf-coat was a particular kind of berserk, stating that 'those berserks who were called *úlfheðnar* wore wolf shirts (*vargstakkar*) for mail-coats'. The poem, *Hrafnsmál*, written about 900 and convincing because of its relatively early date, mentions wolf-coats among the retinue of the historical King Harald Fairhair, who ruled Norway in the second half of the ninth century.

The same poem contrasts the sound made by the two kinds of beast-warrior – 'the berserks bayed', while 'the wolf-coats howled' – and other distinctions between the two groups of animal-skin-clad warrior are certainly intriguing. Some have deduced from the different characters of the two animals in question that the berserk was a lone fighter, assuming the solitary fierceness of the bear, a single champion striding through battle like Bodvar Biarki. The wolf-coats, on the other hand, like their lupine counterparts, were pack animals, warriors of perhaps lesser prestige than the mighty berserks, who hunted the battlefield together, bringing down their prey by ferocity and weight of numbers. There are several descriptions among contemporary observers of the bestial fury with which Scandinavian armies customarily fought, which read like eyewitness accounts of the berserks and wolf-coats in action. Leo the Deacon, for instance, witnessed eastern Vikings fighting with Svyatoslav on the Danube against the Byzantine Emperor in the tenth century, and contrasted their ferocious attacks with the Greeks' scientific approach to warfare. These Vikings, he complained, seemed to have no preconceived plan, simply the ability to fight viciously and intemperately, like wild beasts, 'howling in a strange and disagreeable manner'.[9]

If there were no more evidence than this, however, it would be difficult to argue for the real survival of lycanthropic beliefs among the northern pagans. After all, the ceremonial troops of the British Army still wear bear-skins today, albeit merely as a rather impractical form of head-dress, and selected members of their regiments are often draped in leopard-skins or the pelts of other predators, yet no one argues from this that there are lycanthropes in the ranks, even if they do sometimes howl in a strange and disagreeable manner. The berserks and wolf-coats would not have fought clad entirely in the pelt of the appropriate animal, which offered too great a hindrance to a warrior's free

movement, but more likely girdled with a belt made of the
animal's skin, as had the leopard-hunters of Çatal Hüyük seven
thousand years earlier. A popular figure in Norse art is a dancing
warrior with a horned helmet, armed with a spear or sword,
dressed only in a belt; this may well represent the warrior in a
bear- or wolf-skin girdle. H. R. Ellis Davidson has argued from
a different standpoint that these figures are intended to represent
the champions of Odin, which would certainly be consistent with
them as berserks and wolf-coats.[10] Nevertheless, however practical and undemanding of magical explanation it may be that
warriors should draw their fighting inspiration from the ferocity
of wild animals, it is clear that lycanthropic ideas were deeply
ingrained in the northern European pagan psyche.

Odin, for example, to whom the berserks and wolf-coats owed
particular loyalty, had himself the power of changing shape, as
Snorri spells out in *Ynglinga Saga*: 'Odin could change himself.
His body then lay as if sleeping or dead, but he became a bird or
a wild beast, a fish or a dragon, and journeyed in the twinkling of
an eye to far-off lands, on his own errands or those of other men.'
From this it is clear that Odin has shamanistic powers, the ability
to enter a trance and travel outside his body in animal form. His
shamanistic aspect seems to be expressed in his name: the
Germanic form of it, Wodan, is thought to be related to *wut*,
meaning high mental excitement, fury, intoxication, or possession, and the later Scandinavian form of his name, *Oðinn*, is
derived from the Old Norse adjective *óðr*, also meaning raging,
furious, intoxicated, and sometimes used to signify poetical
inspiration.[11] The notion of intense excitement and rage combined is obviously relevant to the berserks and wolf-coats, while
possession is central to the idea of shamanistic ecstasy. In this
connection, the association with drunkenness is particularly
interesting. It is perhaps no more than a coincidental detail, but
after the two werewolf-Völsungs, Sigmund and Sinfjötli, have
finished their training period in the forest, they enter the castle of
King Siggeir, intending to avenge themselves on him. As there are
only two of them, they are forced to hide at first, and so they
clamber inside huge ale-vats they find sitting near the entrance of
the king's great hall. There is no direct suggestion of them
drinking the ale in order to invoke and induce in themselves the
rage of Odin, their family ancestor, but some vestigial trace of the

connection may have had something to do with their choice of hiding place. Northern werewolves were to appear again in closer and more explicit association with barrels of ale at a later date.[12]

Odin is far from being the only figure in Norse mythology with lycanthropic powers. The trickster-god Loki, for example, was reported to have changed into a mare to lure away the marvellous stallion, Svaðilfari, owned by the giant who built the walls of Asgard. As a result of Svaðilfari's attentions, Loki gave birth to Sleipnir, the supernatural eight-legged horse which Odin rode on his shamanistic journeys to the underworld. Loki himself begot on a giantess the terrible wolf Fenrir, which at Ragnarok, the time of the destruction of the gods, would break free of his bindings to defeat and devour Odin, only to be killed in turn by Odin's son Vidar. In the many stories in which he features, Loki is endlessly mutating: in order to steal apples, he changes into a bird; at various other times he is a flea, a fly, a seal, an old woman. The goddess Freyja is several times described in myths as having a 'feather' or 'falcon' shape, which on one occasion Loki is able to steal in order to fly about. The apparently ridiculous idea that a shape could be stolen depends on the complex meaning of the Old Icelandic word for 'shape', *hamr*, which could be used to refer to an animal skin, the wings and feathers of a bird, and for any non-human shape used in ecstatic transport, or *hamfarir*, 'shape-journeys'.[13] The connection between Odin's shamanistic powers and the wild rages of his berserk followers is hinted at in the related verb *hamask*, meaning to fall into a state of berserk fury: someone who has done so is referred to as *hamrammr*, 'out of his shape'. Interestingly, one of the longest Icelandic family sagas, *Eyrbyggja Saga*, which like all early Icelandic literature was written down in the Christian era, uses the phrase *eigi einhamr*, 'not of one shape', to describe someone not yet converted to Christianity, an early hint of what was to be the Church's attitude to those who persisted in pagan beliefs in the power of shape-shifting.

Nor were these beliefs confined to the world of heathen myths and storytelling. The strongest evidence that the pre-Christian peoples of the north practised what their myths and legends indicate they believed centres around the well-documented craft of *seiðr*. This was recognizably a form of witchcraft specifically linked to the goddess Freyja, she of the 'feather-shape', who was said to have been the first to pass on the secret knowledge. The rituals necessary for practising *seiðr* involved the construction of a raised platform or seat, on which the female practitioner, or *völva*, sat, dressed in a costume of animal skins: one description in *Eiríks Saga* specifies that she wore calfskin boots and gloves of catskin, which chimes with Snorri's statement that Freyja's carriage was drawn by cats. The seated position of the *völva* is reminiscent of that of the Mothers of Celtic, Roman, and Anglo-Saxon imagery. The same source also describes an unpleasant-sounding sacrificial meal eaten by the *völva*, stewed up from the hearts of all the living creatures the locals could muster. The *völva* then encouraged the singing of certain spells, after which she fell into a state of ecstasy, from which she emerged with messages from the spirit world. The trappings of the cult make it clear that the whole concept is again shamanistic: the *völva*'s spirit-journey is done in animal-shape while her human body remains in a trance on the platform. On emerging from the trance, she was able to answer questions concerning people's personal destinies, about their loves and marriages, and about the success of their crops. These functions were inextricably intertwined, and related to the powers of her patroness, the goddess Freyja, who was especially linked with fertility, both in the sense of childbirth and marriage and of the productivity of the fields. Another saga[14] tells of one *völva* in Iceland who was said to have worked *seiðr* so that a sound would fill with fish, while the description of a ceremony in Greenland tells how the *völva* would be consulted about matters of human fertility, childbirth, betrothals, and the like.

Thus at the very moment these pagan ideas were submerged beneath the oncoming wave of Christianity, two already distinct figures were emerging in the north from the mass of ancient concepts about shamanistic shape-shifting, each drawing inspiration from a god, one female, the other male. The followers of Freyja had taken on for themselves alone the functions of prophecy and divination, particularly in relation to fertility, while the followers of Odin, the berserks and wolf-coats, were restricted to using the shamanistic trance to endow themselves with the strength and imperviousness to pain of wild animals. This division of the shamanistic gift along the line of gender interestingly foreshadows the breakdown by gender of the victims of the later continental witch-craze; the overwhelming majority of the people who were later to be accused of witchcraft – practices obviously similar in several crucial respects to *seiðr* – were to be women, while practically all of the alleged werewolves were men.

5

The Wolf in Sheep's Clothing

The hungry sheep look up, and are not fed,
But, swoln with wind and the rank mist they draw,
Rot inwardly and foul contagion spread;
Besides what the wolf with privy paw
Daily devours apace, and nothing said.

MILTON,
Lycidas

Although the Celtic-Germanic figure of the werewolf-warrior had a violent, aggressive, even murderous, aspect, he had a specific social utility in the Heroic Age – to put it at its simplest, the berserk rages of the wolf-coats helped win battles. For the Christian church, seeking to spread the new message of universal benevolence and love, such an atavistic figure from pagan belief would prove intolerable. Yet there is irony in that in its earliest years the Christian church should have suffered very much the same kind of official disapproval as surviving pagan ideas were to encounter during the centuries succeeding the triumph of western Christendom. Presenting itself as a continuation of, and successor to, Judaism, Christianity had emerged from a morass of Hellenistic mystery cults and Gnostic ideas current in the later years of the Roman Empire to stake its claim as the universal religion, eschewing as it did so the whole panoply of animal (and, of course, human) sacrifice, divination, spell-casting, and other forms of magic, which were so congenial to the pagans of the Empire.

In place of these heathen nostrums, Christianity offered the concept of 'salvation' through the death of the divine figure, Jesus Christ. Many of the rival cults which flourished at this time were

extraordinary affairs, combining animal sacrifice, personal initiation ceremonies, and a preoccupation with secrecy reminiscent
of the Lykaian ritual. In the famous *taurobolium*, for example,
which is known to have taken place from the second century AD
onwards, a deep pit was dug into which the would-be initiate was
cast. Wooden beams were laid loosely across the mouth of the pit,
and a bull was then slaughtered on top of this platform. The lucky
initiate emerged, having been in some danger of drowning one
might think (a full-grown bull contains about fifty litres, eleven
gallons, of blood), and was worshipped by his fellows as someone
now in a state of grace. Like all initiation rites, this had the pattern
of a spiritual rebirth – one rendered as literal as possible by the
participant emerging from a dark hollow place besplattered with
blood. The exalted condition resulting from this rebirth was
recognized as lasting for twenty years only; after that, the rite had
to be undergone again. The reciprocal influence between Christianity and the mystery cults is shown by a famous *taurobolium*
inscription, the dedication of Aedesius, which claims that he is
'eternally reborn', *in aeternum renatus*, as a result of undergoing
the rite. The inscription dates from AD 376, two generations after
the victory of Christianity but at a time when the pagans had
organized a brief and ultimately unsuccessful backlash. Most
authorities agree that it is an attempt by the *taurobolium* initiates
to appropriate for their own cult the Christian claims to offer
eternal salvation.[1]

The early Christian leaders wanted nothing to do with such
bloody rites. In a famous passage in Augustine's *Confessions*, the
great Church Father laments the temporary downfall of his friend
Alypius, who has been dragged off by his pagan friends to see the
Roman gladiatorial games. Alypius is confident in his own will-
power and thinks that he can resist the frenzied bloodlust of the
place simply by keeping his eyes shut, but the noise and excitement arouse his curiosity. He opens his eyes for a moment and is
lost: 'For, directly he saw that blood, he therewith imbibed a sort
of savageness; nor did he turn away, but fixed his eye, drinking
in madness unconsciously, and was delighted with the guilty
contest, and drunken with the bloody pastime.'[2] In short, Alypius
is driven to a berserk fury by the triumph of the pagan ceremonial
over his frail human resolve, and is only saved when God teaches
him to put his trust in Him rather than his own will. This chapter,

one of the most striking passages in all patristic literature, shows
how fervently the Church distrusted all forms of pagan savagery,
associating it directly with possession of the senses. Nevertheless,
until such writings had made the Church's attitude clear, the
authorities of the Roman Empire treated Christianity as only one
cult among many. Far from being accepted at their own estimate
as practising an austere, abstemious religion, Christians were
widely accused by pagan writers of holding sexual orgies, and of
committing incest and cannibalism. Early Christian writers
refuted the charges, and even turned them back to accuse the
pagans. More noticeable was their habit of using exactly the same
kind of accusation against Christian heretics. Already by 150
Justin Martyr was accusing heretics of orgies, incest, and
anthropophagy, committed under cover of darkness.[3] The Christian terror of the dark had begun early.

Christianity retained a few faint traces of primitive animal-
based religions – three of the four Evangelists are represented by
an animal, the third member of the Trinity is represented in art
as a dove, and so on – but these were purely symbolic. In all other
ways, the religion was ostensibly as far removed from pagan
practices as could be imagined. And yet at the heart of the new
religion was the symbol of the dying god, killed in order that
mankind might gain eternal life – a human sacrifice, in fact. And
the most important ritual of the new religion was the regular
holding of a sacrificial feast at which the celebrants shared out
among themselves the body of the god, eating his flesh and
drinking his blood. Both these ideas, the killing of the god and the
eating of his body, are also found in the mystery cults, in the
deaths of the gods Attis, Adonis, and Osiris, and in the Dionysiac
ritual in which an animal, usually a bull, was torn apart and eaten
raw, apparently to commemorate the mythical occasion on which
the Titans, the ancestors of man, had eaten Dionysus, whom they
had killed, then boiled and roasted.[4] The Pauline reinterpreta-
tion of Jesus's participation with his disciples in the Jewish
ceremony of Kiddush, in which a festival or Sabbath meal is
prefaced by simple blessings made over bread and wine, is clearly
coloured by these ideas of 'eating the god' imported from the
mystery cults.[5]

The Church's placing of the Eucharist as the central event of
daily worship meant that Christian worshippers were constantly

reminded of the sacrificial aspect of their religion. The gospel text was unambiguous: 'Verily, verily, I say unto you, Except that you eat of the flesh of the Son of man, and drink his blood, ye have no life in you. Whoso eateth my flesh, and drinketh my blood, hath eternal life; and I will raise him up at the last day . . . He that eateth my flesh, and drinketh my blood, dwelleth in me, and I in him.'[6] Nor was the god-figure understood as being represented in a purely symbolic fashion in the bread and wine of the mass. The Catholic doctrine of transubstantiation, which was generally accepted by about the ninth century and fully adopted by the Council of Lateran in 1215, took great pains to spell out that the bread and wine *actually were* the body and blood of Christ at the moment of their ingestion by the communicant, and the priest murmured the words *hoc est corpus Christi*, 'this is the body of Christ', as he distributed the wafer to underline the point.

By the twelfth century, visions were occasionally recorded of Christ appearing at the Eucharist, usually in the form of a child or a lamb. These were frowned upon by those in authority, as were the practices sometimes found of imprinting the communion wafer with an image of Christ, or of breaking the wafer up and arranging it on the platen to resemble the human form. When asked why Christ did not visibly appear at the Holy Communion, a popular preacher of the thirteenth century, Berthold von Regensburg, replied that it was to spare the sensibilities of the congregation, who would hardly like it if they could see that they were biting off the head, hands, and feet of Jesus, an answer indicating that awareness of the cannibalistic theme inherent in the Eucharist was by no means confined to the unsophisticated or ill-educated.[7] The whole issue of the real presence of Christ in the Eucharist was to become one of the chief points of difference between the traditionalists and reformists at the Reformation, and the early Church's refusal to recognize that this central rite shared themes of sacrifice with those religions it supplanted sowed the seeds of the intolerant, repressive attitude exhibited by the medieval and early-modern Church towards any and all survivals of ancient popular beliefs.

In the early years of Church evangelism the process of eradicating pagan superstition was undertaken in a piecemeal way. Wise counsels recognized that forcible conversion would not inspire confidence in the new Church among those who had so

recently worshipped the old gods. Pope Gregory, writing to an
abbot on his departure for England in 601, made clear the tactics
he approved:

> [We] have come to the conclusion that the temples of the idols
> among that people should on no account be destroyed. The
> idols are to be destroyed, but the temples themselves are to be
> aspersed with holy water, altars set up on them, and relics
> deposited there. For if these temples are well-built, they must
> be purified from the worship of demons and dedicated to the
> service of the true God . . . And since they have a custom of
> sacrificing many oxen to demons, let some other solemnity be
> substituted in its place, such as a day of Dedication or the
> Festivals of the holy martyrs whose relics are enshrined there.
> On such occasions they might well construct shelters of
> boughs for themselves around the churches that were once
> temples, and celebrate the solemnity with devout feasting.
> They are no longer to sacrifice beasts to the Devil, but they may
> kill them for food to the praise of God, and give thanks to the
> Giver of all gifts for the plenty they enjoy.[8]

The effect produced by this softly-softly approach was complex: on one hand, the tactics were certainly effective in increasing the numbers of Christians, ensuring that the new creed was
grafted onto local patterns of worship and could therefore be
accepted painlessly; on the other, they helped perpetuate old
practices and beliefs, with the crucial proviso that these were now
to be understood in a different way. Gregory's letter, casually
denigrating Anglo-Saxon animal sacrifices as having been made
to 'demons' and to 'the Devil', is characteristic of Christian
attitudes to the old gods of the pre-Christian era. Where a Roman
governor might have referred to 'other gods' or 'their gods' when
speaking of local religious practices which differed from Imperial
ideas, the Christian instinct was always to diabolize all pre-
Christian beliefs, recasting them in a moral hue of purest black.

Notwithstanding this moral rigour, the Church, in the earliest
years of its northward expansion, had to be content with some
fairly shaky converts. The Emperor Constantine is the most
famous example of these: there can be little doubt that he never
grasped the finer points of the new religion he nominally
espoused, but regarded Christ as a kind of solar deity who

happened to bring him luck in battle – and yet his conversion, however superficial, was the most important of any single man's in the history of the religion. In the west the conversion of Clovis was to prove almost as significant. His baptism at Reims in 496, a grand spectacle held in public immediately after his defeat of the Alamanni and accompanied by the simultaneous baptism of three thousand of his men, effectively delivered the whole Frankish nation, and therefore ultimately France, into the arms of the Catholic church, with important implications for papal power in medieval Europe. Clovis may have been a sincere convert – like Constantine, he was said to have been evangelized by his Christian wife – but it seems unlikely to say the least that his fearsome Frankish warriors, after a quick dip in the river, should have returned home with their hearts brimful with the spirit of charity and the joy of Christian forgiveness. The old pagan gods would prove harder to eradicate than that.

By about the beginning of the twelfth century, the Church had succeeded in establishing hegemony over all of western Europe, yet without by any means extirpating all traces of former indigenous beliefs. One of the major festivities openly expressing shape-shifting beliefs was the feast of the January calends, when throughout Europe, particularly in the Celtic-Germanic area, great processions took place during which people dressed themselves as animals. As Bishop Burchard discovered to his dismay at Worms, tables groaning with food were customarily left out overnight as offerings to invisible female beings who controlled fertility. Writing in the sixth century, Cesarius of Arles condemned the practices he saw at the January calends: he complained that some of the participants disguised themselves as stags, others donned the skins of sheep and goats, or wore animal-masks. The meaning behind these ceremonies is clear enough: they are fertility rites plain and simple, intended to simulate and stimulate plenitude of game, domestic stock, and crops for the forthcoming year, undertaken at just that time of year when fertility is at its lowest ebb. Also lying behind the animal disguise is the shamanistic concept of travelling in animal-shape to the other world in which such matters as fertility are decided. Cesarius was particularly disgusted that the participants at Arles exulted in their disguises as if delighting in their loss of humanity, which suggests that something at least approaching ecstasy was

experienced during such ceremonies.[9] On the Gregorian principle of assimilating heathen festivities to Christian festivals, the
celebrations became synchronized with the twelve days between
Christmas and the Epiphany, the German *Zwölften*, and some of
that atmosphere of riot and plenty in the midst of winter still lives
on in the modern secular Christmas, even the feeding of the
supernatural fertility-figure surviving in the piece of cake and
glass of wine left out for Germanic Santa Claus.

Another related phenomenon, said to occur particularly frequently during these same twelve nights, was the Wild Hunt,
references to which occur from about the eleventh century
onwards throughout Europe – France, Spain, Italy, Germany,
England, and Scandinavia. The Wild Hunt was a nightly caval-
cade of the dead, led through the forests by some mythical figure
riding on a horse, sometimes Wotan or Odin, in which case
wolves would naturally run beside him, or more often a female
figure, Perchta, Berhta, or Berta, 'the bright one', or her male
equivalent, Berthold, Herlechin, or Herne, clearly related to the
ancient concept of a lunar hunting deity. Many texts add the
name of Diana to the list of leaders of the Hunt, perhaps because
their educated authors noticed the parallel between the classical
and the Celtic-Germanic figures, but also because the parallel
was preserved in the syncretistic melting-pot of surviving folk-
beliefs in northern Europe. Such images of the Wild Hunt
reinforced the old Mediterranean fear of the moonlit forests of
northern Europe as infested with bestial figures of the night.
Christian commentators could not but help imbuing these images with the taint of diabolism.

Meanwhile the moonlit forests of northern Europe had been
undergoing something of a transformation. Possibly the most
significant agent in these changes was the Black Death, that
deadly cocktail of bubonic, pneumonic, and septicaemic plague
strains which in its most virulent outbreak ravaged the western
world from 1347 to 1351, when it is estimated that somewhere
between 25 and 45 per cent of Europe's population died –
Froissart's apocalyptic estimate that 'a third of the world died',
which he probably took from the Book of Revelation, is close
enough.[10] Plague epidemics continued to recur in shorter and
longer cycles throughout the rest of the fourteenth and for the
whole of the fifteenth century. Under this constant onslaught the

population of Europe declined dramatically. Whole rural villages were abandoned as a flight to the towns took place throughout the period, although towns offered no protection from plague, only economic opportunities for the survivors. The environmental changes were dramatic: many areas which by 1200 had been deforested, especially in the north German plain and in parts of England and France, recovered their covering of woodland over the next two centuries. Most of the twentieth-century forests in Europe date from this late medieval period.

Accompanying the return of the forests was the return of wolves. During the agrarian expansion of the early Middle Ages, wolves had been hunted rigorously throughout Europe. Specialized huntsmen, like Charlemagne's *luporii*, had tracked and killed them, and new breeds of dog big enough to defend their owners' flocks from the lupine menace had been sent out to prowl alongside the shepherds. Wolf-hunting edicts such as that issued in 1114 by the synod of San Diego de Compostela were routine in this period. All priests, knights, and peasants who were not working were ordered to spend every Saturday, except Holy Saturday and Pentecost Eve, hunting down wandering wolves and setting up traps. Anyone refusing to take part was to be fined.[11] In England this programme of extermination was easier to carry out than on the continent. Edgar is the king most renowned for his efforts to wipe out the wolf population: during the tenth century he insisted that the king of Wales pay him an annual tribute of 300 wolf-skins, which must have had a considerable effect on the wolf population there (always assuming that the Welsh king did not import the skins from Ireland). In the thirteenth century Henry III made grants of land to several individuals on condition they destroyed all the wolves they found there, although by the time of Edward II's reign at the beginning of the fourteenth century wolves were still recorded as being troublesome in thickly wooded areas like the king's forest of the Peak in Derbyshire. Nevertheless, the wolf was extinct in all parts of England by about the end of the fifteenth century, although it lingered on in isolated highland regions elsewhere in Britain, being recorded in Scotland (somewhat unreliably) as late as 1743.

The success of the English campaign against the wolf depended almost entirely on England's being part of an island, the most heavily populated part. While not usually nomadic when in possession of secure territories of their own, wolves are capable of travelling in a pack at a rate of over 100 miles a week,[12] and so a wolf-pack wiped out in the mountains of eastern France, say, might well be replaced by one escaping harassment in the forests of Germany within a very short time. In England such migrations were less likely to succeed in replenishing numbers, and wolves steadily decreased as a threat to the livelihood of English farmers as the end of the medieval period drew near. It is almost certainly for this reason that werewolves scarcely feature at all in medieval and early-modern English folklore. Different conditions prevailed in Ireland, and the wolf survived there longer. A famous Cromwellian law of 1652 forbade the export of Irish wolfhounds from the island in order not to deplete the numbers of man's best weapon against wolves, while a few years later the English writer John Dunton, staying in County Galway, was 'strangely surprised to hear the cows and sheep all coming into my bedchamber. I enquired the meaning and was told it was to preserve them from the wolf, which every night was rambling about for prey.'[13] But once again the fact that Ireland is an island seems to have been the deciding factor in the success of the wolf hunts: by the eighteenth century wolves were extinct there too.

However, on the continent, in the aftermath of plague and reforestation, wolf populations grew rapidly during the later medieval period, so that whereas in 1300 wolves had largely been confined to the Far North, Russia, and mountainous regions, they made a distinct comeback in the succeeding centuries, featuring often in fourteenth- and fifteenth-century chronicles as marauders and predators through France and Italy. In one instance in the 1420s wolves were allegedly seen roaming through the suburbs of Paris. In general, wolves were nocturnal creatures (ironically it was human persecution that made them so; in wilderness areas where they remain undisturbed by man, wolves prefer to hunt during the hours of daylight), whose noticeable depredations were increasingly aimed at the numbers of sheep now spreading across the pastures of Europe. For a variety of reasons – among many others, higher labour costs and higher standards of living among the post-plague survivors, and cheaper wheat and other grains grown in the East – sheep farming became one of the most popular and profitable forms of agriculture in western Europe in the late medieval period. Sheep were simple to keep: they required only rough grazing rather than expensive fodder, and a flock could be looked after fairly easily by one man and a few mastiffs. (England, where a shepherd needed only a single small dog bred for rounding up sheep rather than fending off wolves, did particularly brisk trade.) Mutton kept well compared to other meats, which was a consideration in the days before refrigeration, and wool could be collected from the animal every year, which was more than could be said for cowhide. Wool quickly became one of the most popular commodities of the era, and increased manufacture of woollen cloth led to the displacement of traditional materials: bed-blankets, for example, which had formerly been made from animal skins and furs, could be replaced with manufactured woollen blankets that were cheap and easier to clean. The price for this progress was that man was now one further remove from intimate contact with the animal world.

While it would be an exaggeration to say that all western Europeans regarded themselves as shepherds, there was a sense in which most regarded themselves as sheep. The image was biblical: Christ was the Good Shepherd, Christians the flock he tended, a metaphor given special emphasis in the gospel of John. The image was one of the most commonly reiterated of the medieval era, used by everyone from the pope to the lowliest scribe. The usual term for a humble clergyman, 'pastor', punningly acknowledged that the functions of the shepherd and the priest were analogous: both had their pastoral duties. And yet Christ was not only the Shepherd, he was also himself the Lamb of God. As Paul wrote to the Corinthians, Christ was to be identified with the sacrificial Paschal lamb: 'For indeed our Passover has begun; the sacrifice is offered – Christ himself.'[14] The author of the Book of Revelation worked up a rather more powerful vision of the Lamb, 'having seven horns and seven eyes, which are the seven Spirits of God sent forth into all the earth', but medieval artists preferred to portray the Lamb of God as a small defenceless thing, meek and mild, radiant with the light of innocence. The image of Christ as lamb indicates a curious shift in the iconography of Christ in the western tradition, in which Christ was increasingly seen in infantile terms, either as the helpless baby lamb or as the equally helpless infant at his mother's breast.

Earlier Christian iconography had taken as its central image an adult Jesus, Christ Pantocrator, Christ the powerful, ruler of the universe. More or less apocryphal episodes in his career, such as the Harrowing of Hell, in which Christ descends to the underworld to defeat the powers of darkness and release all human souls, were in this earlier era given a prominence which often surprises modern Christians, while missionaries attempting to convert the northern heathen found it useful to portray Christ as a great hero capable of defeating the old gods of strength like Thor in open combat. But from about the twelfth century a noticeable growth in the cult of Christ as lamb or infant took place, with a concomitant increase in devotion to the Virgin who nurtured the infant. To some authorities, the persistence of the image in the popular imagination was to be deplored, as it detracted from the truly remarkable feature of the Christian divine figure, his humanity. The thirteenth-century liturgist William Durand, bishop of Mende, sought to offer guidelines on this point: '. . . because Christ was a real man, Pope Adrian declared that we must paint him in human form. In fact it is not the Lamb which should be painted on the Cross, but after the man has been depicted, there is nothing to prevent one from showing the Lamb either at the foot or on the back of the Cross.'[15]

The eternal enemy of the lamb is of course the wolf, and the shift towards Christ the lamb naturally led to the growing use of lupine imagery in Satanic iconography. The Christian conception of the devil had become a complex affair: Satan, who had previously been a shadowy figure with no pronounced personality, emerged by about the ninth century as the ultimate personification of evil, exhibiting in his physical appearance traits which are descended from Pan, the Greek rural semi-deity, and Cernunnos, the antlered Celtic god. This new universal enemy was usually depicted with horns and a goatish rump and tail, and the wolf added another layer of influence, so that Satan might be pictured with a wolf's hindquarters, or with a wolf's snarl and fangs. In images of the Day of Judgement, the jaws of Hell, gaping wide to receive fallen sinners, were often pictured as those of a wolf. In the Book of Revelation, the Lamb is set against an even greater beast than the natural wolf, the apocalyptic Beast with 'seven heads and ten horns, and upon his horns ten crowns, and upon his heads the name of blasphemy', and these three figures of the Beast, Satan, and the wolf tended to become interlinked. For the average Christian worshipper in the Middle Ages the ancient opposition between wolf and lamb, proverbial among pastoral cultures from time immemorial, had now been elevated to cosmic proportions in the battle between Christ and Antichrist.

It is with just these biblical overtones that the word 'werewolf' first appears in English. In the Ecclesiastic Ordinances of Cnut, the Danish king who ruled England from 1017 to 1035, 'werewulf' is used in a passage which has little apparent connection with the folkloric motif of a man transformed into a wolf. The key text is Matthew 7:15: 'Beware of false prophets, which come to you in sheep's clothing, but inwardly they are ravening wolves', and the author of the Ordinance, the interestingly named Wulfstan, warns bishops and priests to be diligent in protecting their flocks *'thaet so wodfreca werewulf to swidhe ne slyte ne to fela ne abite of godcundse heorde'* ('in order that the ravening werewolf should not too widely devastate nor bite so many of the spiritual flock'). The alliterative pairing of *wodfreca werewulf* here is fascinating: *wodfreca*, used for the Hebrew adjective the Authorized Version renders as 'ravening', is not an exact translation of it. Anglo-Saxon *wod* is cognate with Germanic *wut*, meaning madness, rage, fury, intoxication, possession, hence related to Wodan/Odin, while the adjective *frec* means bold, grasping, greedy. Although used adjectivally here, the word *freca* could also be employed as a noun in poetic use to mean warrior.[16] *Wodfreca*, a rare adjective recorded only a few times in the whole canon of Anglo-Saxon literature and variously translated by different authorities, seems therefore to contain within it much the same ideas as the Scandinavian concept of *berserk*. By employing this particular word to qualify *werewulf*, Wulfstan conflates the Norse idea of a werewolf, derived from the berserks and wolf-coats who fought inspired by Odin, with the biblical concept of the wolf as the embodiment of moral danger, an appropriate cluster of symbolic usages for an eleventh-century Christian document prepared in Anglo-Saxon England under the rule of a Danish king.

Wulfstan's choice of words can be compared to an English paraphrase of the same biblical passage which appears in *Pierce the Plowmans Crede*, written at the end of the fourteenth century, where Matthew's wolves are still seen as 'wer-wolves, that wiln the folk robben'. Here, however, the term, now with a significant change of spelling, has lost the specific allusion to berserks and wolf-coats, and seems to relate to the more general concept of the werewolf as human outlaw and robber. This concept had also been expressed by the Old Norse *vargr*, but the idea of the werewolf as brigand was not confined to northern folklore: the *hirpi*, the wolf-priests who served the Sabine god of death in the classical period, claimed to have chosen their particular way of life after receiving an oracle to live 'in imitation of wolves', in other words by banditry (*lupos imitarentur, i.e. rapto viverent*).[17] The wolf was a recognized emblem for the outlaw throughout medieval Europe. It is worth pointing out that Wulfstan's use of the prefix *were-* rather than *wer-* to form *werewulf* has puzzled many etymologists. Gervase of Tilbury, writing at the beginning of the thirteenth century for a continental audience, noted that '*Anglice* werewolf *dicunt*, were *enim anglice virum sonat*, wolf *lupum*' ('In English they say *werewolf*, for in English *were* means man, and *wolf* wolf')[18] but he is wrong in thinking that *were* ever meant man in English. It is a more attractive but unprovable hypothesis that the 'were-' prefix derived instead from the Old Norse *vargr*, by way of the German *warg*.

At this stage in medieval Europe, by about the eleventh and twelfth centuries, there appears to have been no widespread fear of the werewolf as a lycanthropically transformed monster. The popular revulsion was primarily against the real wolf, the forest-dwelling, sheep-slaughtering predator, and secondarily against those men who, by leading lives of brigandage and violence, chose to behave like wolves, the man-wolves of *Pierce the Plowmans Crede*. The word 'wer-wolf', in English at least, denoted merely this latter category. The fact that it was the real wolf that bore the brunt of symbolic denigration in the medieval era helps to explain what would otherwise be fairly surprising instances of sympathetic treatment of the animal in literature at the same time as it was being hunted so assiduously in the forests. The terrible wolf of Gubbio, for example, was a famous beast in popular legend from the thirteenth century onwards, tamed by Francis of Assisi. Saint Francis was a remarkable figure, whose band of 'little brothers' (originally just twelve of them) set out to practise humility and absolute poverty. Distrusted by the Church, and forced to moderate his potentially subversive practices, Francis was nevertheless an excellent subject for the hagiographers. Legendary tales grew up around him, most of them featuring beasts of one kind or another, for so great was his empathy with all of God's creation that he was credited with the ability to communicate with animals. It is clear that the reason the wolf was chosen for the Gubbio legend is precisely *because* it was so widely feared; its murderous notoriety only served to emphasize the greatness of Saint Francis's powers in taming it.

The same kind of thinking stands behind similar appearances of ostensibly sympathetic wolves in medieval chronicles. In 617, according to Baronius, a pack of wolves appeared at a monastery and tore to pieces a number of monks who held heretical opinions. Wolves similarly attacked the members of the army of Francesco Maria, duke of Urbino, who were attempting to sack the treasure of the holy house of Loreto. A wolf was said to have sat guard over the head of the ninth-century Anglo-Saxon king, Saint Edmund, which had been cruelly struck off by the Vikings.[19] These wolves are all acting for the good, but this does not imply that contemporary attitudes to the animal were less antipathetic than otherwise suspected, for in each of these cases a polemical point is made by reversing the normal moral order and bringing the villains of the piece into ironic contrast with wolves. Heretics are more deserving of death even than the most worthless of animals, is Baronius's implication; the Vikings who martyred the king are no better than pitiless wolves, according to the bereaved Anglo-Saxons.

It would appear then that both the classical concept of the werewolf, as laid out by Petronius (albeit with his authorial tongue toying gently with the inside of his cheek), and the old Germanic idea of the wolf-warrior were pretty well laid to rest by the high point of the medieval period. The fear was no longer of the beast within, for the average Christian had external threats enough to be getting on with: plague, famine, Jews, lepers, Muslims, heretics, to name but the most widely feared. Predators like the wolf were only another external threat, and the figure of the wolf had become cloaked with all manner of diabolical associations. Yet it is important to note that it was the real wolf that suffered such denigration. The categories of 'man' and 'animal' were understood to be separate, and no power (excepting always God's) was regarded as sufficient to confuse the two.

Indeed, at this period, it was held to be heretical to believe that a man could be changed into a wolf, or to believe in any of the supernatural phenomena – shape-shifting, night-flight, magical bewitchment – that the classical authors had described. The famous *Canon Episcopi*, a Frankish capitular probably issued about the year 900 (although it was widely believed to be much earlier), condemned such beliefs in fairly specific terms: 'Some wicked women are perverted by the Devil and led astray by illusions and fantasies by demons, so that they believe they ride out at night on beasts with Diana, the pagan goddess, and a horde of women.' The capitular explained that these delusions were caused by Satan and that such ideas as lycanthropic transformation and transvection, flying out at night, were illusory: 'It is only the mind that does this, but faithless people believe that these things happen to the body as well.'[20]

The very fact that it was felt necessary to speak out against such ideas implies that pagan beliefs remained deeply embedded in Christianized western Europe. It would require two things – a general acceptance that the categorization of man and animal could be blurred, particularly through Satanic influence; and increased fear of the extent of that influence – before the popular imagination would combine the almost hysterical fear aroused by the real wolf with the moral obloquy with which the wolf-like bandits of medieval Europe were regarded, thus revivifying the ancient and terrible figure of the werewolf.

6

Monsters, Dog-Heads, and Old Irish Tales

'Tis like the howling of Irish wolves against the moon.

SHAKESPEARE,
As You Like It

In the beginning God created heaven and earth, and luckily for the medieval world somebody bothered to set down exactly how He did it. This was something to be thankful for, as it solved the potentially troubling question of how man was to be distinguished from the rest of creation. The narrative of Genesis laid down clearly the exact chronological order of that creation, and nobody could doubt that this order had significance: on the fourth day the waters had begun to teem with countless living creatures and the vault of heaven had been filled with birds; on the fifth day cattle, reptiles, and wild animals were added to the scene. In the honoured position, last of all creation, like a prelate whose grand arrival is heralded by a preceding gaggle of choir boys and minor clergy, came Man, made in the image of the Creator to rule over His work. According to this scheme, the distinction between man and animal was sharp: man was given the role of steward of all creation, even down to the job of giving names to the animals – a necessary task this, as they had been created, not in the Creator's perfect image, but in a bewildering variety of less dignified shapes 'according to their kind'.

Even so, the dividing line between human and animal proved dangerously narrow on occasion. Man walked on two legs and thought of God, but it was hard to deny that he was largely occupied with the same imperatives of eating, defecating, copulating, and sleeping as the lower animals. There were always plenty of examples of men who failed to live by the higher ideals,

and medieval man was acutely aware that through sin an individual might descend all too easily into bestiality. There was
biblical precedent for such a fall in the story of Nebuchadnezzar,
the mighty king of Babylon, whose transformation was prefig-
ured in a dream which only Daniel could interpret. As divine
punishment for his kingly arrogance, 'he was banished from the
society of men, his mind became like that of a beast, he had to live
with the wild asses and eat grass like oxen, and his body was
drenched with the dew of heaven'.[1] Although this story could be
interpreted (and was) as a metaphorical description of an episode
of ordinary human madness inflicted on the king, the horror of
his transformation is constantly underlined in the biblical narrative by the bestial details. His hair grew long, like that of a goat,
and his nails became eagle's talons, the chronicler points out,[2]
and the fact of his living with asses and eating grass like oxen is
reiterated five times in the book. Medieval book illustrators took
the hint and pictured him, not as a deranged lunatic, but hairy
and crouching in the bushes, clearly half man, half wild animal.

The medieval observer would also see the dividing line blurred
in his own world – at the edges of it, to be exact, for there it was
everyone knew dwelt the monstrous races. Lurking at the edges
of the *mappaemundi*, or listed in the great illustrated encyclopae-
dias, occasionally peering out from the swirling fronds of marginal book illumination, were monsters, races of men so different
from the European norm that their very existence threatened the
stable order of creation. There were races of abnormal dimen-
sions, like the Giants and Pygmies, or with peculiar physical
features, such as the Himantopodes with strap-like feet, the
Panotii with giant ears, or the Amyctyrae with grossly distended
lower lips. Some were distinguished by their unusual diets, like
the Astomi who had no mouths and lived on the smell of apples,
or the Anthropophagi, who ate human flesh. Some are still
familiar to us today, like the Amazons, fierce women who lived
without men in a martial society and cut off their right breasts to
make drawing a bow easier, or Troglodytes ('hole-creepers'),
mute creatures who lived in caves in the deserts of Ethiopia. Still
others seem beyond the realms of imagination, like the Sciopods,
one-legged creatures who lay around protecting themselves from
the sun with the shade of their single huge foot, or the Blemmyae,
who had no head or neck but had their facial features on their

chests. (These are the 'men whose heads do grow beneath their shoulders' of whom Othello told such charming traveller's tales.)

That these creatures were believed to exist at the edges of the known world, in those exotic, almost mythical lands of India, Ethiopia, Albania, and Cathay, obviously suggests something of the intellectual milieu in which the werewolf myth could thrive; but the history of the belief in the monstrous races themselves makes a wider point about the transmission of information from antiquity to medieval times, and sheds light on the way in which the medieval temper might have read the werewolf and metamorphosis stories of Petronius, Virgil, Apuleius, Ovid, *et al.*

It has been a commonplace for many years now to observe that we live in an age in which each generation brings some new scientific or technological advance. Constant research brings new facts to light, while the economic world order disseminates products of that new advance, so that in a short time startlingly complex inventions such as the personal computer can become ubiquitous (and relatively cheap) throughout the industrialized world. Medical knowledge can be put into practice so effectively that, for example, smallpox has been eradicated from the human population in the short space of two hundred years. In these two areas – frequency of discovery of new data, and efficiency of dissemination of information – the medieval world lagged far behind us. It also lagged behind the classical age that had preceded it. The discoveries of Pythagoras or Euclid, for example, could never have taken place in the medieval schools, and intelligent men knew as much. Bernard of Chartres realized that medieval thinkers stood in relation to the classical world as 'dwarfs on the shoulders of giants, so that we can see more than they, and things at a greater distance, not by any virtue or any sharpness of sight on our part, or any physical distinction, but because we are carried high and raised up by their giant size'. Even this summation, with Bernard's subtle implication that, despite the disadvantages of the medieval era, progress was being made, was somewhat optimistic. Given a paucity of new information, the Middle Ages often had to make do with unquestioning repetition of the information passed on to them by antiquity. As they had lost knowledge of the Greek language (and, with the sacking of Constantinople in 1204 by the hooligans of the Fourth Crusade, a great many of the actual texts), they were confined in

most cases to secondary sources available in Latin. The unfortunate result of this was stagnation in a number of areas of
knowledge: the standstill in the field of medicine was only one
example.

It can hardly be thought surprising, therefore, that all the
stories of monstrous races which circulated so widely throughout
the Middle Ages turn out to have come from a tiny selection of
classical sources. In his book *The Monstrous Races in Medieval Art
and Thought*, John Block Friedman[3] goes so far as to name them
the 'Plinian' races, after the classical author in whose *Natural
History* most of the races are first listed. Pliny did not discover
these races for himself by travelling to the edges of the world. He
was no great experimental investigator in the post-medieval
scientific tradition, although his death while inspecting the
eruption of Vesuvius at too close a quarter argues something of
an investigative urge in him. Instead, Pliny was content to travel
in the realms of literature. He had a book by him at all times, his
nephew Pliny the Younger tells us, and he never read one without
making extracts from it. His pleasant maxim was that no book
was so bad as to have nothing of interest in it. The result of this
obsessive reading and note-taking in both Greek and Latin
authors was thirty-six volumes of his *Natural History*, which he
states in the preface to the first book represented 20,000 facts
extracted from some 2000 volumes.

Such an undertaking – representing a treasure house of information culled from many sources no longer extant in the Middle
Ages – simply could not be repeated, and the medieval encyclopaedists like Isidore of Seville, Vincent of Beauvais, and the many
others who wrote about the monstrous races, did not try. Instead
they took most of their information directly from Pliny. An
appearance of progress, of the unearthing of new facts, was given
by the medieval authors' habit of combining the characteristics of
two or more Plinian races to produce what seemed to be entirely
new monsters, so that the numbers of races gradually increased.
A few others could be incorporated from other sources in order
to swell the list still further. A growing awareness of the reality of
the world outside Europe, as gathered by travellers like Marco
Polo, and the many merchants, missionaries, and crusaders who
travelled beyond the bounds of western civilization throughout
this period, did little to dampen belief in such creatures. This may

have been because the habits and appearance of the tribes these well-travelled Europeans encountered were so far removed from their own cultural experiences that they defied the imaginative leap of sympathy required to understand them. To the medieval European, many native peoples really were monstrous.

The modern westerner, in contrast, thinks very little monstrous. He has no difficulty in conceiving of tribes taller or smaller than the average in his own culture; indeed he still refers to some native peoples such as the Baku as 'pygmies', much to their irritation. Through such modern eyes it is easy to see how the cannibalistic habits of any number of tribes could have given rise to the Anthropophagi, or how other tribes' facial decorations and self-mutilations could generate the distended-lipped Amyctyrae or the huge-eared Panotii. A number of plausible explanations for the origins of the apparently impossible monstrous races suggest themselves. The Sciopod who uses his foot as an umbrella could well be based on the strange contortions of a practitioner of Yoga. Even the Blemmyae with their faces on their chests have a conceivable origin in direct observation: a tribe with that name are recorded as having attacked Christian settlements in North Africa between the middle of the third century and the fifth.[4] If they had used chest armour, perhaps painted with ferocious faces, the beleaguered Christians watching from above and at a distance could be forgiven for thinking their attackers had their heads below their shoulders.

Humankind comes in so many forms that examples can be found which could explain even the most bizarre of the Plinian monsters. Two of the monstrous races are distinguished by their unusual pedal extremities: the Himantopodes have elongated, strap-like feet, and the Hippopodes have feet like horses. In the modern Zambesi valley on the border of Zimbabwe there can be found a tribe among which a number of members suffer from an unusual deformity: instead of five small toes, their feet are divided into two giant toes. Their neighbours call them 'ostrich-feet', although doctors prefer the equally animalistic 'lobster-claw syndrome'. The condition is hereditary and is thought to be transmitted via a single mutated gene. The tribe's isolation, and the inevitable inbreeding that has resulted from it, have produced a high incidence of the deformity.[5] An encounter with such a tribe would be a memorable occurrence indeed.

The fact that a belief in the existence of the monstrous races continued in the face of growing evidence that the human race was managing to thrive in a variety of non-European guises the world over suggests that the belief filled some emotional need in medieval man. These monsters were usually seen as vile, barbarian, deformed, unclothed, speechless beings, and it became a common theme to trace their descent from Cain, the murderer of Abel and universal outcast. Not all writers, however, chose to emphasize the moral implications of the existence of these monsters: some seem to have genuinely enjoyed the exercise of their powers of fantasy and imagination, very like twentieth-century science fiction writers festooning their creations with absurd complements of extra eyes, giant crania, features taken from animals, TV aerials protuding from their heads, or anything else they can think of. The medieval encyclopaedists must have given their readers similar pleasures. When medieval writers did take up moral attitudes towards these monstrous beings, they were not necessarily entirely censorious. One race of particular relevance to the re-emergence of the werewolf myth in the late medieval and early modern era illustrates something of this surprising moral complexity.

The Cynocephali were the best-known of the monstrous races, probably because of their memorable appearance, combining the homely and the grossly outlandish. Their Latin name is explicit – they are Dog-Heads, creatures with the bodies of men but the heads of dogs. Pliny's Greek source located their habitat in the mountains of India. The Cynocephali could not talk, but barked to communicate with each other. They wore animal skins, lived in caves, and hunted efficiently, using swords, bows, and javelins. In another of the sources for information about the monstrous races circulating in the Middle Ages – the cycle of marvellous tales about Alexander the Great and his travels in India – the Cynocephali are more frightening, with enormous teeth and breathing fire. Several accounts make them cannibals. All accounts emphasize that the Cynocephali combine the natures of man and beast.

As with other monstrous races, there are a number of rationalist theories to explain the origin of the Cynocephali. Any ferocious cave-dwelling aboriginal, clad in animal skins and screaming threats in an unknown language, would be likely to impress a Greek traveller, fresh from the decorous civilities of the *polis*, with his bestial appearance. As for his barking to communicate, the very word 'barbarian' has come down to us because the Greeks thought the language of foreigners sounded like the meaningless 'bar-bar' (which is noticeably like the childishly imitative 'bow-wow' of modern English). An alternative explanation sees baboons or other anthropoid apes as the originals of the Cynocephali; the baboon in particular, with its dog-like muzzle and simian body, is a likely candidate. The celebrated medieval schoolman Albert the Great certainly thought so, mentioning during his discussion of the great apes that 'they are those who are called dog-men in the mappaemundi'.[6]

But for the majority of Christian writers who believed in their existence, the Dog-Heads had a special place in creation. The tales of travellers had confirmed what Jesus' words as quoted by John (10:16) seemed to imply, that there were other non-Christian flocks in the world needing the services of the Good Shepherd. It followed that it was every Christian's duty to help bring them into the fold, in answer to the command implicit in the story of the Pentecost. That story was told in the Acts of the Apostles: after the death of Jesus, the apostles and their colleagues, including Jesus' mother and brothers, were gathered together. Tongues like flames of fire descended on them, and they were given the gift of talking in strange languages. The chronicler notes that there were at that time 'men[7] of every nation under heaven' living in Jerusalem, the point being of course that these men were naturally amazed to hear the apostles speaking in their own languages. He then gives a list of these foreign witnesses of the supernatural event: they were inhabitants of Parthia, Media, Elam, Mesopotamia, Judaea, Cappodocia, Pontus, Asia, Phrygia, Pamphylia, Egypt, the districts of Libya around Cyrene, Rome, Crete, and Arabia. This can hardly be called a comprehensive list of 'every nation under heaven'. In fact it is a list of the lands clustered around the eastern end of the Mediterranean in the first century AD. 'Asia', for example, is not the modern continent, but the contemporary name for the western seaboard of what is now Turkey. To the medieval mind, however, accustomed to the vague, near-mythical geography of Pliny and his followers, many of the names of these countries had a wider, more resonant meaning. 'Arabia' especially could be read as implying a far greater geographical range than the chronicler himself was likely to have known existed. Indeed, it would have to, if the notion of 'every nation under heaven' being present were to be taken seriously.

Depiction of the nations present at the Pentecost was a popular theme in medieval illustration, particularly in eastern Christian art. Only those who fail to keep in mind the medieval desire to read the list in Acts as literally representing 'every nation under heaven' will be surprised to recognize the frequent appearance of Dog-Heads in Pentecostal illustrations. One such illustration, done in 1262 in an Armenian gospel book,[8] shows a Dog-Head in a group of figures being preached to by Christ. Above the group is the quotation 'Medes, Parthians, and Elamites', implicitly including the Cynocephali among the Pentecostal nations. An earlier manuscript – the eleventh-century 'Theodore' Psalter now in the British Library[9] – also depicts Christ preaching to dog-headed men, and such illustrations are far from uncommon in Byzantine art. If the description of the nations in Acts was not enough to sanction the appearance of Dog-Heads in these illustrations, medieval scholars were happy to fall back on the Old Testament. As always, the events of the Old Testament were seen as prefiguring those of the New, and Psalm 22 was an obvious typological representation of the Passion of Christ. After all, its arresting opening words were those quoted by Jesus in his final agony – 'My God, my God, why hast thou forsaken me?' It was verse 16, however, which was relevant to the Cynocephali: 'For dogs have compassed me: the assembly of the wicked have inclosed me: they pierced my hands and my feet.'[10] More than one commentator[11] explained that allegorically the dogs in this passage represented the Jews, because just as a dog barks at anything strange, so the Jews rejected the new doctrines of Jesus and 'barked' against them. Despite this depiction of the Cynocephali as the type of the heretic who knowingly rejects the truth, Christian missionaries were eager to show the power of the Word in overcoming such obstacles. Their most famous Dog-Head convert was one of the major saints of the Christian world.

The stories of the missionary activities of the apostles were of course recorded in the books of the New Testament, but these were too few to satisfy the curiosity of all the faithful, and a number of non-canonical Acts of the Apostles were in circulation throughout the Middle Ages. One such, the *Contendings of the Apostles*, probably translated into Ethiopic in the fourteenth century from earlier Coptic and Arabic material, purported to describe the Acts of Andrew and Bartholomew among the Parthians, a Pentecostal nation which – as the 1262 Armenian gospel book shows – was sufficiently outlandish to the medieval Christian world to be thought of as monstrous. There the two apostles meet a giant cannibal called Abominable. As his name suggests, he was a terrifying sight, 'four cubits in height, and his face was like unto the face of a great dog, and his eyes were like unto lamps of fire which burnt brightly, and his teeth were like unto the tusks of a wild boar, or the teeth of a lion, and the nails of his hands were like unto curved reaping hooks, and the nails of his toes were like unto the claws of a lion, and the hair of his head came down over his arms like unto the mane of a lion, and his whole appearance was awful and terrifying.'[12] Luckily for the two apostles, when they chance upon him Abominable has just been vouchsafed an angelic visitation in which he has been promised a human nature if he accepts their teaching. He does so; the relieved apostles rename their tame dog-headed cannibal Christianus, and he becomes their guide as they continue their evangelistic mission in that heathen land.

The outline of this story, in which the power of the Word converts even the hideous and scarcely human Cynocephalus, strongly influenced the legends of two major saints. Saint Mercurius is not well-known in the western tradition; he appears chiefly in Egyptian and Greek accounts in which he uses converted Cynocephali as fiercesome soldiers, very like the berserks of Odin, in the fight against the pagan hordes. Although, as with Abominable, conversion has rendered Mercurius' Dog-Heads gentle, their savagery and cannibalism can be usefully revived in the service of Christianity at the saint's command. Much better known is Saint Christopher, patron saint of travellers, although the fact that he was a Dog-Head has been silently edited out of the versions of his life circulated in the west. A very popular version of his story in the eastern Christian tradition follows every detail of Abominable's story in the *Contendings of the Apostles*: Christopher is born a pagan Dog-Head called Reprobus. Like Abominable, he regrets his bestial nature, and is overjoyed when his conversion to Christianity allows him to lose his Cynocephalic nature.

In the western tradition, this version of Saint Christopher's life was best known in Ireland and the Celtic periphery of Britain. This could have arisen from the presence in Ireland of monks who still knew Greek, although it may have had more to do with the fact that Irish Celtic culture had escaped Romanization.[13] The *Libar Breac* glosses an eighth-century Irish kalendar, or list of saints, noting of Christopher that he 'was one of the Dog-heads, a race that had the heads of dogs and ate human flesh. He meditated much on God, but at that time he could speak only the language of the Dog-heads.'[14] A near-contemporary Anglo-Saxon martyrology has much the same account.[15] Walter of Speyer, writing in the tenth century, gives two versions of Christopher's life, one in prose, the other in verse, in which the saint's dog-headedness is alluded to more delicately. The verse account states that 'he took his origins from the race of Cynocephali, a people in speech and countenance dissimilar to others'. References to Christopher as a Dog-Head are harder to find in western literature and art after this date, although the image persisted in icons in eastern Christian art until the nineteenth century. Western art usually prefers to depict Saint Christopher as a giant carrying the infant Jesus on his shoulders. There are two points to make about this. First, in western iconography Christopher is still a member of one of the Plinian races, the Giants, less threatening in appearance, yet very much a monster to medieval thinking. Secondly, the word Christopher actually means 'Christ carrier', and the name may well have supplied the details of the west's favoured alternative narrative – the pagan earning his salvation literally by being a Christ carrier – rather than the other way round.

Although Saint Christopher was gradually ousted from their ranks, the Cynocephali remained a feature of western Christian medieval thought. One of the most important churches in medieval France was that of the Madeleine at Vézelay. Built as a pilgrimage shrine to contain the relics of Mary Magdalene, the church stood on the crossroads of the routes to Jerusalem and the shrine of Saint James of Compostela, which meant that it was among the most frequently visited churches in France and probably western Europe. Its fame was further increased in 1145 when Saint Bernard preached the Second Crusade there. The most notable feature of the church interior is the tympanum, the vast bas-relief sculpture above the central portal. The scene is once again Pentecostal: Christ, with arms outstretched, stands amid the apostles, upon whose heads the tongues are descending, preaching their Mission to go out and convert all the races of the earth.[16] Above them in an arched frieze, as if at the edge of the world, are the monstrous races, including, at Christ's right hand, a group of Cynocephali. Small wonder that the medieval French peasant who had either seen for himself or had heard of this impressive vision of the world from some close neighbour, perhaps his parish priest who had undertaken a pilgrimage to Vézelay, should continue to believe that there were half-canine creatures at its edges.

The complex of ideas surrounding the Cynocephali throughout most of the Middle Ages was ambiguous. On one hand, they were potential converts who might be used as awe-inspiring soldiers against the forces of pagan darkness, like Saint Christopher. On the other, if they resisted the Christian message, just as the Jews had rejected the idea that Jesus was the son of God, they were to be abhorred; their monstrosity was the physical mark of their heresy. Jews were not the only targets for this moralizing metamorphosis; Muslims too were identified with the Cynocephali. Christians routinely referred to their rivals for the Holy Land as 'dogs', and the Pentecostal artists of the east often gave their dog-headed figures Islamic dress. Indeed, in the 1262 Armenian gospel the dog-headed figure wears pagan dress and stands in front of a crowd. The only other figure so distinguished is a figure in Jewish dress, which suggests that these two are meant to represent the principal religions which opposed Christianity, the Cynocephalus here, as elsewhere, to be understood as standing for Islam. A world map of 1430, which shows a people called Beni Chelib, has a rubric that reads 'Ebinichebel is a Saracen Ethiopian king with his dog-headed people'. The name of the king and of his people comes from a Latin transliteration of the Arabic *banu kalb*, meaning 'sons of a dog'. The fact that this king is a Muslim and an 'Ethiopian' (i.e., black) shows how the term 'dog-head' was gradually becoming an all-purpose insult intended to cover any degree of geographical, physical, or theological remoteness from the norms of Christian civilization.

It is hardly surprising, therefore, that travellers to the remoter parts of the world should persist in finding these and similar monsters when they got there. One such traveller was Giraldus de Barri, called Giraldus Cambrensis (Gerald of Wales) from the place of his birth. Giraldus was a member of the Norman ruling class which had come over to England with William the Conqueror in the eleventh century. His family had taken a leading role in the conquest of Ireland a little over a hundred years after their arrival in England, and he had visited the new territory for the first time in 1183. Giraldus revisited Ireland two years later at the command of Henry II, and wrote the first account of Ireland and its early history, his *History* or *Topography of Ireland*. Giraldus and his contemporaries thought Ireland to be the furthermost point in the world, and it seemed natural to them that he should devote the whole second part of his three-part book to the 'Wonders and Miracles of Ireland', the place where, almost uniquely in the west, the legend of dog-headed Saint Christopher had flourished.

Giraldus divides his Irish wonders into ancient and modern, and is very careful to give a date for the first of his modern wonders: he states specifically that it occurred three years before their expedition's arrival in Ireland; that is, in 1182 or 1183. A priest, travelling from Ulster to Meath, had camped down for the night in a forest on the borders of Meath. He and his only companion, a small boy, were sitting up late by their fire when they were greatly shocked by the sudden approach of a wolf. More shocking still was that the wolf spoke to them, although it kept telling them they need have no fear of it. Despite the wolf's reassurances of its good intent, the priest was naturally terrified, but he questioned the animal closely and was relieved to hear Catholic answers to all his questions. At length the priest managed to establish the facts: the wolf was a man, one of a pair of inhabitants of the village of Ossory which had been cursed by a saint, the abbot Natalis. As a result of his curse, every seven years two people of Ossory, a man and a woman, were exiled and forced to assume the shape of a wolf. If they survived for that length of time they were allowed to return to the village and to their human forms, but two others must take their place.

But now it seemed as if this werewolf's companion was not going to see out her seven-year stretch. She was dangerously ill, and the werewolf begged the priest to come and administer to her in her final illness. Still fearful, the priest followed him and found the she-werewolf groaning in the hollow of a tree. She too behaved in a reassuringly human way, thanking the priest profusely for coming. Nevertheless the priest was still uncertain. Was he justified in performing the divine offices for a creature that looked so clearly inhuman? Deciding that he should err on the side of caution, the priest administered all the last rites except for the final communion. But the werewolf-husband saw that his wife was being denied, and came nearer. Using his huge wolf's paw like a hand, he delicately peeled back the pelt of the she-wolf from the head down to the navel, revealing to the astonished priest the shape of an old woman. The priest was convinced by this demonstration of her essential humanity and gave her the sacrament, which she received devoutly. The coda of Giraldus' story has the author himself called upon by the bishop and synod of Meath to deliver his learned opinion as to whether or not the priest did right.

Despite Giraldus' concern to date this story precisely there are a number of familiar elements in it. The seven years of the saint's curse, for example, is reminiscent of the Lykaian nine-year period of werewolfism; seven and nine are both numbers which recur frequently in folklore, seven being rather more popular in the western tradition. The whole story is yet more familiar still to those with any knowledge of early texts on Ireland, for the story is not entirely Giraldus' own. Like many others of his wonders of Ireland, this story belongs in a tradition of oral history going back into the Old Irish period that is available in several other independent versions. More or less the same story, for example, turns up in the thirteenth-century Norse *Kongs Skuggsjo* (*Speculum Regale*), where the saint is said to be Saint Patrick, and the werewolfism a punishment heaped on the descendants of those who opposed his teachings; some of them turn into wolves every seven years. The theme is also present in a number of other versions of early Irish history. One can certainly connect this recurring motif with the legend of Saint Christopher as Dog-Head being circulated here in Ireland. Whichever came first, one was likely to have been instrumental in preparing the way for belief in the other.

One notable feature of Giraldus' telling of the story is that his werewolves are innocent victims. Their werewolfism is a punishment invoked by a curse, just as in the Lykaon myth, but while the inhabitants of Ossory may originally have been guilty of something vile enough to arouse the saint to such a ferocious imprecation (although if he knows what their crime was, Giraldus is not telling), the feature of this curse is that it falls on the population as a whole regardless of individual guilt or innocence. In this respect it resembles God's curse on Adam and his descendants, or its parallel – some might say its antithesis – God's curse on Cain and *his* descendants, in that the punishment has fallen on more than just the perpetrator of the original sin. Giraldus' werewolves, however, are clearly Adam's rather than Cain's kin: they are good Christians, more worried about fulfilling the sacramental requirements of dying well than in grieving over their own sad situation. Not once do they express resentment at the saint's Old Testament vindictiveness, and in this they express true Christian fortitude. This feature of the story is significant, as it demonstrates that although a twelfth-century werewolf story is likely to be told to some moral purpose, the werewolf himself – the person trapped inside the pelt – need not be depicted as evil, debauched, or in a pact with the Devil.

Much the same moral attitude can be found in one of the lays of Marie de France, another Norman writer of this era. Her *lai* of *Bisclavret* opens with a brief definition of terms. Marie says that *bisclavret* is the Breton name for the werewolf, the creature known as *garwaf* by the Normans. The Breton word has intrigued linguists: some derive it from *bisc*, 'short', and *lavret*, 'wearing breeches', which would bear some relation to the importance of the motif of clothing in the story that follows; others prefer to relate it to the Breton *bleiz lavaret*, 'speaking wolf', or *bleiz laveret*, 'rational wolf'. Whatever the derivation, the hero of this particular story lived in Brittany, a brave knight, well considered by his fellows, and, we later find out, particularly beloved of the king. He was married to a beautiful lady, who had, however, one great sorrow: for three whole days each week her lord went missing. Naturally she was intrigued to find out his secret, and where he went during those three days, but when she finally plucked up enough courage to ask him, he told her that she must not put such questions to him. Nothing but evil would befall them if he were to reveal his secret. Furthermore, he feared that her love for him would cease if she found out. But she insisted, using all her feminine powers of persuasion, until at last he revealed the truth:

> 'I become Bisclavret. I enter the forest and live on prey and plunder. I run as naked as a beast.'
> 'What do you do with your clothes?'
> 'I cannot tell you that. If I should lose them, or even if anybody were to catch me in the act of undressing, I would be doomed to wander as a werewolf forever.'

But his wife insisted on knowing where he put his clothes, asking him how he could doubt her faith in him, so that in the end he told her of his secret hiding place: a hollow stone concealed by a bush, near an ancient chapel, deep in the heart of the woods. By now she was convinced of the truth of his explanation of the missing three days. She was horrified to think that her husband was a werewolf and began to plot how she might get away from him. Luckily she had a would-be lover, a knight who had for some time been paying her tribute in the approved courtly manner. She wrote to him, telling him that he could at last have what his heart desired. There was just one little thing he could do for her . . .

A year passed. Bisclavret had not been seen since his sudden disappearance. The woods had been searched, but nothing was found. His wife, apparently despairing of his ever returning, had married her suitor. And now the king set out on a hunt, his hounds running before him, sniffing through the undergrowth of the same wood in which Bisclavret lurked. At once the hounds picked up a scent, the horn was blown, and the whole pack raced off in full cry. They chased Bisclavret from dawn to dusk, until he was finally cornered, torn and bleeding, terrified with the realization that his final moment was upon him. But as he crouched there shivering, the king rode up to see the kill. Bisclavret recognized him and ran over to him, making piteous motions for the king to spare his life. Although frightened by this prodigious display, the king realized that the animal was a marvel: 'Here is a beast with the sense of a man,' he told his courtiers, and proposed to take the werewolf back to his hall.

Bisclavret followed the king home, trotting along beside his horse as obediently as a dog, and showed no signs of wanting to return to the wood. In fact he settled into castle life easily, doing no harm to any of its inhabitants, and earning their trust and affection by his good nature. He even came to win a place in the king's chamber. Everyone could see that the king loved him as a friend. One day, however, the king gave a great feast, and among the guests was the husband of Bisclavret's former wife. Bisclavret caught sight of him as soon as he entered the hall and could not restrain himself: in the sight of everyone, including the king, he raced over and sank his fangs into the unsuspecting knight. The king managed to ward him off by threatening him with a stick, but twice more during the feast Bisclavret attacked the knight. Everyone was naturally amazed because the wolf had, until then, displayed only a sweet disposition. Knowing him to be a reasonable creature, the company began to have their suspicions.

The feast ended without further incident, and the treacherous knight was able to make his escape. Some time later, however, the king was again hunting in the forest where Bisclavret was originally found, and the wolf trotted by his side, as always. The day wore on, and eventually the company made for their customary hunting lodge in the woods to spend the night there. In the morning, the local nobility came to pay their respects, including Bisclavret's former wife. When she entered the chamber, nothing could restrain the wolf's wild fury. He burst his leash and sprang up at her, biting off her nose in his ferocious attack. The courtiers managed to beat him off, and were about to set about him with their swords when a wise counsellor intervened, pointing out that the wolf had never attacked anybody except this woman and her second husband. He pointed out that this woman was once the husband of the king's favourite who had disappeared in mysterious circumstances.

The king agreed that the matter should be looked into further, and the knight and his paramour were questioned under torture. At last the lady confessed that she had organized the theft of Bisclavret's clothing from the hollow stone. The king demanded the return of the garments, and, when they had been brought, laid them in front of Bisclavret. But the wolf shied away from them, and once again the wise counsellor spoke up, taking the king to one side and telling him that the transformation from wolf back to man must be done in secret, as Bisclavret would have to shoulder a heavy burden of shame as he abandoned his bestial shape forever. So the king took the wolf back to the regal bedroom and left him there alone with the garments. After a short while he re-entered, and found the long-lost knight sleeping on his bed like a little child. He rushed to him and greeted him joyously on his return to humanity. Bisclavret's lands were restored, and his treacherous former wife and her lover banished from the kingdom.

Although Bisclavret, like Giraldus' inhabitants of Ossory, is treated sympathetically – indeed, he is the hero of this knightly tale – Marie leaves in a number of details which indicate the unpleasantness of the werewolf *per se*. Right at the beginning she emphasizes that a werewolf is a horrible creature, a 'beste salvage', which hides in the woods by night, does evil, and seeks to devour humans. She also notes the king's fear when first importuned by the wounded wolf, and never lets her audience forget that the wolf is allowed into the castle on sufferance. His few displays of feral violence are, understandably enough, carefully discussed by the castle's inhabitants, and the courtiers have their swords drawn ready to kill him after his nose-biting assault on his faithless wife. But the most significant detail in this network of signs pointing to the vileness of the lycanthropic state is the face-saving ritual the wise counsellor works out towards the conclusion of the story in order to avoid embarrassing Bisclavret on his return to human form. Although the *lai* allows the hero to be a werewolf, it is never forgotten that a werewolf is a loathsome thing, and that any noble knight would be desperately ashamed of having been one, no matter how innocently the transformation came about.

The question of Marie's attitude to the notion of a werewolf is of significance in judging how far the appearance of such creatures in the literature of the period reflects actual belief in them among the intended audience of the work. Giraldus, for example, evidently believed in his Ossory werewolves. Indeed, he would look pretty foolish, blasphemous even, if his audience did not share his belief, for he puts his own ecclesiastical dignity on the line by stating that he was asked to adjudicate in an episcopal review of the case. Marie gives fewer clues to her own views, although she does end her tale by emphasizing its truth (*L'aventure ke avez oïe / Veraie fu, n'en dutez mie*). This might be disregarded as a formulaic expression of little evidential value, but it is noticeable that this is one of only two occasions in her twelve *lais*

when she insists on the truth of the 'aventure'. Some critics refer
to the 'supernatural' subject matter of *Bisclavret*, but it is clear
that Marie herself failed to recognize any distinction between
what modern sceptics distinguish as the supernatural and the
realistic.[17] On the contrary, *Bisclavret* appears to be based on a
generally accepted belief in the possibility and reality of
lycanthropy, a belief evidently current among the educated
Anglo-Normans of the twelfth century.

Marie de France was a close contemporary of Giraldus
Cambrensis. Her *lais*, although evidently based on sources dating
back before her time, were composed at much the same time as
his *Topography of Ireland* – the usual *terminus ad quem* given is
1189, the year of Henry II's death (the same king who had
launched the Norman invasion of Ireland and for whom Giraldus
wrote his book). She shared with Giraldus what might anachro-
nistically be called an Anglo-French culture. It can be deduced
from her work that she was a native of France (possibly specifically the Île-de-France, as distinct from the other regions which
eventually came under the rule of the French crown), and that at
some time she lived and wrote in England. The 'Breton' *lais* she
wrote down for her Norman audience and for posterity were a
traditional form of narrative read or sung to the accompaniment
of the Breton *rote*, a sort of harp. As such they preserved a clear
line of storytelling with roots stretching back into the Celtic past,
by no means restricted simply to stories from the region of
Brittany. The British (Celtic) bard Hyvarnion had sung at the
Frankish court of Childebert I as long ago as the sixth century,
and he may even have sung of the same *matière* as Marie. Her *lais*
are rich in place names and specific geographical locations,
transporting the reader from Brittany to England, from Nor-
mandy to Wales, and as far afield as Salerno in Italy, and critics
have noted elements of classical, eastern, and Scandinavian
origin in her works. It is difficult to maintain that these were all
her own additions: more likely they are evidence for the remarkable richness of the culture she shared with Giraldus, a culture
which preserved a notably large element of the pre-Christian past
and which was wide-ranging and eclectic. The Dog-Heads made
their way from the east to France and Ireland by the most
circuitous of routes, and it is hardly surprising that their close
cousins, the werewolves, should join them there.

There are several other werewolf stories found in Celtic-influenced culture in this period. A fourteenth-century manuscript gives a Latin version of a Welsh tale called *Arthur and Gorlagon*, which bears a close relationship to *Bisclavret*. In this version of the story, King Arthur is challenged by his queen to discover, if he can, the heart, the nature, and the ways of women. Arthur sets out alone, and rides to the castle of a neighbouring king, Gargol. This king cannot help him, but directs him to the castle of his brother, King Torleil. The second king is no more help than the first, and Arthur is forced to continue his journey until he reaches the castle of the third royal brother, King Gorlagon. Here at last he is promised a story that will shed some small light on his quest, although Gorlagon warns that Arthur will be only marginally the wiser at the end of his tale.

Gorlagon's story concerns a king who had a garden in which there grew a magical sapling. Whoever cut this sapling, struck his head with it, and repeated a certain formula would at once become a wolf. The king's treacherous wife discovered this secret, cut down the sapling, and used it to transform the unfortunate king. She then married a handsome youth, son of a pagan king, and let him rule the kingdom. The werewolf-king fled to the forest, where he met a real she-wolf, and started a wolf family of his own. One day, with his cubs and wolf-wife, he entered the town and attacked the two princes, who were the spawn of his adulterous wife and her lover. The citizens were alerted by this attack, and when the werewolf and his family returned and attacked two noble counts, the queen's cousins, they managed to catch the cubs and kill them, although the werewolf escaped.

Maddened by the slaughter of his offspring, the werewolf wrought terrible havoc on the flocks and herds until at last he was chased out of the country, but he was no more welcome across the border. Eventually he found refuge in a wood in a third country where he seemed to be safe. One night, however, he overheard two locals saying that the king was determined to hunt down the frightful wolf that had been terrorizing the country. Here the story closely parallels *Bisclavret*: the wolf waylays the king and manages to persuade him not to kill him, and is then installed in his castle as a favourite. The faithless woman at this point of the story is the queen, who was cuckolding her husband with one of the castle servants. When the king was away, she mistreated the wolf, to whom she had taken an instinctive dislike. One day he pounced as she was engaged in love-making with her servant in the king's bed, and inflicted deep wounds on the servant. The queen locked away her own son in the dungeon, and swore that the wolf had eaten her son and attacked the servant who had tried to defend him. But the wolf managed to get the king to follow him to the dungeon where the prince was discovered unharmed. The servant eventually confessed his crime, and was flayed alive and hanged; the queen was torn limb from limb by horses, then burnt.

Reviewing this whole unpleasant episode, the king naturally voiced the suspicion that the wolf was so intelligent that it must be a man bewitched, at which the wolf wagged its tail, licked the royal visage, and generally showed its approval. The king decided to let the wolf wander wherever it wanted so that it could lead them back to the site of its bewitchment. The werewolf duly led them to his native country where they discovered a land groaning under a dreadful tyranny. The king invaded, won a great military victory against the tyrant and his wife, and forced the usurped queen to fetch the magic sapling and restore the wolf to human shape.

Arthur is impressed by this story, but says that he has one more question to ask of Gorlagon: Who is that strange, sad-looking woman who sits opposite you, with a bloody head on a platter which she kisses whenever you kiss your wife? That is the faithless queen, says Gorlagon, for I was the werewolf in the tale I have just told you. The two foreign countries in the story were those of my brothers, Gargol and Torleil. I spared her life on one condition, that when I had remarried, she should always carry the head of her lover for whom she betrayed me, and that every time I kissed my new wife, she should kiss the head of her lover, so that everyone could be reminded of her great wickedness.

The first modern editor of this story, Professor Kittredge, noted the significant detail that the three kings in the story were at one stage the same person, and that each of their names signifies Werewolf. Gorlagon is a barely changed version of *Gorgalon*, an expanded form of *Gorgol*, which is *Guruol* or *Guorguol* in Old Welsh, meaning werewolf (the first syllable means *man*; the second, *wolf*). It is cognate with the Norman *garwaf.* The Arthurian element, which Professor Kittredge thinks is a comparatively late addition to the structure of the story, needed three kings (for reasons which need not concern us here), and so the original werewolf-king was divided into three. The name Torleil, which is the furthest from the Old Welsh original, may simply be an error in transcription made by the fourteenth-century Latin clerk, or an attempt to disguise the triple-elaboration.[18]

Very similar parallels to both these werewolf stories may be found in other contemporary works: the *Lai de Melion*, which like *Bisclavret* styles itself a 'Breton lay', dates from not after 1250 (it may be even earlier), and like *Arthur and Gorlagon* features the mythical figure of King Arthur. The werewolf-hero is hunting in the woods, where he meets a beautiful woman from Ireland with whom he falls in love. They marry but she learns his lycanthropic secret, transforms him, and departs for Ireland with one of the werewolf's servants as her lover. The wolf follows and rages throughout the country. The wife's father hunts him down, but the wolf succeeds in endearing himself to the father-in-law. Arthur then arrives in Ireland, and takes over the role of the werewolf's protector. One day, the wolf sees the faithless servant, attacks him, is threatened by courtiers, and is protected by Arthur. The servant is forced to confess, the hero is returned to human form, and leaves for England in Arthur's company, abandoning his faithless wife.

One contemporary werewolf story which perhaps fails to sit quite so neatly in this collection of Celtic tales, and yet was probably the most widely circulated version of them all, is the Old French romance of *Guillaume de Palerne*, the earliest known version of which was apparently written about 1194–7. It was translated into Middle English alliterative verse about the middle of the fourteenth century, and an early-modern English prose version taken from the Middle English was printed by Wynkyn de Worde, Caxton's successor, in the 1520s, from which in turn an Irish translation was made some time in the same century. Meanwhile a modernized French prose *Guillaume* was printed at Lyon in 1552, a printing which was to carry the werewolf legend nearer to an audience disastrously receptive to its more monstrous aspect.

Much of the scholarly debate about the Celtic element in

Guillaume stems from the Old French poet's statement that he took the story from a Latin source. It is virtually impossible to say whether this is true or whether he was simply trying to be impressive by giving his story a largely spurious antiquity and cultural background. The poem has a different setting from *Bisclavret* and its analogues, being set in the Kingdom of the Two Sicilies: that is, southern Italy and the island of Sicily. This is less of a cultural distance than might at first be apparent; the ever-expanding Normans had taken over the kingdom in the early part of the twelfth century after a period of Saracen influence, and looked on it as their golden Kingdom of the South. The poet crams in plenty of local Sicilian colour, the story moves from Sicily to Rome, and the werewolf has a subsidiary role to play in the story, yet still the familiar elements are present.

The plot of *Guillaume* is rather more complex than its northerly Celtic cousins. Briefly, and putting the werewolf plot to the fore, the werewolf is Alphonse, son of the King of Spain, who has been transformed by his wicked stepmother. She uses an ointment to effect the transformation, and swears that Alphonse has been drowned. The werewolf rescues the young son of the King of Sicily, Guillaume, from a plot against his life. He is chased across Sicily, but manages to swim across the Straits of Messina to the mainland, carrying the child with him. He hides the child, who is found by shepherds and brought up as their own. Guillaume is then discovered by the Emperor of Rome, who recognizes his innate nobility and takes him back to the palace, where he falls in love with the Emperor's daughter, Melior. The lovers elope, and the werewolf brings them food and drink, and disguises them, first in a pair of white bear-skins, and later in the hides of two deer he has caught. He escorts them to Sicily, and when they are almost discovered in a barge, he leaps into the water to distract the sailors. Guillaume is able to defeat his enemies and inherit his late father's throne, and the werewolf is eventually returned to human form and marries Guillaume's sister. His disenchantment is performed by the repentant queen, who places a red cord with a talismanic ring around his neck and reads out the appropriate spells from a book of magic. Alphonse is then returned to human shape, but he is naked, and the queen has to bathe him and find clothes for him before the transformation can be regarded as complete and irrevocable.

Alphonse is perhaps the most sympathetic werewolf to appear in any of these medieval narratives. He only shows any sign of cruelty twice, once attacking the wicked queen immediately after his transformation, the second time just before his restoration to human shape, and these are obviously excusable displays of ferocity. Far from being in league with Satan, Christ is on his side, as the poet remarks when Alphonse and the lovers are approaching Palermo. And those who say that the werewolf's moral stature is belittled because Alphonse is not the true hero of the romance perhaps overlook the strong elements of lycanthropy attached to the two royal lovers as they dress themselves in bear- and deer-skins, and deceive even close observers into thinking that they are those animals. Guillaume and Melior are honourable shape-shifters too.

All four versions of the werewolf legend seem to be relatively independent of each other (although *Melion* arguably shows signs of influence by both *Bisclavret* and *Guillaume de Palerne*), which has suggested to some analysts that behind them all lay a common prototype, which is now unfortunately lost. These werewolf stories have numerous details in common, not least their persistent anti-feminism. Another less immediately apparent shared feature is that in most of the stories the werewolf crosses a large body of water. In the final movement of *Arthur and Gorlagon*, for example, the werewolf is left by the king to wander where he will. He indicates where he has come from by leading the king to the shore, and running into the waves to show that his country of origin is across the water. The king accordingly builds a navy and takes the wolf across. This causes a problem for the storyteller, who suddenly has to account for the fact that the wolf travelled from the first country to another and on to a third without ever having to cross water, so he inserts a quick explanation at this point: the three countries were indeed joined together on one land mass, but the land curved around in such a way that the quickest way from the third kingdom back to the first was across the sea. This whole episode has an unfortunate effect on the pace of the narrative, since it kills off the dramatic urgency which had been building up as the werewolf was nearing his goal of restoration to human shape. The reader is forced to imagine a pause in the action while the king gathers together a fleet, a pause which, realistically speaking, would have lasted weeks or, more likely,

months. As *Arthur and Gorlagon* is the latest and most obviously
clerkly of the medieval Celtic werewolf tales, it might be imagined
that the storyteller would have been tempted to leave out this
awkward detail of the sea-crossing simply on the grounds of
plausibility. That it is retained at all suggests that it is a significant
episode in the original. The action in *Melion* passes back and forth
across the Irish Sea, while water is a constant motif in *Guillaume
de Palerne*, with Alphonse alleged to have been drowned, crossing
the Straits of Messina twice, hurling himself into the water to save
the lovers, and having to be bathed (and clothed) before he can
at last return to human form.

This motif is not, of course, found here for the first time.
Euanthes' ancient Greek werewolf story featured the metamorphosing lake in Arcadia across which members of the Antaeus
family swam; and liquid turned up in Petronius' werewolf story,
although somewhat facetiously in the form of the soldier's urine.
It is possible that this aspect of the legend of the werewolf – water
as enabling agent for, and symbolic representation of, the passage
from man to animal – was transmitted from these classical
sources through to early Celtic culture, and thence into the
Anglo-Norman mainstream. Of the four major medieval werewolf romances, three feature the water motif. *Bisclavret* does not,
but instead features clothing very strongly; if some linguists are
correct, the very name of the *lai* may draw attention to this aspect
of the story. Euanthes' story, too, features clothing: the young
man chosen from the Antaeus family must leave his garments on
a tree by the lake's edge. When he returns eight years later (having
eaten no human flesh), he may don his clothes and resume
human shape. It is remarkable that all four of these medieval
examples should exhibit either one or other of the water and
clothing motifs found in the ancient Greek tale, and it is particularly interesting that probably the most widely circulated version
– *Guillaume de Palerne* – has them both. Remarkable too is the fact
that Euanthes' story was not known to medieval audiences in the
Greek original: it was known only via its inclusion in Pliny's
Natural History, the same book that spawned the monstrous
races.

By the twelfth century the werewolf had found itself in company with the Plinian monstrous races, in the lands under
Norman influence at least. This is clearly apparent in Giraldus'

Topography of Ireland, for immediately after his tale of the Ossory werewolves he parades for the reader's delectation a variety of similar monsters. He had managed to imbue his werewolf legend with qualities of pathos and moral sympathy, and the whole subject of these and similar monstrous aberrations clearly stirred his creative imagination. But, like the good churchman Giraldus was, he sought to reconcile his fondness for their ability to liven up his *Topography* with his interest in discovering the moral root of this disorder. His monsters are indeed a disorderly lot: a woman who had a beard down to her waist and a mane of hair running down her spine; a man whose extremities were those of an ox; a cow with the hindquarters of a stag; a goat that had sexual intercourse with a woman; and a lion that loved a woman. Disappointingly, not all these turn out to be Irish monsters: the cow-stag comes from Chester, in north-west England, and the amorous lion from Paris; but Giraldus had been educated at Paris and had travelled to Chester, and he was apparently loath to waste good monstrous material.

The monster that most aroused Giraldus' interest was the half man, half ox. He describes its physical appearance carefully. The were-ox had hooves instead of hands and feet, and was able to use his forehooves to bring food up to his mouth. He was entirely bald, although a light down covered his scalp. His eyes were huge (like an ox's, Giraldus points out), and his nose did not protrude: he simply had two nostrils in the middle of a flattened face. He could not speak; he could only low. Giraldus says that this man was resident in Wicklow at the time when his own cousin Maurice fitzGerald, one of the chief leaders of the Norman invasion, took possession of the county and the castle – that is, in 1174 – and that he attended Maurice's court for a short time before his death. This suggests that Giraldus did not arrive in Ireland soon enough to have seen the were-ox, yet something in the detail of the description rings true, and his relative in the castle could certainly have provided him with a closely observed description. If this were the case, it may be that this were-ox was simply a man suffering from congenital deformities, that the usual contemporary thought-processes were applied, and an animal was chosen that bore some physical relation to his deformities in order to 'explain' them. Even Giraldus seems not to doubt the were-ox's essential humanity. The story ends sadly, however: the Norman

youths of the castle taunted the local Irish with accusations of
having sired the were-ox themselves by having sexual relations
with their cattle, infuriating the Irish so much that they killed
him, 'a fate', Giraldus adds thoughtfully, 'which he did not
deserve'.

Giraldus cannot take much credit for an enlightened attitude,
however, for he follows up this story with another 'man-calf',
which he says was born to a cow in the mountains around
Glendalough. This, he explains, was due to the Irish predilection
for committing sodomy on their livestock, precisely the same
accusation that had sealed the Wicklow were-ox's fate. In fact, it
becomes clear from Giraldus' list of monsters that the chief moral
lesson he wishes to draw from them is that bestiality is sinful. He
rages against the two women in his stories of the goat and the lion
for submitting to the beastly desires of the animals in question,
and ends his fiery peroration with Leviticus 20:16: 'If a woman
approaches any beast to have intercourse with him, ye shall kill
the woman, and let the beast die the death.'

Giraldus's treatment of them is a good indication how, by the
twelfth century, monsters were passing from being regarded as
objects of delightful curiosity to creatures arousing fear and
abhorrence of sexual deviance. The theory that monsters could
be engendered by sexual relations between man and beast was a
long time dying. In 1580 an eight-year-old Shrewsbury boy was
rumoured to be the result of bestiality committed on a sheep, the
evidence for this accusation being that he had 'both his feet
cloven and his right hand also cloven', a deformity reminiscent of
Giraldus' Wicklow were-ox. In an equally grisly case, at Birdham
near Chichester about 1674, the dead body of another supposed
were-sheep was nailed to a church door so that all church-goers
could be reminded of the vile consequences of bestiality. In the
same era Anthony Wood reported seeing the deformed child of
an Irishwoman, which he thought had been 'originally begot by
a man, but a mastiff dog or monkey gave the semen some
sprinkling', and such ideas have lasted long since.[19] The best-
known example in more recent times is the nineteenth-century
story of John Merrick, the so-called 'Elephant Man'. He suffered
from congenital deformities which led others to give him his
animal nickname, and he himself spread the story that his
condition had come about because his mother had been knocked

down by a circus elephant while she was pregnant with him. This version avoids the stigma of bestiality, but only just, and it may represent Merrick's attempt to give a sanitized version of the crude stories broadcast about him when he was exhibited as a fairground freak. His physician, Frederick Trevers, was certainly aware of such talk, referring in his memoir to 'the loathing insinuation of a man being changed into an animal'.[20]

Interestingly, of the medieval werewolf romances, only the latest – *Arthur and Gorlagon* – tackles this theme: Gorlagon marries a real wolf and fathers two cubs. This action is not criticized within the story, but it is noticeable that he is the most formidable werewolf in this group of narratives. His violent rampages around the countryside are vividly depicted, and, unlike the rather dog-like Bisclavret or the Christ-aided Alphonse, he attacks many more people and animals than merely those who have wronged him. Since it cannot be known how the Welsh original treated the sexual aspect of the story, or whether it was even mentioned at all in that earlier version, it is difficult to draw any firm conclusions, but it is possible that the fourteenth-century cleric who wrote down the story for posterity found it hard to accept the essential goodness of a werewolf who indulged in sexual relations with a real wolf, and coloured his accounts of the werewolf's deeds of violence accordingly.

Once brought into alignment with the monstrous races, little stood between the werewolf and the judicial fires of the witchfinders of the early modern era. Monsters were no longer a cause of mild amusement or curiosity; they had become signs of disorder and sinfulness. As religious controversy began tearing at the fabric of medieval Europe, the tendency to stigmatize the monster as heretic, begun with the dog-headed Jews and Muslims, quickly gained momentum. Symptomatic was Martin Luther and Phillip Melancthon's influential pamphlet *Deuttung der czwo grewlichen Figuren, Bapstesels czu Rom und Munchkalbs czu Freyerbeg ijnn Meysszen funden*, first published in 1523. This contribution to the literature of monsters, which was translated into French in 1557, and into English in 1579 with the title *Of Two Wonderful Popish Monsters*, announced the discovery of two revolting aberrations: a pope-ass found on the banks of the River Tiber in 1496, and a monk-calf born on 8 December 1522 at Freiburg. The polemical points the two reformers make are readily apparent. The pope-ass is the image of the Church of Rome, Melancthon says, implying that it is equally as disgusting that the pope should be head of the Church as it is that a human should have the head of an ass. Luther elaborates on the physical monstrosity of the monk-calf to a similar end: God is revolted at the practices of the monks, and so the monster's huge ears are His denunciation of the pretensions of monks to hear confessions, and its lolling bovine tongue shows their doctrine to be idle gibberish.

It is tempting to dismiss this as robust satire, albeit somewhat distasteful, that can bear little relevance to the problem of understanding the catastrophic switch from the romantic Celtic werewolf tradition to the nightmarish fears revealed in the later view of the werewolf as heretic and cannibal. The English translator evidently felt rather differently. He is clear that Luther and Melancthon's purpose is to generate fear and horror by writing of these prodigies, 'the which the most times do note and demonstrate unto us the ire and wrath of God against us for our sins and wickedness, that we have and do daily commit against him'. He specifically warns his readers not to regard these monsters as mere fables, and hopes that all his readers will 'repent from the bottom of our hearts of our sins, and desire him [God] to be merciful to us, and ever to keep and defend us from such horrible monsters'.[21] Such attitudes were to be expressed more commonly as western Christendom found itself gripped in a paroxysm of monster-hunting.

7

The Werewolf Trials

He that goes by the law (as the proverb is) holds
a wolf by the ears.

BURTON,
Anatomy of Melancholy (Democritus to the Reader)

1598 was another cold, wet year in a terrible sequence of cold, wet
years. The rains smashed down from an iron sky onto the fields
of France, bending ears of wheat, retarding growth, rotting the
grain before it could be brought in from the field, so that even
now, at harvest time, people were hungry. The poor and starving
were everywhere. Priests distributing charitable bread were becoming used to seeing collapse and deaths among the pushing,
frantic crowds. Men and women, young and old, shivered in the
streets, skin hanging and stomachs swollen. Others lay stretched
out in final exhaustion, the remains of a desperate last meal of
grass sticking out of their mouths. Famine was, as always,
accompanied by epidemic: plague carts clattered through the
larger towns, while out in the country those still strong enough to
shovel earth laboured to bury the dead. Sensitive observers,
educated men with minds full of the high-minded debates of the
humanists and the neo-Platonists, were frankly shocked to see
how quickly hunger reduced the standards of their fellow men to
those of brute animals. Having no bread or other food, the
ravening peasants were reported to fall on dead horses, asses, or
any other carrion, leading one churchman to note that 'the
pasturage of wolves has become the food of Christians'.[1]

There is, however, worse fare than carrion. One day in the
middle part of that year, a soldier and some peasants walking
through fields near Angers, north-west France, came across a

wild beggar, cowering half-naked in the bushes. Pulling him out, they saw blood smeared across his hands and face and shreds of flesh embedded under his filthy nails. Nearby lay the mutilated corpse of a fifteen-year-old boy.

There is no way of knowing how this beggar, Jacques Roulet, was interrogated on first being taken into custody. Some modern writers have read his testimony in court as suggesting that he was both retarded and epileptic, and so perhaps his inquisitors had no need for the instruments of torture routinely used in witchcraft cases at this time. Certainly he was easily led through his confession in court by Judge Pierre Hérault:

Judge Hérault: What is your name and what your estate?
Roulet: My name is Jacques Roulet, my age thirty-five; I am poor and a beggar.
Judge: What are you accused of having done?
Roulet: Of being a thief; of having offended God. My parents gave me an ointment; I do not know its composition.
Judge: When rubbed with this ointment, do you become a wolf?
Roulet: No. But for all that, I killed and ate the child Cornier. I was a wolf.
Judge: Were you dressed as a wolf?
Roulet: I was dressed as I am now. I had my hands and face bloody, because I had been eating the flesh of the said child.
Judge: Do your hands and feet become paws of a wolf?
Roulet: Yes, they do.
Judge: Does your head become like that of a wolf – your mouth become larger?
Roulet: I do not know how my head was at the time; I used my teeth. My head was as it is today. I have wounded and eaten many other little children. I have also been to the sabbat.[2]

La peste – the plague – was indisputably the devil's work, and it seemed in 1598 as if another plague of diabolical origin was reaching its peak in France: for this was the year of an apparent epidemic of lycanthropy. In the same year a tailor of Châlons was also found to have committed cannibalistic horrors: he attacked children, either at his place of work or wandering through the woods, and ate their flesh. The children's bones were found in a cask at his shop. Like Jacques Roulet, the lycanthrope of Châlons was sentenced to death, and the court records ordered to be burnt, so vile were the details of his crimes.

In Franche-Comté, the region shadowed by the heavily forested Jura mountains rising west to Lake Leman and the Swiss Alps, a whole family of werewolves had been discovered earlier that same year. Perrenette Gandillon was the first of these *loups-garoux* to meet justice. A sixteen-year-old, Benoît Bidel, was picking fruit near the town of St Claude, and had left his sister at the foot of the trunk while he climbed into the branches. Suddenly a tailless wolf attacked the unprotected girl. Benoît leapt to the ground to defend his sister, but the wolf – which Benoît now saw had human hands covered in thick fur – snatched his knife away from him and dealt him a fatal blow to the neck. Hearing the commotion, peasants working nearby came rushing to him, and Benoît was able to pass on the crucial detail of the wolf's human hands before he died. Perrenette Gandillon was found wandering in the area, and the enraged mob tore her to pieces.

The other Gandillon werewolves were found guilty after more orthodox treatment. Perrenette's sister, Antoinette, was accused of being a werewolf, and of being able to make hail. She was also alleged to attend the witches' sabbat, and to copulate with the devil, who came to her in the shape of a goat. Pierre Gandillon, her werewolf-brother, stood similarly accused. He had been seen lying in his bed in a cataleptic state on Maundy Thursday: when he awoke, he spoke of attending a sabbat of werewolves. His confession told how 'Satan clothed them in a wolf's skin which completely covered them, and that they went on all fours, and ran about the country, chasing now a person and now an animal, according to the guidance of their appetite. They confessed also that they tired themselves with running.'[3] Pierre's son Georges also confessed to using a salve to turn into a wolf and, in the company of Perrenette and Antoinette, killing two goats – although in one case this had been a mistake.

The good citizens of St Claude were fortunate in being protected from such *diableries* by the famous lawyer, Henri Boguet, whose fund of case histories involving witchcraft, *Discours des sorciers*, became a standard text for witch-hunters, with twelve editions in twenty years. He was proud of his record of vigilance in eradicating witchcraft from the Jura, claiming in his later writings personal responsibility for 600 executions from 1598 to

1616. To the second edition of his book, published in 1602, Boguet added a long chapter dealing with lycanthropy that dealt with some of the cases in which he himself had been involved, in which he recorded his visit to see the wretched werewolf-family in gaol: 'In company with the Lord Claude Meynier, our recorder, I have seen those I have named go on all fours in a room just as they did when they were in the fields; but they said that it was impossible for them to turn themselves into wolves, since they had no more ointment, by being imprisoned. I have further noted that they were all scratched on the face and hands and legs; and that Pierre Gandillon was so much disfigured in this way that he bore hardly any resemblance to a man, and struck with horror those who looked at him.' Boguet noted that the three surviving Gandillon werewolves were convicted and burnt.

Nor were these the only werewolves to have been discovered in the Jura: the whole mountainous region was set to become the *locus classicus* for the werewolf of modern imagination. Boguet himself retold the story of the three werewolves discovered some seventy years earlier at nearby Poligny. The leader of this diabolical trio was Michel Verdung (or Udon), whose wolfish *alter ego* had come to light when a traveller passing through the district was attacked by a wolf. He wounded the animal and tracked it to a hut, where to his amazement he found a woman bathing Verdung's fresh wounds.

This was clearly a matter for the Inquisitor-General at Besançon, and his investigation soon produced more information. Under torture, Verdung implicated his friend Pierre Bourgot, known as Big Peter, in his devilish crimes, and in his turn, Bourgot confessed how he had been started on the road to lycanthropy. Twenty years earlier a fierce storm had scattered his flocks and he had set out to search for them, only to encounter three black horsemen. Bourgot told them his troubles, and one of them promised aid if Bourgot would agree to serve him as lord and master. Pierre promptly accepted and soon found his lost sheep. A few days later he met the black horseman again to seal the bargain. The horseman revealed himself as a servant of the devil. He made Pierre deny Christianity and take the feudal oath of loyalty by kissing his left hand. Pierre felt it against his lips as black and cold as ice.

But as time passed Pierre felt himself sliding back to Christianity, and Michel Verdung was deputed by the devil to put some backbone into this newest recruit to the Satanic cause. Verdung accordingly promised Pierre gold if he would attend a sabbat with him. There Verdung made Pierre strip and apply a magic ointment; Pierre found himself a wolf. Verdung was able to restore him to human form by applying another ointment, but meanwhile Pierre was able to run around and commit the horrible crimes to which he confessed. He had attacked a seven-year-old boy, he told the Inquisitor-General, but had been forced to put his clothes back on quickly to return to human shape because the boy had screamed too much. He had eaten the flesh of a four-year-old girl and found it delicious, and he had broken the neck of a nine-year-old and eaten her. One element common to the confessions of these two lycanthropes was that they had mated with real wolves. Boguet affirmed that each said 'they had as much pleasure in the act as if they had copulated with their wives'. Such horror stories seemed all too feasible in the region which had also produced Gilles Garnier.

Gilles Garnier had been the *bête noire* of an earlier generation in Franche-Comté. In the early 1570s, in the countryside around the town of Dôle, attacks on children were becoming alarmingly regular, and several witnesses spoke of seeing children carried off by a werewolf. Responding to these stories, the local *parlement* issued the populace with sweeping powers 'to assemble with pikes, halberds, arquebuses, and sticks, to chase and to pursue the said werewolf in every place where they many find or seize him; to tie and to kill, without incurring any pains or penalties'. These vigilantes soon found their prey. In November 1573, only two months after this proclamation, a little girl was rescued from a huge wolf in the meadow of La Poupée, between Authune and Chastenoy. She was already badly bitten in five places, and the shocked peasants who saved her thought they recognized human features in the great animal they chased off. Some were sure these were the features of a misanthropic recluse who lived with his wife in remote poverty near Armanges: Gilles Garnier, originally from Lyon, known as 'the hermit of St Bonnot'. Six days later another child went missing, and Garnier and his wife were promptly arrested.

Garnier's subsequent confession was detailed, and included confirmation of the last two incidents. The second child, a ten-year-old boy, he had strangled while in the shape of a wolf; he then tore off one of the boy's legs with his fangs, and ate the flesh of the thighs and most of the belly. In addition Garnier confessed that in August of that year he had killed a twelve-year-old boy in a pear orchard near the village of Perrouze. He was seized by an urge to eat the child's flesh 'despite of the fact that it was Friday', but had been interrupted by the approach of some men. As he and these witnesses agreed, he had done this, not in the shape of a wolf, but in human form. Early in October he was luckier: in a vineyard near a wood called La Serre, no more than a mile from Dôle, he came across a ten-year-old girl. He was in wolf-shape this time – there were no witnesses – and tore at the girl with his teeth and claws. Once she was dead, he stripped her naked and ate her. Her flesh tasted so sweet, he testified, that he took some home to his wife.[4]

The usual practice in Europe at this time was to burn those convicted of sorcery. In France, as also in Germany and Scotland, it was customary to temper the severity of the sentence in cases where a confession had been made by strangling the victim first, either by garotting or hanging, before the pyre was ignited. This allowed the authorities an additional refinement to their interrogation methods: in cases where sorcerers and heretics recanted their confessions, the privilege of strangulation could be withheld. Knowledge of this kept the number of last-minute changes of heart to a minimum. Although Garnier had confessed his crimes, even to the extent of corroborating the statements of eyewitnesses, a comparatively rare occurrence in trials of this kind, his crimes were considered so horrible and the popular clamour against him was so great that, like an eve-of-execution recanter, he too was denied this final mercy of strangulation before burning.

Such popular clamour against werewolves was not confined to this particular corner of France. All Europe knew the case of the werewolf of Cologne, Peter Stubb (variously spelled Stump, Stumpf, or Stube), whose trial took place in 1589. Pamphlets giving the details of his crimes were translated into a number of languages, and contemporary authorities such as Del Rio, Rowlands, and Fairfax added their own comments. The article around which much of Stubb's trial revolved was a magic belt, which was said to transform him into 'a greedy devouring wolf, strong and mighty, with eyes great and large, which in the night sparkled like brands of fire; a mouth great and wide, with most sharp and cruel teeth; a huge body and mighty paws. And no sooner should he put off the same girdle, but presently he should appear in his former shape, according to the proportion of a man, as if he had never been changed.'[5] Stubb would don his magic belt and attack people who strayed into the countryside, using his animal strength to bring them down: 'such was his swiftness of foot while he continued a wolf that he could outrun the swiftest greyhound in that country.' If he could not find human prey, it was alleged, he would take lambs and kids to feed his appetite for blood and raw meat. In addition to his animal diet he was reckoned to have murdered thirteen young children and to have attacked two pregnant women, ripping the foetuses from their wombs in order to devour them. He was also accused of incest with his sister and daughter, and of murdering his own son and eating 'the brains out of his head as a most savoury and dainty delicious means to staunch his greedy appetite'.

Stubb's fate was sealed when a pack of dogs was set on a wolf in the fields near the town of Bedbur. According to his accusers, this was Stubb in wolf-shape. When he realized that he could not outstrip the huge mastiffs chasing him, he removed his magic girdle so that he suddenly appeared as a normal traveller, staff in hand, walking towards town. But his pursuers insisted that they had never taken their eyes from their prey. They had seen the transformation from man to wolf, and duly apprehended the protesting Stubb. Taken to town, he was put on the rack where he 'voluntarily confessed his whole life'. When asked why he could not produce the magic girdle he used in order to assume his feral guise, Stubb stated that he had abandoned it 'in a certain valley' at the moment of his arrest. The magistrates gave orders for this valley to be searched but nothing was found. This was not regarded as surprising, 'for it may be supposed that it [the girdle] was gone to the Devil from whence it came, so that it was not to be found. For the Devil having brought the wretch to all the shame he could, left him to endure the torments which his deeds deserved.'

If Gilles Garnier had suffered unusually harsh punishment, Stubb was to feel the full force of the era's detestation and fear of every detail of his crimes. He was strapped to a wheel, and chunks of his flesh were torn from the bone in ten places with red-hot pincers. While he was still conscious, Stubb's arms and legs were then smashed with a wooden axe, after which he was finally dispatched by having his head struck off and his corpse burnt on the same pyre as his daughter and mistress. 'After the execution, there was by the advice of the magistrates of the town of Bedbur a high pole set up and strongly framed, which first went through the wheel whereon he was broken, whereunto also it was fastened; after that a little above the wheel the likeness of a wolf was framed in wood, to show unto all men the shape wherein he executed those cruelties. Over that on the top of the stake the sorcerer's head itself was set up, and round about the wheel there hung as it were sixteen pieces of wood about a yard in length which represented the sixteen persons that were perfectly known to be murdered by him.'

With a wealth of stories like this passed on both through local oral tradition and through the pamphlets which were beginning to circulate among an increasingly literate population, the peasantry of Franche-Comté had strong reasons to believe in the existence of werewolves. But if it is possible to see why, in 1598, the local peasantry might believe in the reality of lycanthropy, it is far less easy for the modern enquirer to discover anything in these case histories that he can treat as ascertainable fact; it is impossible to tell whether these alleged criminals were guilty of anything at all. One can certainly speculate to one's heart's content. Gilles Garnier, for example, was seen by witnesses having killed a child. This was the only time he could possibly have been positively identified in the commission of his crimes, as he was not then in wolf-shape. If it were not for this incident, one might be tempted to think that his chosen role of misanthropic beggar made him particularly susceptible to accusations of lycanthropy and that he may have been entirely innocent. But, if the witnesses are to be believed, the dead child convicts him as a murderer. The other murders to which he subsequently confessed may have been actual, or they may have been lurid fantasies concocted under the pressure of torture. It is natural to imagine that his inquisitors, hearing his confession and finding it hard to contemplate the inhuman and sadistic horrors of the crimes he enumerated, should prefer to think of them as having been committed by a true monster, half man, half wolf, in league with the devil.

But in general the modern reader is always left at sea by the gap between his and the sixteenth century's notions of admissible evidence. In the case of Peter Stubb, for example, the crucial matter of the apparent non-existence of his magic belt is entirely sidestepped by the court. If the belt cannot be found, they argue, is that so surprising when it is an object of the devil? Visiting the wretched Gandillons in their death cell, Boguet notes that they cannot transform themselves into wolves in front of their accusers, but, he reasons, that is simply because they are imprisoned and cannot get any of the necessary ointment.

It is also relevant that all of the crucial evidence in these trials, the 'confessions', the whole-hearted admissions of culpability made by the defendants – all of these have been made under torture. As lycanthropy involved a pact with the devil, and was therefore heretical, torture was the recommended practice in werewolf cases. Merely to undergo the *question préparatoire*, the first stage in the procedure, in which the victim was taken to the torture chamber to be shown each instrument and have its particular pains described – the thumbscrews and Spanish boots used to crush the extremities; the pulleys used to hoist the prisoner into the air by his or her arms in the procedure known as *strappado*, a comparatively mild method of torture in which the prisoner's shoulders were sometimes pulled from their sockets; the ladder to which the new prisoner might be strapped for a short time just to demonstrate how painful it would be when the torture was begun in earnest, with the bindings twisted tighter and the prisoner's whole body agonizingly stretched out – merely to undergo this gruesome preliminary tour of the inquisitor's place of work was enough to make some start confessing there and then.

Nor was too much reliance put on the prisoner's loquacity under such conditions. The interrogators routinely used previously prepared lists of questions, to which a simple 'yes' was all that was required by way of an admission of guilt. In this way, the beliefs of the interrogators inevitably imposed themselves on the confessions. This process can be clearly seen at work in the confession of Jacques Roulet. It is clear that it is the judge, not he, who has the clearest idea of the exact nature of what he is supposed to have done. Did the ointment transform you into a

wolf? asks the judge. No, says Roulet, but I committed the crime
anyway: 'I was a wolf.' If he is speaking metaphorically here, it is
lost on the judge, who presses on with werewolf questions until
Roulet is simply confused: 'I do not know how my head was at the
time,' he protests. The effect of this kind of questioning was
cumulative: the more alleged werewolves were required under
torture to agree with the authorities as to what exactly a werewolf
was and did, the more the authorities became alarmed at the
apparent epidemic of lycanthropy they had themselves helped
create.

And yet it is easy for the modern enquirer, indignant at these
recorded displays of legal barbarity, to get carried away with the
notion of an epidemic of lycanthropy. Writers may speak carelessly of the Inquisition condemning 'hundreds of alleged werewolves to burn at the stake'[6] but the truth about this era of legal
prosecution of werewolves is both less melodramatic and more
interesting. It has been shown that the great Jura witch-hunter
Boguet, for example, who claimed to be responsible for 600
executions in witchcraft and werewolf cases combined in the
period 1598–1616, probably exaggerated the true number by a
factor of 120: a French historian[7] has calculated that he had tried
fewer than thirty witches of any kind before 1603. Unlike some
other witch-hunters, Boguet had a special interest in werewolves,
but in his extensive treatment of the subject in his book he refers
chiefly either to earlier cases previously recorded by other authorities (the werewolves of Poligny, Gilles Garnier) or to tales of
werewolves who were not brought to trial and so cannot be
included in any statistical survey. Other witch-hunters were no
less immune from this tendency to exaggerate: Judge Nicolas
Rémy, Boguet's neighbour in Lorraine, claimed that his *Demonolatry* (Lyon, 1595) was based on the court cases of 900 people
he had sentenced to death; the actual records suggest a figure
about one-seventh of this total.

Nevertheless the witch-craze of this period of European history
can hardly be written off as the unsubstantiated boastings of a few
scribbling lawyers: it is a matter of known historical fact. In the
Jura alone official records show that over 500 people were
executed for witchcraft between 1570 and 1670, and the figures
for the whole of Europe run into many thousands. Yet it is
noticeable how few werewolves are to be found among their

number. Franche-Comté is almost unique in providing so many examples. To the north lay the larger region of Lorraine, its dark forests just as fertile breeding ground for tales of werewolves, one might think, yet only five instances are recorded there.[8] Werewolves are remarkably thin on the ground elsewhere in Europe. Most German territories, including Peter Stubb's, can only muster a single occurrence of the phenomenon each, and England and Scotland were almost entirely free of werewolves in this period.

Naturally, folk-belief in werewolves may survive in times and places where trials involving them were unknown, but it must be asked what particular factors may have led to France in the late sixteenth century being the epicentre of belief in, and legal process relating to, werewolves. Unlike some other areas of Europe at this time, France can legitimately be spoken of as a country. By the end of the previous century, with the expulsion of the English and the marriage of Charles VIII to Anne of Brittany, France had become a single nation settled more or less into its present-day borders, a fact which seemed to promise a far better outlook for the French people. After the miseries of the Hundred Years' War, the first half of the sixteenth century was a time of almost unalloyed economic recovery and progress. The seemingly endless war conducted by his Valois king against the Hapsburgs hardly affected the average Frenchman. The population was growing at a steady rate: in François I's reign it was more than twice the size of Spain's, and five times that of England. In Paris and Lyon, France had two of the largest and richest cities in the world, while all along the Loire valley the great châteaux were either being built or acquiring expensive Italianate facelifts. These self-confident Renaissance constructions – Chabord, Blois, Azey-le-Rideau, Amboise, and the rest – spoke eloquently of France's renascence to the outside world.

Yet behind this glittering façade lay the reality of everyday life for the vast mass of society, an existence eked out in small rural communities often isolated from the culture of the great cities, still dependent as for time immemorial on the gathering in of the harvest and the avoidance of death and disease. And in this world disturbing movements were afoot, movements such as the somewhat misleadingly titled 'German peasants' revolt' of 1525, a vast inchoate protest which spread beyond the borders of the German states to affect – among other parts of northern Europe – Franche-Comté, Lorraine, and Burgundy. The impulse to rebellion was not confined to Germany, nor to the rural peasantry, as was shown by the events in Lyon in 1529. Lyon was by this time the largest industrial city in France, if not the world; prosperous chiefly from the silk industry but also from all manner of burgeoning mercantile activity, a city rich enough to finance the 1524 expedition of the Florentine Giovanni da Varrazano which claimed Newfoundland for France. And yet in April 1529 the urban poor in Lyon rioted for food. Their *Grande Rebeyne* began when a crowd of 2000 rallied under the leadership of a swordsman and a baker, and set off to ransack the houses of the city's merchants. Some church images were also attacked, but in general the thrust of the protest was clear, and the Lyonnaise bourgeois took the message. When the rioting had been quelled, they established soon afterwards the Aumône Générale, in order 'to nourish the poor forever' and so prevent social disaster.

Events like these were alarming enough in a period of economic success, but acquired apocalyptical overtones after the mid-point of the century, when events took a freakish and disastrous turn. The First of July 1559 was the day fixed for a tournament to celebrate the Treaty of Câteau-Cambrésis, the treaty which would finally end half a century of fighting between France and Spain. The chief author of that long war, François I, was dead, and his young successor, Henri II, joined enthusiastically in the jousting to celebrate the peace. During one of his matches, a lance shattered and a sliver of wood from it pierced his eye; within days it moved to his brain and killed him. The Valois monarchy was irredeemably weakened by this unlucky accident. Henri's two elder sons came to the throne as minors and each reigned only briefly; their successor and youngest brother, the feckless Henri III, was to be the last Valois king of France.

The key to France's problems after 1559 lay not so much in the ages or personalities of her kings as in the economic realities which were only beginning to be dimly understood even by the keenest minds in the kingdom. The treaty between France and Spain which looked like a triumph of diplomacy and good sense was in fact inevitable; both countries had driven themselves into bankruptcy in their prosecution of the war. In 1557 both kings were obliged to admit to it publicly: Henri II had taken out a huge series of short-term loans at an annual rate of interest of 16 per cent only two years earlier, and now, like Phillip II of Spain, found himself having to default on them. By the time of the truce, the French debt was 40 million livres; this represented approximately £4 million in contemporary English money, or about fifteen times the annual income of Elizabeth I at the beginning of her reign. Such prodigality had been maintained in the past only by resorting either to the expensive services of usurers or to increased taxation of the populace, and it was becoming clear that high taxation meant serious social instability.

The crisis set Catholics against Protestants. The Reformation had, after all, offered freedom to all from the tyranny of the Catholic church, and to most French peasants, the most important aspect of this was freedom from having to pay tithes, the ecclesiastical 10 per cent. Too late the Protestants realized the genie they had uncorked in encouraging non-payment: the Huguenot nobility met at Nîmes in 1562 to condemn those who refused to pay tithes as 'sowers of sedition, disturbers of the public order', but riots against all forms of taxation could now be expected at any time. In Aquitaine in 1548 the subject of the protest was the imposition of the salt tax (gabelle); in 1560 in Languedoc it was tithes. The protesters in Agen in 1560–1 threatened even more subversive behaviour: 'They are beginning in some places not to pay their tithes, and proclaim that they will no longer pay the tailles or their seigneurial dues.' Any rebellion was deeply disturbing to the government, but an attack on secular taxes was the worst kind.

One such attack, in the town of Romans, in Dauphiné, the region to the south of the Jura, sheds an interesting light on werewolf beliefs at the time. This was a Protestant area, and in 1580 the rural peasants of the surrounding countryside came together with the artisans of the town under the leadership of a man called Jean Serve or Paulmier. Their rebellion was as subversive as could then be imagined. The peasants first refused to pay either their tithes or tailles, then broke into the local châteaux and burnt the terriers, the manorial records from which all the details of each peasant's tax liabilities would be calculated. Together with the artisans, they ran riot through Romans, threatening the rich in the streets. Their cry was 'Before three days Christian flesh will be sold at sixpence a pound!' Their

commune took over the government of the town and installed
Paulmier as a parodic mayor. During the winter festival, he sat in
the mayor's chair, wearing a bear's skin and chewing lumps of
what was supposed to be human flesh, as the common people
paraded by, adorned in the stolen ceremonial robes of civic and
religious dignitaries, crying 'Christian flesh for sixpence!'

The horror of these gestures can be gauged by the ferocious
response they aroused. The richer classes of the town organized
themselves into a small army which burst upon the rioters on the
eve of Mardi Gras, Shrove Tuesday, 15 February 1580, and
slaughtered them. The massacre continued for three days, while
peasants from the surrounding countryside fought in vain to save
the revolutionary cause. Most interesting are the symbols by
which the rioters chose to express their rebellion. The eating of
human flesh, the greatest of the werewolf's transgressions against
nature, was deliberately used by the rioters to taunt and infuriate
the law-abiding Christian bourgeois. The raising of the rebel flag
of cannibalism, as it were, was not unique to this town: a
somewhat similar uprising in Naples in 1585 culminated in a
magistrate being lynched, mutilated, and pieces of his flesh being
offered for sale. In Romans, Paulmier chose to defile the seat of
civic authority with a public display (albeit faked) of this most
heinous of crimes while clad in a bear's skin, the universal sign
both of the outlaw and of the shape-shifter.

Acts such as Paulmier's were, of course, the outrageous
exception. Most of the poor of France were too busy with the
daily struggle against hunger and disease to contemplate such
gross gestures against the *status quo*. Nor was that struggle
becoming any easier. As the century progressed, the religious
conflict between Catholic and Protestant worsened, the Valois
line petered out in the face of more powerful rival claims to the
throne, and the politics of France collapsed into a series of civil
wars which were to occupy the country for the last four decades
of the century. By now the optimistic outlook of the early part of
the century had evaporated. The economic consequences of the
prolonged war against Spain had made themselves felt, and were
made worse by the general inflation that struck Europe in the
sixteenth century. The cost of food rose alarmingly, the price of
wheat in France, for example, increasing by 651 per cent between
1500 and 1600. Such economic trends were still imperfectly

understood. The more sophisticated thinkers took the line popularized by the French writer (and witch-hunter) Jean Bodin, who advanced the theory that the price rise was caused by '(a reason that no one has yet suggested) the abundance of gold and silver' from America.[9] Ordinary people were more inclined to point to human greed and to the accumulation of excessive wealth by the rich. Still others were inclined to see inflation as God's punishment on a wicked society.

Such economic trends were greatly exacerbated by the civil wars. Output declined throughout France as the wars raged on. In the Paris region production was down by a quarter in the 1590s, in Auvergne and Burgundy by 40 per cent, in the Cambrésis by a half. Bad harvests caused by bad weather in the mid 1580s and again in the 1590s joined with already soaring prices to create a situation that was catastrophic for the peasantry. The most cohesive protest movement of the century, the uprising of the *Croquants* in southern France, sprang up in the years 1593–5, the bonds of their common situation yoking together Catholic and Protestant, rural peasant and urban artisan, in one great cause. Their grievances were real, and their protest was profoundly anti-war. They spoke of the soldiers of both armies 'who had reduced them to starvation, violated their wives and daughters, stolen their cattle, and wasted their land'.

The French civil wars unleashed a carnival of ferocity that would stay imprinted on the collective consciousness for years to come. In one incident Protestants captured a Catholic monastery and forced the monks to hang one another; in another, at Orléans, Catholic mobs burnt down a gaol packed with Huguenot prisoners. The most infamous atrocity of the wars, indeed of the century, took place in Paris on St Bartholomew's Day, 24 August 1572, when Henri III ordered the slaughter of all the Huguenots who were crowded into the town for the feast day and subsequently attempted the wholesale massacre of every Protestant in France. When by the early 1590s the pendulum of war had swung the other way, and the Huguenot leader Henry of Navarre had emerged as sole contender for the throne, the Catholic citizens of Paris held out against a Protestant king. Under siege they ate anything – dogs, cats, vermin of any description, grass – rather than surrender. In an attempt to make bread, the bones of animals and of human corpses were ground down for flour.

It is in a world like this, a world inured to religious hatred, civil war, famine, plague, and economic disaster, that the werewolves of Franche-Comté begin to make sense. Their alleged cannibalism touched a particular chord in a society in which the taboo against the eating of human flesh was tested to breaking point. One contemporary commentator writing of the 1637 famine in Franche-Comté noted that 'posterity will not believe it: people lived off the plants in gardens and fields; they even sought out the carcasses of dead animals. The roads were strewn with people . . . Finally it came to cannibalism.' Even if such evidence is dismissed as anecdotal and actual incidents of cannibalism are reckoned to have been as rare in sixteenth-century as in modern France, there can be no doubt that a person starving to death, surrounded by potential nourishment in the shape of plentiful human corpses, will begin to question the validity of such a taboo. And it is when taboos are beginning to be questioned that the prohibitions against the breaking of them become ever more elaborate and terrifying. The werewolves of Franche-Comté were the receptacle into which a tormented peasantry was able to cast fears that its own system of morality was breaking down under the intolerable pressures of that sad and terrible era.

Such a theory ascribes a great deal of importance to the beliefs and actions of the peasants, and there are a number of sensible reasons why this should be so. After all, the accusations against werewolves came primarily from peasants and the alleged werewolves themselves were almost exclusively from rural peasant or urban artisan stock. In the cases of Jacques Roulet and Gilles Garnier they were outcasts of even these lowly strata, a beggar and a hermit respectively, while the three Gandillons visited by Boguet in their prison cell seem, like Roulet, to have suffered from some form of mental abnormality which helped make them an obvious target for the hatred and violence of the people of St Claude. But it is clear that such accusations would have failed had not the prevailing climate been in some way disposed to accept lycanthropy as fact. There were courts and lawyers and due processes of law involved in the execution of these werewolves, and the judges and advocates were not generally drawn from the ranks of the peasantry, even if in this respect they appear to have shared their beliefs.

Central government can easily be absolved of responsibility for these trials. The uniformity of administration which had been established in France by the first half of the sixteenth century was considerably disrupted by the civil wars; indeed the Bourbon monarchy would spend much of the following century installing absolutist structures in an attempt to ensure that such a break-down never occurred again. At the end of the sixteenth century authority resided locally, with the representative provincial Estates or with aristocratic governors. Legal decisions were made locally and any precedents thereby established could be expected to have force only in that particular region. It is for this reason that the theories of those judges who published the famous demonologies have come under particular scrutiny. Many writers on the subject have argued that legal judgements in witchcraft cases were chiefly influenced by the publication of demonologies, and that published theories of the existence of werewolves and other manifestations of witchcraft determined legal practice. Evidence for such a correlation is certainly there in relation to werewolves. Franche-Comté had by far the highest concentration of werewolves in sixteenth-century Europe, and it also had a jurist in Henri Boguet who devoted a long chapter of his demonology to the subject and who argued for their existence. Lorraine had a far lower number of werewolf cases, despite apparently similar conditions, and it had Judge Rémy who had stated categorically in his *Demonolatry* that it was 'absurd and incredible that anyone can truly be changed from a man into a wolf or other animal', although he went on to consider that 'there must be some foundation for the opinion so obstinately held by so many'.[10]

Yet, as Judge Rémy's equivocation here suggests, the demon-ologists were often curiously at sea in discussing the truth or otherwise of lycanthropy. The Jura demonologist Boguet begins his chapter by asserting the truth of lycanthropy with reference to specific examples, but most of these turn out to be either classical or legendary. Of course he uses the rich history of werewolves involved in legal cases in Franche-Comté to bolster his list, and these give his chapter a certain weight, but he also includes a number of stories which he hardly attempts to corroborate at all. He tells of 'the three wolves which were seen on the 18th of July, 1603, in the district of Douvres and Jeurre about half an hour after a hailstorm had very strangely ruined all the fruit of that country. These wolves had no tails; and, moreover, as they ran through herds of cows and goats they touched none of them except one little kid, which one of them carried a little distance away without doing it any harm at all. It is apparent from this that these were not natural wolves, but were rather witches who had helped to cause the hailstorm, and had come to witness the damage which they had caused.' He states that one larger wolf led the rest, and explains this by referring to the confessions of various convicted lycanthropes who claimed that 'when they ran about in the shape of wolves, Satan used also to assume the form of a wolf and led and guided them'.

Practically all of the details of this uncorroborated story can be explained as an eyewitness account of an authentic event. First, nothing could be less strange than that a hailstorm should ruin fruit. Nor is Boguet's suggestion that these are 'not natural' wolves credible: it is far from unusual for wolves to pass through herds of animals without attacking all of them; the singling out of one animal from the herd is a classic lupine hunting technique, and it is often a conspicuously weaker member of the herd which is picked out. The only question is how the kid could have escaped unharmed, and this may have been the one apparently supernatural element in the scenario which called for a mythopoeic explanation. The large 'Satanic' wolf at the head of the pack would, of course, be what animal behaviourists usually refer to as the lead or 'alpha' wolf (often the largest wolf in the pack, for obvious reasons). If the alpha wolf were more concerned with leading the pack elsewhere rather than attacking the herd, and a wolf of lesser status had taken the kid, this might explain why the pack as a whole did not join in the attack and the kid was able to escape.

Boguet concludes his list of contemporary examples with another tale which

> happened in the year 1588 in a village about two leagues from Apchon in the highlands of Auvergne. One evening a gentleman, standing at the window of his château, saw a huntsman whom he knew passing by, and asked him to bring him some of his bag on his return. As the huntsman went on his way along a valley, he was attacked by a large wolf and discharged his arquebus [an early kind of gun] at it without hurting it. He was therefore compelled to grapple with the wolf, and caught it by

the ears; but at length, growing weary, he let go of the wolf, drew back and took his big hunting knife, and with it cut off one of the wolf's paws, which he put in his pouch after the wolf had run away. He then returned to the gentleman's château, in sight of which he had fought the wolf. The gentleman asked him to give him part of his bag; and the huntsman, wishing to do so and intending to take the paw from his pouch, drew from it a hand wearing a gold ring on one of the fingers, which the gentleman recognized as belonging to his wife. This caused him to entertain an evil suspicion of her; and going into the kitchen, he found his wife nursing her arm in her apron, which he took away, and found that her hand had been cut off. Thereupon the gentleman seized hold of her; but immediately, and as soon as she had been confronted with her hand, she confessed that it was no other than she who, in the form of a wolf, had attacked the hunter; and she was afterwards burned at Ryon.

Boguet liked to end his werewolf stories with a judicial burning, but this is so obviously a folk-tale that even he cannot disguise it as anything which really culminated in any kind of legal proceeding. No names or specific locations are given, so that verification would have been impossible even to Boguet's contemporaries, and the whole story abounds with folkloric motifs: the faithless wife, the exchange of hunting trophies between guest and host, the sympathetic wound which gives away the werewolf. The description of the fight between man and werewolf is purely formulaic – the expression 'holding a wolf by the ears' is proverbial, used to express the idea that it is equally dangerous to keep hold as to let go. As a strategy in a real fight with a real wolf it would be little short of disastrous. Boguet concludes rather limply: 'This was told me by one who may be believed, who went that way fifteen days after this thing had happened.' His 'one who may be believed' sounds remarkably like the 'friend of a friend' of modern urban myth whose identity always remains so tantalizingly elusive.

It is easy to mock Boguet for credulity, but at least he is consistent to this point. However, after his long litany of case histories, he suddenly makes a startling admission: 'It has always been my opinion', he says, 'that lycanthropy is an illusion, and that the metamorphosis of a man into a beast is impossible.' He goes on to explain that his objections to the truth of lycanthropy are theological in origin: it is impossible for the body of a brute beast to contain a reasoning soul, he argues, and so if a man is truly metamorphosed, what happens to his soul in the meanwhile, and how is it returned to him when he resumes human shape? To credit the devil with being able to juggle man's immortal soul in this way would be to grant him the ability to perform miracles, and that can never be. Furthermore a council of the Catholic church has proclaimed belief in lycanthropy heretical.

How then does Boguet reconcile these theoretical reservations with his crusading zeal against such creatures? 'My own opinion', he states, 'is that Satan sometimes leaves the witch asleep behind a bush, and himself goes and performs that which the witch has in mind to do.' Satan gives himself the appearance of a wolf, but he deliberately befuddles the mind of the witch, who consequently believes that it was himself who has become a wolf and run about attacking men and beasts. Boguet explains away the sympathetic wound – the classic 'proof' of lycanthropy, which is fatally undermined by this reasoning – by arguing that Satan is able to transfer any blows he receives while in wolf-guise to the body of the sleeping witch. But, without apparently discarding that ornate explanation, Boguet then goes on to expound a completely contradictory theory: 'It is the witch himself who runs about slaying: not that he is metamorphosed into a wolf, but that it *appears* to him that he is so. And this comes from the devil confusing the four Humours of which he is composed, so that he represents whatever he will to his fantasy and imagination.' Thus Boguet succeeds in having it both ways: the sorcerer does not commit the deeds of a werewolf, Satan does, but – on the other hand – the witch may commit the crimes himself, although only because Satan has taken temporary hold of his mental powers.

It is an attractive notion that the intellectual poverty of Boguet's book led to the decline in the prosecution of werewolves in France, but the sad evidence of the many editions of his book published into the seventeenth century suggests otherwise. Nevertheless, he was riding the crest of a wave that was about to break abruptly. The first sign of a changed attitude was the treatment of Jacques Roulet, sentenced to death by Judge Hérault in August 1598. Roulet was allowed the final resort of an appeal to the *parlement* of Paris, which commuted his death sentence to two years in the insane asylum of St Germain-des-Prés, with the stipulation that, while there, he should receive instruction in religion, 'which he had forgotten in his utter poverty'. That this *parlement* was the same authority which later that year sentenced to death the tailor of Châlons on apparently overwhelming evidence of infanticide and cannibalism suggests that its members were learning to distinguish between the genuine psychopath, whose crimes might as well be categorized as 'lycanthropic' as anything else, and the vulnerable, mentally disturbed victim of aggressive and prejudiced interrogation.

The case which in retrospect seems ultimately to have ended the late sixteenth-century werewolf craze in France was that of Jean Grenier. It is ironic that the fullest account of his trial should come from Pierre de Lancre, a witch-hunter who is often regarded as having been every bit as credulous as Boguet. In 1609, after investigating witchcraft in the Pays de Labourd, a Basque-speaking country in the south-west of Guienne, he concluded that the entire population of the area, some 30,000 people, was infected. Like Boguet and Rémy, he was proud of his judicial zeal, and claimed 600 executions in this particular witch-hunt, but like Boguet and Rémy he exaggerated somewhat: the real figure was something in the region of eighty.

The Grenier case had come earlier in his career, while he was a lawyer for the *parlement* of Bordeaux, and had been referred up to that authority from smaller courts in the St Sever district of Gascony and at Coutras. The case hinged on the confessions of Jean Grenier, a strange, stunted, fourteen-year-old boy who liked to frighten girls with boasts of being a werewolf. He claimed that a man had given him a wolf-skin cape which, used in combination with a magic salve, transformed him for about an hour at dusk every other day. He said that in wolf-shape he had killed dogs and drunk their blood 'but little girls taste better, their flesh is tender and sweet, their blood rich and warm'. One girl to whom he told these stories, a thirteen-year-old named Marguerite Poirier with whom he often tended sheep, accused him of attacking her in his werewolf guise. One day when Jean was not with her, a wolf had jumped out at her. She had beaten it off with her staff, she told the authorities, but it had only retreated a little, sat back on its haunches, and glared at her so fiercely that she fled. The creature she had seen was smaller than a wolf, and stouter; its hair was red, like Jean's, its tail was a mere stump, and its head was smaller than that of a natural wolf.

Jean Grenier seemed determined to agree with such accusations by confessing openly to many similar crimes. A number of children had gone missing in the area, and so his confessions were paid close attention. The superior court at Coutras spent a considerable amount of effort in checking his evidence, including searching his house for the magic salve, although nothing was found. Jean's father and their neighbour, del Thillaire, were both imprisoned on the basis of Jean's incrimination of them and were tortured; they soon confessed that they had sought out little girls, but only *pour en jouir et non les manger* (to enjoy and not to eat). Several children who had seen their playmates seized by a wolf came forward with details which linked Jean's confessions to these incidents. In the face of all the circumstantial evidence, the judge at Coutras convicted Jean Grenier in June 1603, and sentenced him to be hanged and burnt.

Nevertheless Jean Grenier's case was taken before the *parlement* of Bordeaux for review in September of the same year. Jean told his story all over again, how at the age of ten or eleven he had been introduced by his neighbour, del Thillaire, to a 'black man' he called the *Maître de la Forêt*, how the *Maître* had signed him with his nail and given him the salve and pelt necessary to become a wolf. He was questioned about the children he was supposed to have killed and eaten; he told the court that he had once entered an empty house in a village, the name of which he could not now remember, and had dragged a baby out of its cradle and eaten it. He had given what was left over to a wolf. On another occasion, in the parish of St Antoine-de-Pizon, he attacked and ate a little girl-shepherd who was wearing a black dress. Six weeks before his arrest he had fallen on another child, near the stone bridge, in the same parish. He had attacked a dog in Eparon, and would have killed it, had the owner not chased him away with a rapier.

One result of the three investigations into Jean Grenier was that the authorities succeeded in disentangling a good many threads of a confused story. It had been quickly established that Jean Grenier was not the son of a priest, as he had first claimed in his boastings to the young girls, but of a poor labourer. His father had remarried, had put Jean out of the house, and Jean had been forced to wander around the country, often reduced to beggary. Doctors who examined him found him to be malnourished and of restricted growth. Whenever he had managed to find casual work tending the flocks, he was usually dismissed shortly afterwards for negligence. Given these circumstances, it was hardly surprising that he should repeatedly attempt to implicate his father in his crimes: on one occasion he said that his stepmother had separated from his father because she had seen him vomit the paws of a dog and the fingers of a child. Significantly, when confronted with his father in court, his testimony began to falter and the limitations of what was surely a meagre intelligence become obvious to all. The charges against his father were summarily dismissed.

Yet the circumstantial evidence that Jean had committed these crimes was felt to be overwhelming. But it was the sentence of the court that set such an astounding precedent. Taking 'into account the young age and the imbecility of this boy, who is so stupid and idiotic that children of seven and eight years old normally show more intelligence, who has been ill fed in every respect and who is so dwarfed that he is not as tall as a ten-year-old . . . [and that] here is a young lad abandoned and driven out by his father, who has a cruel stepmother instead of a real mother, who wanders over the fields, without a counsellor and without anyone to take an interest in him, begging his bread, who has never had any religious training, whose real nature was corrupted by evil promptings, need, and despair, and whom the Devil made his prey', the court sentenced him to life imprisonment in a local monastery, where he might be educated in his Christian and moral obligations.

Grenier's trial marked the end of the werewolf fever in the French judicial system. The judge summing up at his trial had been careful to distinguish between the likelihood of his having committed the crimes and the possibility of his having made a pact with the devil in order to commit them. While allowing that the devil had made him his prey, the court insisted that lycanthropy was merely an hallucination, and that the change of shape existed only in the mind of the insane. Therefore, as an illness, lycanthropy deserved treatment rather than punishment. This was to be the predominant note in later werewolf trials. Confessions of lycanthropy were not often taken seriously in seventeenth-century courts, but in those areas where werewolves traditionally roamed free, the idea was longer dying than elsewhere. In the 1630s the provincial *parlements* organizing wolf hunts in the Franche-Comté found it necessary to redraft a number of clauses in their edicts several times as arguments broke out as to the reality or otherwise of werewolves, and as late as the 1650s a member of the *parlement* could be found defending the peasants of St Claude who still believed in them, although he and his colleagues no longer convicted lycanthropes for any crime.[11] The age when the courts of France took seriously confessions of diabolical pacts, magic salves, and metamorphosing animal pelts had passed forever.

8

Journey to the Land of the Dead

... a cursed past in which man was wolf to
the man.

BARTOLOMEO VANZETTI

A little under a hundred years after the Jean Grenier case, on the
other side of Europe, an eighty-year-old man was interrogated on
charges of being a werewolf. This alleged idolator, a man named
Theiss, was questioned at Jürgensburg, a town in Livonia, on the
eastern side of the Baltic Sea, some two thousand or so miles
north of Franche-Comté, in the year 1692. This is a considerable
distance both in space and time from the sixteenth-century
French trials, a fact consonant with a pattern detectable in the
continental witch-craze as a whole, in which trials started from an
epicentre roughly in the Alpine region of western Europe and
died out earliest in the same area. In countries at a geographical
distance from the epicentre, the witch-craze lingered longest: one
of the last large-scale trials in continental Europe occurred at
Mora in Sweden in 1670, when eighty-five witches were burnt.
The furthest of all manifestations from the epicentre, the famous
transatlantic outbreak of witch hysteria at Salem, Massachusetts,
took place in the same year as the interrogation of Theiss. What
makes this Livonian werewolf's confession so interesting, however, is not its relative lateness but its remarkable content, for
Theiss's confession threatened to turn the inquisitors' accepted
definition of the early-modern werewolf upside down.

Theiss said that he and the other Livonian and Russian
werewolves, both male and female, went out on three nights of
the year, on St Lucy's night before Christmas, on St John's night,
and on the night of the Pentecost, and visited hell, which was

located 'at the end of the sea'. The werewolves were the dogs of God, he said, armed with iron whips. In hell they battled with the devil and sorcerers, who were armed with broomsticks wrapped in horse tails. The sorcerers had stolen the shoots of the grain, and it was the werewolves' job to battle for them back, otherwise famine would sweep the land. Their battle that year had been successful, Theiss said; the harvest of barley and of rye was going to be plentiful, and there would also be enough fish to go around. Naturally Theiss was pressured by the judges to admit that, far from fighting the devil, he had made a pact with him, but he resisted all such suggestions. His only concession to his interrogators' cosmology was eventually to agree that hell was located underground.[1]

Theiss's confession is not the only evidence that werewolves in this area of Europe were remarkably different in character from those who found themselves at the mercy of Judge Boguet. Another werewolf, imprisoned at Riga some time in the middle of the sixteenth century, was interviewed by a Livonian professor named Witekind.[2] Far from being cowed by his imprisonment, Witekind's werewolf laughed and skipped about happily inside his cell. On the night before Easter, he said, he had changed himself into a wolf and escaped from prison. He had only returned because his 'master' wished him to do so. Like Theiss's interrogators, Witekind and the prison authorities attempted to persuade the werewolf that this master was an evil one. The werewolf replied only that if they could tell him of a better one, he would follow him.

These cases have traditionally been regarded as rather inexplicable exceptions to the rule. The Franche-Comté werewolves of the sixteenth century have always been thought of as classic werewolf cases, and there is a clear line of descent between such alleged cannibals as Gilles Garnier and the werewolves of Hollywood horror films. The French werewolves are allegedly involved in occult practices, having made a pact with the devil; they are transformed periodically and wreak terrible crimes on their peasant neighbours; and they are identified and hunted down amid the dim lights of fear, superstition, and terror. Although today they are usually regarded as innocent victims of superstitious persecution (just as the hero of a werewolf film exhibits a touching innocence while in the guise of his human *alter ego*), there is no doubt that the Franche-Comté werewolves represent the apotheosis of the werewolf as a wicked, destructive creature. Conversely, these Baltic werewolves hint at the survival of the contrary idea, evident previously in the medieval Celtic werewolf romances, of the beneficent werewolf. Although their beliefs are not the same as their Christian interrogators' and so open to wide misunderstanding, these werewolves claim not to worship but to fight the devil and his witches on behalf of their own community.

Another Livonian treatise of the same era, written by Caspar Peucer, includes details equally alien to the Franche-Comté werewolf stereotype.[3] Livonian werewolves boast of fighting witches, Peucer notes. They change shape only during the twelve days between Christmas and Epiphany, and are driven by a tall man who is armed, like Theiss's dogs of God, with an iron whip. He leads his followers towards an enormous river, and with a lash of his whip parts the waters for them to cross. As they do so, they are transformed into wolves. Although they attack cattle, these werewolves cannot do harm to human beings. Of course the sheer numbers of these Livonian werewolves are potentially alarming and they are regarded as a menace to livestock, yet they are noticeably less horrific than the French loner-werewolf who captures and eats young children. Another clue that the image of the werewolf was much more ambiguous in this part of the world is the description by Olaus Magnus, Bishop of Uppsala, of the behaviour of his local werewolves, given in his *Historia de gentibus septentrionalibus* of 1555. He gives a similar picture to Peucer, adding the detail that the werewolves of Prussia, Livonia, and Lithuania expended a good deal of their demonic energy on breaking into cellars and stealing wine and beer. Some commentators have been so baffled at this departure from the traditional werewolf legend that they assume the good bishop is really describing the activities of a secret society of drunken hooligans, who perhaps took the wolf as the emblem of their illicit activities.

What characterizes this Baltic evidence, particularly in the cases of Theiss and Witekind's werewolf, is a considerable gap between the werewolves' perception of themselves and that of the inquisitors. Although it is only natural that the defendant and the prosecutor should have different viewpoints, here in the Baltic region the two opposing camps could not even agree what constitutes a werewolf. By contrast, the question of the precise nature of a werewolf seems never to have arisen in the French trials: the confessions of Pierre Bourgot or of Gilles Garnier, even of the hesitant Jacques Roulet, all reinforce the stereotypical image of a werewolf as a shape-shifting murderer, cannibal, and devil-worshipper. The Baltic cases pick out threads from an alternative skein of ideas woven around the werewolf legend, ideas which had begun to unravel under the pressure of the spread of Christianity. Peucer's werewolves, for example, are seen enacting rites in which a significant body of water is crossed, familiar from the classical Arcadian stories repeated by Pliny as well as from the medieval werewolf romances. Theiss regards himself as something of a shamanic figure: he travels in animal-shape to the other world, which is at the end of the sea, where he fights on behalf of his community for the fertility of the fields. Both he and Witekind's werewolf evidently regarded themselves as able to travel in their wolf-shapes while their human bodies remained behind.

Yet the traditional argument of most historians has been to deny that anything resembling ancient shamanic practices or fertility cults could possibly have managed to survive as late as the end of the seventeenth century. That argument was at least partially demolished when the Italian historian Carlo Ginzburg unearthed evidence of a previously-ignored fertility cult in the Friuli, an Alpine region of north-eastern Italy. There, in the records of some fifty inquisitorial witchcraft trials held between the last quarter of the sixteenth and the last quarter of the seventeenth century, Ginzburg came across a number of local men and women who called themselves *benandanti*. They believed themselves to be marked out from the ordinary by being born with the caul, the amniotic membrane still attached to the heads of some infants at birth, which they preserved and wore around their necks in later life. As adults, the *benandanti* went out on four nights of the year 'invisibly in spirit', to battle, like Theiss's dogs of God, *against* witches. Their spirits left their bodies, sometimes in the shape of a mouse or a butterfly, sometimes riding on hares, cats, or other animals. While their abandoned bodies lay lifeless, their spirits rode out to fight with bundles of fennel against their witch-enemies, who wielded stalks of sorghum, for the fertility of the fields. The Friuli inquisitors, like their counterparts in Livonia, were astonished by these stories, and tried to reconcile them with the accepted pattern of the diabolical sabbat, but, as Ginzburg makes clear, it took some fifty years before the *benandanti* began to make grudging and incomplete changes towards orthodoxy in their testimonies.[4]

Although the Friuli *benandanti* did not assume the shape of wolves during their ecstatic swoons, there is a remarkable similarity between their evidence and that of the Baltic werewolf Theiss, a similarity equally unacceptable to the witch-beliefs of their orthodox Christian inquisitors and to modern-day historians vehemently opposed to the idea of the continuing existence in this period of ritual activity designed to ensure fertility. Some historians have argued that the *benandanti* were a purely local, idiosyncratic phenomenon, but Ginzburg has answered by pointing to connecting factors between the *benandanti* and roughly contemporary werewolf beliefs elsewhere. To their east, for example, in the Slavic world stretching from the Baltic and Russia in the north to Serbia in the south, to be born with the caul was the traditional sign of the werewolf. The ruthlessly bloodthirsty Prince Vseslav of Polock, who died in 1101 after a short reign as King of Kiev, had been born with the caul and wrapped in it, and in the epic poem *Igor's Tale* he is portrayed as a werewolf. The hero of another of these epics, Volch Vseslav'evič, could transform himself into a wolf, a falcon, and an ant.[5]

That the *benandanti* were not unique has also been shown by the tracing of analogous beliefs in the Balkan countries along the far coast of the Adriatic, outside the ambit of the western continental witch-craze, where men were believed to be marked out at birth to fight in spirit on behalf of the community. In Istria, Slovenia, and Croatia, the *kresnik* (or *krestnik*; *krsnik* in Croatia) was born with the caul, as was the *zduhač* of Montenegro, Bosnia, and Herzegovina. In Southern Dalmatia the *negromanat* was recognized by having been born with a tail, while the *mogut* of northern Croatia was the son of a woman who had either endured an unusually long pregnancy or who had actually died giving birth to him. The idea that someone whose mother had died in childbirth had special powers was widespread in European folklore: Macduff, in Shakespeare's most witchcraft-ridden play, was uniquely qualified to fulfil the witches' prophecy and vanquish the evil of Macbeth by having been 'from his mother's

womb untimely ripp'd'. More pertinent from the point of view of
the werewolf legend is that Völsung, titular head of the Germanic
werewolf clan in the old saga, was also born in this way. In the east
these remarkable men were destined to fight witches and vampires, often on fixed days like the Ember-week festivals or on
Christmas night, and these fights usually took the form of clashes
between animals, the spirit-representatives of the opponents.
These animals – boars, dogs, oxen, horses – were often distinguished by colour: black for the witches, white or dappled for the
community's spiritual champions.

In Greece the equivalent figures were (and still are today in the
Peloponnese and the Greek islands) the *kallikantzaroi*, envisaged
as monstrous, bestial creatures, sometimes small enough to use
a cockerel as a mount, sometimes awesomely large. The
kallikantzaroi usually have an assortment of animalistic limbs –
donkeys' ears, goats' forelegs, horses' hooves – as well as being
said to ride abroad on animals, and to be capable of transforming
themselves into animals. Once again, as with the Celtic-
Germanic traditions of the Wild Hunt and the medieval midwin-
ter animal festivals, the time of their nocturnal marauding is
linked to the twelve days of the Christmas festival. The scholar
Leone Allacci, who wrote deprecatingly of superstitious beliefs in
the *kallikantzaroi* among the inhabitants of the Greek island of
Chios in the middle of the seventeenth century, mentioned that
children born on Christmas Day were believed to be fated to
become *kallikantzaroi*. Such a destiny was abhorrent to their
parents, and children born on that day would be held over a fire
by their heels to scorch the soles of their feet and so prevent the
terrible claws of the *kallikantzaros* from growing. If this were not
done, the *kallikantzaros* would grow up to join his peers in their
wild routs, entering houses and spoiling the food and drink there,
or attacking travellers with their long claws. Although the
kallikantzaroi are not lycanthropes, nor indeed any specific were-
animal, the analogy with the werewolf is recognized in the fact
that in Messenia, southern Laconia, and Crete, an alternative
name for them is *lykokantzaroi*.

The significance of these related folk-beliefs across a wide
band of countries, running from Livonia and the Baltic in the
north, through Russia and Hungary, to the Balkan states and
Greece in the south, is difficult to assess. Although there are

connections between them, these areas are usually regarded as culturally disparate. At first sight, their only connecting factor is that they form a fringe along the demarcation line between those areas of continental Europe which fell prey to the Renaissance witch-craze and the east which did not. The question might be put: did these folk-beliefs at an earlier date obtain over a wider area, perhaps the whole of Europe; or were they later arrivals, moving by diffusion westwards from the shaman-saturated Asiatic world through Orthodox eastern Europe, before coming up against the 'hard' theology of western Christianity, which was unwilling to tolerate such ideas? By this latter reckoning the *benandanti* of the Friuli would be seen, not as a manifestation of native folk-belief deeply buried in the western tradition, but as the western-most protrusion of ideas common in the east, assimilated via their close neighbours in Slovenia. The strongest argument against this view are the few but significant similarities between the Baltic evidence and the medieval werewolves of Celtic-influenced literature, an otherwise unbridgeable gap of distance and time which is surely best explained by accepting that a common inheritance of folk-beliefs informed both cultures.

Yet on returning to the sixteenth-century French werewolves, it is hard to detect many beliefs comparable to the ecstatic night-battles of Theiss or the *benandanti*. Perhaps one hint occurs in the earliest of the Franche-Comté cases, the werewolves of Poligny, executed in 1521. The most important witness, Pierre Bourgot, confessed that he had fallen into devil-worship after the loss of some of his cattle during a storm. After agreeing to worship the devil, Pierre had his herd returned to him. It is possible to detect here an echo of some fertility rite; but if it is an echo, it is only a very faint one. Of course, the evidence in this case is distinctly second-hand: the local witch-hunter Boguet wrote about the case some seventy years after it happened, and seems to have been aware of it largely because there were paintings of the three werewolves on the wall of the Church of the Jacobins at Poligny, while even the rigorously investigative Johann Weyer, who published an examination of the case in 1563, wrote about it from the safe distance of Germany. He almost certainly never visited Besançon, but instead relied on court records circulated throughout Europe in the succeeding decades for his description of the case.

It is important to remember, however, that the French were-wolves were at a great disadvantage compared to their Baltic counterparts in that they had the full rigour of the law levelled against them. The western tradition of using torture to extract confessions from alleged werewolves, well-established in witch-trials by the sixteenth century, meant that the learned, ridiculous ideas of the demonologists were all that were allowed to remain in the final depositions to the court – all else had been stretched and beaten out of the alleged werewolf beforehand in the privacy of the local gaol. Ironically, the one French case in which it is certain that the defendant confessed more or less voluntarily to all manner of stereotypical werewolf crimes, that of Jean Grenier, was ultimately decided, not by demonologists, but by doctors who plainly disbelieved the boy's confession. By contrast, as Carlo Ginzburg points out, the authentic voices of the alleged werewolves ring out clear in two of the Baltic cases: Theiss, stubbornly denying the foolish ideas of his inquisitors with the detachment of a man who has lived long enough; Witekind's werewolf, mockingly asking his questioners to find him a better master if they can. For this reason, their evidence is all the more compelling.

The idea that alleged werewolves might actually have believed their own confessions, and had coherent reasons for doing so, is one which strikes at the heart of what most historians regard as the most puzzling question about the continental witch-craze: why should so many people have confessed to doing things that are patently impossible, of which transforming themselves into a wolf by the use of a bewitched wolf-skin or a magical ointment is not even the most bizarre? In the whole period of the craze, usually taken to run from 1300 to 1700, a substantial number of people were brought to trial on charges of witchcraft. Only a few of them were charged with lycanthropy: the majority of charges centred instead on the ritual of the witches' sabbat. To get to this unholy gathering, witches were supposed to apply their magical ointment to themselves or to their household objects – broom-sticks, stools, fenceposts – and fly off to the sabbat, which met at night in some secluded place, in a cave, or a cellar, or, like Macbeth's witches, on a deserted heath. Sometimes witches rode on animals to get there, and occasionally the animal used in this way was a wolf. Richard Kieckhefer has pointed out that the witch-trial records suggest that witches riding on wolves was a distinctively Swiss tradition. In a trial at Zürich in 1494 children testified that they had seen a woman riding over fields, hedges, and graveyards on a wolf, keeping dry even in a storm, although adult witnesses said the animal was an ass. Five years later at Lucerne, an alleged witch defended herself against similar accusations, saying she had actually been walking her dog. Any such explanation provided by Else of Meerburg, who was also tried at Lucerne around 1450 on charges of riding on a wolf, is not recorded.[6] Having arrived at the sabbat whether by wolf or by broomstick, the witches might induct a new member, forcing her, or more rarely him, to renounce Christianity and defile a crucifix or consecrated host, usually by stamping or defecating on it. The new member's pact with the devil was sealed with the *osculum infanum*, a kiss on the behind of the devil, or his representative, sometimes a goat. The witches then proceeded to the main business of the meeting, which characteristically involved cannibalistic feasts and sexual orgies, before flying off to their separate homes in time for sunrise.

The usual response to this has been to regard the whole story as nonsense from the tip of its Satanic horns to the last twitch of its goatish tail, fit only for repetition in a Dennis Wheatley novel. Many historians, incredulous at the farcical nature of these allegations, have started from the assumption that witches simply did not exist and that the many women who were brought to trial for witchcraft confessed more or less the first thing that came into their heads. Once a pattern had been established by the earliest trials, inquisitors then attempted to get all alleged witches to conform to it, and a new myth was born. The most cynical form of this view puts the blame for the content of the witches' confessions entirely on the ecclesiastical authorities, who supposedly wished to repress witches in order to enhance their own temporal power and, by the by, fill their purses with the proceeds of confiscations. (This motive does not appear to have been a factor in any of the werewolf cases, since most of the accused were too poor to be worth picking on.) Others have noted that many of the accusations against witches – especially human sacrifice, cannibalism, and sexual licence – were exactly those that had been made against the Christian church in her earliest days, which the Church had always used in turn against her own enemies and internal dissenters: the dualist Gnostics and Manicheans in the early period, the Cathars from the 1140s on, the Waldensian heretics of the thirteenth century, and the Knights Templar at the beginning of the fourteenth century, as well as those perennial supposed enemies of Christ, the Jews and, to a lesser extent, the Muslims. According to this view, the witch-craze was only a later efflorescence of the repressive, doctrinaire spirit of western Christendom in general.

In the opinion of many, the key document of the witch-craze was the infamous *Malleus Maleficarum*, first published in 1486. The *Malleus* (the Latin title is usually translated as 'The Witches' Hammer', although 'Mallet against Malefactors' would preserve the alliteration) was the inspiration of a German Dominican named Heinrich Kramer, styling himself 'Institoris'. Appointed inquisitor in southern Germany in 1474, he had ceased to concern himself with ordinary heresy by 1476, and concentrated almost exclusively on witchcraft thenceforth. A deeply corrupt and venal man, Institoris was helped in his work by a fellow Dominican, Jakob Sprenger, who later repudiated his master and testified against him. Together they compiled the *Malleus*, which was issued with the approval of the pope, Innocent VIII, and a preface which reprinted a recent papal bull confirming the inquisition's new powers against witches. It was to become one of the most popular books of the early era of printing, reaching a fourteenth edition by 1520. In some ways the *Malleus* is a defensive document, for Institoris and Sprenger's powers were recently granted and, at first, far from generally accepted by all episcopal authorities. More importantly, the inquisitorial duo had to overturn the centuries-old tradition, represented by the *Canon Episcopi*, that belief in the powers of witches to transform themselves into animals or to fly out at night was itself heretical. That they managed to do so, at least to the general satisfaction of contemporary jurists, marks a turning point in the witch-craze, so that the years 1300–1500 are categorized as a period when persecution of witches was haphazard and the content of their confessions was less monotonously stereotypical, while the period 1500–1700 was one in which the witch-craze spread from its Alpine beginnings to every corner of western Europe (central and southern Italy, Spain, and Portugal notably ex-cluded), with a concomitant increase in the use of torture, prepared lists of questions, and other pieces of witch-hunting artillery supplied by the *Malleus*. That this latter period was also the time of the great Renaissance flowering of humanism, art, science, and religious reform is one of the more disturbing ironies of history.

From the point of view of werewolves, the significance of the *Malleus* is ambiguous. The authors do not specifically treat werewolves or lycanthropy in any great detail, probably because werewolves were at best only a tangential feature of witchcraft trials of the early period. One trial at Basel in 1407, for example, involved several women who had been accused of employing various magical spells and potions, details of which were put before the municipal court. Some spells invoked orthodox images of piety, the saints or the wounds and nails of Christ, but others called upon demons and werewolves to perform terrible tasks, such as sucking the blood from a victim's heart.[7] The werewolves are not envisaged as humans lycanthropically transformed, but as part of an inhuman rabble of demonic personages to be invoked whenever the sorceresses needed a particularly nasty job done. It is probably because werewolves occupied only this diminished role in the earlier trials that Institoris and Sprenger did not deal with them in any great detail. Their book does, however, consider 'Whether Witches can by some Glamour Change Men into Beasts', concluding with that familiar argument that the animal shapes seen by witnesses are not real, only illusory, as the devil does not have the power of true creation. Nevertheless they add a supplementary note detailing 'What is to be Thought of Wolves which sometimes Seize and Eat Men and Children out of their Cradles, Whether this also is a Glamour Caused by Witches', which certainly shows their awareness that supernatural explanations were already accumulating around the figure of the wolf. Institoris and Sprenger argue that the attacks of wolves do indeed have a supernatural explanation, but that the wolves themselves are real, possessed by devils, and that this is done by God's express purpose, in order to punish sinners.

Yet they conclude their examination of the subject with a story they attribute to William of Paris, of a man who thought that he was turned into a wolf and went off to live in a cave. 'For there he went at a certain time, and though he remained there all the time stationary, he believed that he was a wolf which went about devouring children; and though the devil, having possessed a wolf, was really doing this, he erroneously thought that he was prowling about in his sleep. And he was for so long thus out of his senses that he was at last found lying in the wood raving.'[8] This, then, is the single werewolf case-study in the *Malleus*, and it is fascinating to detect in it once more that characteristically shamanistic theme of the man lying lifeless in trance while his spirit travels forth in animal-shape.

If the *Malleus* provided ammunition for the likes of Boguet to argue for the catching and killing of werewolves, it was only because of its general approach to the power of the devil and his minions, the witches: the overwhelming impression it gave, despite attempts to discuss various philosophical issues, was that the devil could do pretty well anything he liked, and that witches were everywhere carrying out his Satanic will. Nevertheless, one other possible area of its influence may have had some effect in diminishing the threat of werewolves, the fact that, according to Institoris, the chief practioners of witchcraft were women. The *Malleus* is one of the most misogynist books ever written, Institoris declaring that most witches are female because women are more stupid than men, fickle, lighter-headed, weaker, and seethe with disgusting carnal desires. The pervasive anti-feminism of the era cannot be laid solely at the door of the *Malleus*, however, nor did the Protestant reformers, who sought to avoid the errors of the Catholic church in so many areas, have any better record in this respect – the writings of Martin Luther, for example, writhe with hatred and fear of women, and the witch-craze raged just as fiercely in Protestant countries like Scotland and Germany as in Catholic France. Women had always been particularly vulnerable to witch accusations from the beginning of the craze, especially single women, widows, and midwives, and the later period was little different. Nevertheless, the concentration on women may possibly have led to fewer accusations being made against men. Not all alleged werewolves were men, of course, but there is no doubt that men as ravening wolves makes some kind of psychological sense. Exceptions to the rule, such as the two witches who, in 1610 at Liège, were condemned for having changed themselves into wolves and having killed and eaten children, are generally late and rare.[9] Boguet, who paid more attention to werewolves than any other demonologist, was keen to implicate a number of female lycanthropes – including the unfortunate Perrenette Gandillon and the heroine of his ridiculous Auvergne tale – but contemporary trial records showing that it was overwhelmingly men who were accused of lycanthropy have much greater evidential weight. Although witches were occasionally said to metamorphose themselves, more or less as Pamphile had done in Apuleius' novel over a thousand years earlier, animals most commonly appear in the witch-trials in the reduced role of the witch's familiar, or as the mount for riding to the sabbat.

The malign influence of the *Malleus* and of the later demonologists like Jean Bodin and Boguet who recycled its arguments and intensified its virulence in the later sixteenth century have left an almost unresolvable confusion at the heart of the werewolf legend. In western Europe, any kind of belief the alleged werewolves may have had in their own powers of riding out in animal-shape was so ruthlessly suppressed, so thoroughly diabolized by Christian inquisitors, that it is now well-nigh impossible to disinter the nature of their beliefs from the rubble of learned opinion, popular prejudice, and universal fear of the unknown under which they were buried. One or two glimpses of the alternative tradition can be seen – William of Paris's werewolf prowling around in wolf-shape while his body lay in a trance in his cave, Pierre Bourgot taking on wolf-shape to ensure the well-being of his herd – but these are too few to allow any accurate reconstruction of what lies underneath. In the east, where the Orthodox church was not nearly so concerned to establish complete uniformity of belief, a wide variety of folkloric ideas was allowed to survive, exhibiting a number of parallels with each other and with the werewolf legend.

Seasoned folklorists will recognize the extension of werewolf beliefs to the east as trespassing onto the territory of that related phenomenon, the vampire, close cousin of the werewolf both in folk-belief and in cinematic ghoulery. Most of the available evidence for belief in vampires during the early modern period relates to the Slavic countries. Unlike the glamorous Byronic aristocrat popularized by nineteenth-century Gothic literature and the twentieth-century cinema, whose pale, gaunt body is swathed in a silk-lined cloak, the folk vampire wore the cheap cloth shroud of the hastily buried peasant. As numerous studies have shown, of which Paul Barber's *Vampires, Burial, and Death*[10] is a recent example particularly emphasizing natural *post-mortem* changes as a basis for the belief, the Slavic vampire was characteristically a person generally unpopular in life who had died in some unusual way, and was said to rise from his or her grave and alarm the populace with all manner of irritating and futile tricks. The belief that this undead creature sucked human blood was by no means universal, although exhumations of alleged vampires revealing bloated, reddened corpses naturally suggested this notion. The usual remedy where vampirism was suspected was to exhume the corpse and try various remedies on it, including in some cases the famous stake through the heart, although a great variety of other methods are also recorded.

One of the best, and funniest, accounts of a vampire exhumation comes from the educated and sceptical pen of the French botanist Pitton de Tournefort, who observed just such a posthumous operation attempted on a Greek vampire, or *vrykolakas*, on the island of Mykonos in 1701. De Tournefort's *vrykolakas* had been a surly and quarrelsome peasant in life, who had come to a mysterious end out in the fields. The islanders complained that he had been seen abroad two days after his burial, and had entered houses, overturned furniture, put out lamps, embraced them from behind, and in general behaved in ways more familiar as those usually attributed to poltergeists. The town leaders, both lay and clerical working in unison, decided to wait for nine days after the burial before exhuming the body of this alleged vampire and carrying him to a chapel, where a mass was said to drive out the evil demon within him.

The ageing town butcher was then brought forward to undertake the removal of the vampire's heart, but he opened the stomach first and rummaged around fruitlessly in the dead man's intestines for some time, until eventually someone pointed out that it was necessary to cut through the diaphragm in order to reach the organ he was looking for. By the time the feeble old man had succeeded in hacking out the heart and brandishing it in view of the congregation, the stench in the chapel was considerable, and de Tournefort notes that the atmosphere was made more stupefying by the great clouds of incense being burnt next to the body. To the Frenchman's bemusement, some of the crowd began to say that the smoke was actually coming from the body, and a great cry of 'Vrykolakas!' was taken up both inside the chapel and among the bystanders jostling in the square outside. Several witnesses swore that the vampire's blood was bright red, and the butcher himself said that the body was still warm, which were taken to be sure signs that the body was not dead. In vain did de Tournefort and his friends protest that the warmth of the corpse was easily explained by its state of putrefaction, and that the stinking brown mess all too visible on the butcher's hands was far from fresh.

In the days that followed, it became clear that the ceremonial removal of the vampire's heart had not been sufficient to prevent night-time disturbances on the island, for complaints about the vampire's nocturnal activities soon started up again. After a bewildering number of remedies had been tried without success, the man's much-violated corpse was burnt on a huge pyre built at the furthest tip of a small neighbouring island, and the vampire's nightly depredations were finally agreed to have ceased. The whole case has a number of interesting relationships with werewolf beliefs. For instance, de Tournefort noticed, and poured some scorn on, one accusation made many times during the scare, that the *vrykolakas* had a great thirst and emptied pitchers and bottles in every house on the island (except the one in which de Tournefort and his friends were staying, the sceptical Frenchman noted). This particular belief is clearly reminiscent of the curious practice of Olaus Magnus' Baltic werewolves, who drank wine and beer from the local cellars, as well as the episode in the *Völsungasaga* when the werewolf-heroes hid in ale-vats on entering the palace of the wicked king. In 1575 one of the *benandanti* of the Friuli had been heard to say that he and his fellows went to nightly revels and, on their return, drank wine from cellars and then urinated into the casks.[11] He implied that the presence of the *benandanti* prevented the level of the wine going down in the casks. The same belief in his own powers of drinking without reducing the level had been advanced by a Cathar 'messenger of souls' as long ago as 1319.[12] Each of these instances seems to relate to a widespread belief in the great thirst of the spirit world, and suggests that in the east, at least, the werewolf was regularly journeying to the land of the dead.

Another area in which de Tournefort's *vrykolakas* is instructive lies in the huge variety of methods used to ward off the vampire.

In the case of the werewolf, the cinema has fixed in the modern mind the idea that the only remedy for the terrible condition is a silver bullet. Likewise in the case of the vampire, the three essential apotropaics recommended by the cinema – largely following Bram Stoker – are bulbs of garlic, representations of the cross, and a good sharp stake. De Tournefort's account, on the other hand, makes clear that folk tradition was not nearly so sure of how to rid the world of these creatures. Most of the remedies tried on the *vrykolakas* have some obvious basis in magical tradition – the nine-day period after the burial, the mass celebrated at the chapel, the clouds of incense, the holy water sprinkled in the dead man's mouth, and so on – but when these remedies failed a frenzy of alternatives was liable to erupt. De Tournefort does not hide his amusement at the arrival on the island of an Albanian, who asserted that the several swords plunged into the vampire's grave by the panicking inhabitants were of no practical use, as their handles formed the shape of the Cross and so prevented the devil from leaving the corpse. Turkish scimitars would be much more efficacious, the Albanian told them.

A similar uncertainty as to the proper procedure is found in the many popular remedies for werewolves found in western folk tradition dating after the decline of the Franche-Comté stereotype. In Gascony, for example, there was a belief that sorcerers who wished to become werewolves had acquired their pelts by laying down a sheet on the ground at a crossroads at midnight. By dawn the devil would deposit a magical wolf-skin in which the sorcerer could then assume lycanthropic shape. But if the werewolf attacked a traveller who was bold enough to challenge him by saying 'take off your skin', he had to return to human shape and fight for his liberty. Whoever lost the fight would have to assume the pelt himself.[13] Other legends stated that one could transform a werewolf simply by recognizing the human inside the skin and calling out his baptismal name. (Was the usual procedure on confronting a real wolf to start desperately shouting out the names of one's neighbours just in case it turned out to be a werewolf?) Such remedies strike those expecting the motif of the silver bullet as disappointingly facile, but they indicate that the western fear of werewolves so prevalent in the sixteenth century lessened significantly in succeeding years, for these later stories all concede that the lycanthropic state is a fragile entity. According to some, a simple blow from an iron implement, a fork, or a blood-rusted key, would split the werewolf's pelt.[14] Others state that mere spilling of the werewolf's blood would suffice to end the condition. This last idea seems like a faint echo of the concept of the sympathetic wound by which the werewolf's identity is betrayed, but with the ancient narrative sequence of wound followed by identification followed by eradication of the werewolf speeded up almost to simultaneity.

At this later stage, in the Orthodox Balkans at least, the werewolf was always likely to become entangled with the vampire in the popular imagination. Often the two monsters were simply regarded as different aspects of the same creature, and someone who had been a werewolf in life was believed to become a vampire after his death. In the Greek islands de Tournefort certainly noticed this concretion of the two categories, specifically referring to the *vrykolakas* as a type of *loup-garou*. In classifying the *vrykolakas* as a subdivision of the werewolf family, he may simply have been trying to find an analogy which his eighteenth-century French audience would recognize, but it seems more likely that the confusion between the two was evident to him on Mykonos, and on the neighbouring island of Santorini, a place traditionally infested with vampires. De Tournefort had particularly noted that these Greek vampires tended to be people who had been sullen and irritable during life, and the word *loup-garou* still has exactly this secondary sense in French, being used figuratively to describe an irascible, reclusive personality. (One immediately thinks back to those irascible recluses such as Gilles Garnier who were regarded quite literally as *loups-garoux* during the sixteenth century.) The English language has no exact equivalent for this punning interplay between the concepts of recluse and werewolf, although *bogey-man* and *bugbear* come close.

The vampire and the werewolf, however, were connected in more than merely figurative ways. Many reports emphasize the widely acknowledged belief that the vampire too was capable of animal metamorphosis. The classic example which the cinema has retained is the bat, but other versions have the vampire transforming himself into a wolf, often being seen in burial grounds attempting to dig up corpses. Once again the connection is expressed between werewolves and death. Of course, this association is ancient, dating back to the classical gods of death and to Paulus Aegineta's later description of the melancholic lycanthropes haunting Alexandrian graveyards, but in the Slavic countries there may have been practical reasons for the connection, in particular the idiosyncrasies of contemporary burial practices. A coffin, for example, was an unusual luxury in eighteenth-century eastern Europe: the more usual method was to cover the corpse in a simple cloth shroud. Graves were often shallow, because of the difficulty and expense of digging very deep holes. In times of famine or plague, graves were even more likely to be hurriedly dug. Lying in its shallow grave under a thin covering of cloth and soil, the integrity of a human corpse was obviously at risk. The gases formed during the natural processes of decomposition might bloat the body, disrupting the surface of the grave; subterranean flooding might waterlog the grave, pushing the swollen body upwards; subsidence might result in part of the body being exposed. All these possibilities seem to have contributed to the widespread fear of the dead rising from their graves, a fear which found its outlet in the vampire legend. They also made life easier for predators, especially wolves who would find little difficulty in digging up such remains.

These real wolves, scavenging for grisly titbits in burial grounds at night, could easily be misinterpreted by local observers as werewolves. A similar tradition existed in France, where some demonologists distinguished a particular kind of werewolf, the *loublin*, whose defining characteristic was that he haunted graveyards and devoured human corpses.[15] But the confusion between vampire and werewolf in the east suggests the possibility that someone seeing a real wolf attempting to dig up a human corpse and then making off into the night, might conclude that the corpse was that of a vampire, which had then transferred its spirit into a werewolf, risen from the grave, and run away to cause mischief elsewhere. Among Romanian gypsies, however, it was believed that a particular kind of white wolf that haunted their cemeteries was actually helping to keep the vampires safely in their graves.[16] This belief that real wolves were the eternal enemies of the vampire was shared by the Orthodox gypsies of Kosovo-Metohija, Serbia, who believed that a vampire was fated to wander far and wide through the world, before meeting a wolf which would attack it and tear it to pieces.[17]

The eastern werewolf provides a number of fascinating clues which might help explain some of the otherwise inexplicable features of the werewolf in the west, particularly in those cases where western werewolves confessed to apparently impossible feats. If the crucial question is asked, whether anyone who was not mentally ill ever seriously believed himself able to take on the physical form of a wolf, the answer must surely be yes, for the werewolves of Livonia, the *benandanti* of the Friuli, the *vrykolakai* and *kallikantzaroi* of Greece, the *kresniki* of the Balkans, all belong to a roughly analogous set of folk-beliefs (and there were yet more, like the *táltos* of Hungary and the *strigoi* of Romania)[18] which may have had their equivalents in western Europe before the spread of Christianity – it is clear, for example, that the pre-Christian Germanic peoples held similar beliefs. As is to be expected when dealing with folklore, there is no absolute cast-iron agreement between these comparable traditions. Certain ideas, like the adopting of an animal-shape, the battle for fertility, the association with the twelve-day Christmas festival, the association with the Ember weeks, occur in different combinations in all of these local variants. One particular idea found in each version is that of the fated person being marked out by some peculiarity: being born feet first, being born by Caesarian section, having six fingers on one hand, being born with teeth or an extra vertebra, or with the caul. The western European tradition that someone whose eyebrows meet in the middle is a werewolf conforms to this basic idea.

An interesting footnote to the eastern werewolf came in 1914, when Sigmund Freud found himself faced with a neurotic patient whom he christened the Wolf-Man.[19] The patient was a twenty-seven-year-old Russian man from an upper-middle-class family. During the course of his analysis, he described a childhood dream in which he saw his bedroom window open on its own and six or seven white wolves sitting in the big walnut tree outside the window. The wolves did nothing, but the boy screamed in terror and woke up, to be comforted by his nurse. Freud himself had made some study of the western continental witch-craze – he was particularly impressed by the work of the great sceptic Johann Weyer – but he evidently knew little of eastern werewolf beliefs. Carlo Ginzburg has pointed out the neglected elements of folklore in the Wolf-Man's dream: as Freud's printed account of the case makes clear, the patient was a Russian, born with the caul, and the date of his birth was 25 December, Christmas Day. Ginzburg notes that his nurse was a pious and superstitious old Russian woman, who may well have told the child that to be born on Christmas Day with the caul was the double sign of being a werewolf. With this in mind, it seems possible to interpret the child's fear of the wolves in the dream as his fear of the possibility of being initiated into the society of werewolves. Of course in the Slavic tradition to be thus marked out was not entirely without its good side, and the Wolf-Man told Freud shortly before the end of his analysis that he remembered having been told as a child that he had been born with the caul and that, as a result, he had always felt marked out from the ordinary, immune to any harm. Freud, having no way of detecting the folkloric ideas behind the Wolf-Man's case, interpreted the caul as a veil which hid the Wolf-Man from the world, and the dream as a wish-fantasy for a return to the womb, and made no connection at all with werewolves. Ironically, Freud himself was born with the caul.[20]

9

All Wolves Are Not of the Same Sort

Wolves do change their hair, but not their hearts.
BEN JONSON,
Sejanus

A woman gave her daughter a freshly baked loaf of bread and some milk, and told her to take them to her grandmother. The little girl set off, but at the crossroads she met the werewolf, who asked her where she was going.

'I am taking a hot loaf and a bottle of milk to my grand-mother.'

'What road are you taking,' asked the werewolf, 'the Needles Road or the Pins Road?'

'The Needles Road,' said the little girl.

'Well, I shall take the Pins Road.'

While the little girl enjoyed herself picking up needles, the werewolf reached her grandmother's house. He killed her, and put some of her flesh in the pantry and a bottle of her blood on the shelf.

The little girl reached the house and knocked. The werewolf told her to push the door, which was only held shut with a wet straw.

'Hello, Grandmother; I'm bringing you a hot loaf and a bottle of milk.'

'Put them in the pantry. You eat the meat that's there and drink a bottle of wine that is on the shelf.'

While she ate, a little cat said: 'A slut is she who eats the flesh and drinks the blood of her grandmother!'

'Undress, my child,' said the werewolf, 'and come and sleep beside me.'

'Where should I put my apron?'

'Throw it in the fire, my child; you don't need it anymore.'

And as the little girl took off each article of her clothing, the bodice, the dress, the skirt, and the hose, she asked where she should put them, and the werewolf gave her the same answer: 'Throw it in the fire, my child; you will need it no more.'

'Oh, Grandmother, how hairy you are!'

'It's to keep me warmer, my child.'

'Oh, Grandmother, those long nails you have!'

'It's to scratch me better, my child.'

'Oh, Grandmother, those big shoulders that you have!'

'All the better to carry kindling from the woods, my child.'

'Oh, Grandmother, those big ears that you have!'

'All the better to hear you with, my child.'

'Oh, Grandmother, what a big mouth you have!'

'All the better to eat you with, my child!'

'Oh, Grandmother, I need to go outside to relieve myself.'

'Do it in the bed, my child.'

'No, Grandmother, I want to go outside.'

'All right, but don't stay long.'

The werewolf tied a woollen thread to her foot and let her go out. When the little girl was outside she tied the end of the string to a plum tree in the yard. The werewolf became impatient and called out:

'Are you making cables?'

When no answer came, he jumped out of bed and saw that the little girl had escaped. He chased after her, but she got back safely inside her house just as he arrived.[1]

The judicial fires of the witch-persecution having burnt out, it was perhaps inevitable that by the eighteenth and nineteenth centuries the werewolf should find himself living on as a stock figure in a folk-tale. It was also practically inevitable that the key themes from the sixteenth-century French cultural stereotype should go forward with him, rather than those associated with the beneficent werewolf of the more marginal twelfth-century Celtic and seventeenth-century Livonian cultures. The werewolf in this tale is the embodiment of evil, and his sole aim is to eat the little girl. In this sense he is the direct descendant of cannibalistic werewolves like Gilles Garnier and Peter Stubb. Variants of this

'Grandmother' folk-tale have been traced in a broad area comprising roughly the basin of the Loire river, the northern half of
the Alps, northern Italy, and the Tyrol, an intriguing but not
perfect conformation to the geographical spread of the werewolf
trials. Although shape-shifting as such is not directly mentioned
and the listener is never for a moment left in doubt as to the true
identity of 'Grandmother', the drama of the story arises from the
little girl being for some considerable time deceived by the
werewolf's human appearance. And in this variant he is specifically a werewolf, rather than a wolf: the folklorist who recorded
this particular French version of the tale noted that the storyteller
used the word *bzou*, which he said was the same creature as the
brou, or *garou*, i.e. werewolf, and that he had never heard anything
other than *bzou* used in that particular story.

Although this version of the tale was recorded in France as late
as 1885, there is little doubt that it is a relatively pure transmission
of a tale belonging to a long oral tradition, and that essentially the
same tale was being told at least by the seventeenth century and
perhaps earlier. Nor is the tale limited to France and the Alpine
region: a similar tale is found in the Chinese, Japanese, and
Korean folk traditions. Rather than the lone *petita* of European
tradition, there are typically two girls in the Chinese version, who
are left alone in the house by their mother. A tiger gets to hear of
this tempting situation, either by meeting the mother on the road
and questioning her (usually eating her afterwards, unless it is a
mother who happens to be telling the story), or simply by
overhearing the parting remarks between mother and children.
The tiger then reaches the house and tries to gain admittance,
calling out for the girls to open the door, pretending to be their
grandaunt come to visit. One of the girls, usually the older,
notices that the tiger's voice is too hoarse to be their grandaunt,
and the tiger modifies its tones accordingly. The children are still
suspicious and ask the tiger to put a hand through the door. The
tiger has to use some further trickery to fool the children, either
by wrapping its paw in a leaf or by putting flour on it to disguise
its roughness and colour. Once admitted, Grandaunt Tiger asks
the children to come to bed with her. In the middle of the night
she eats one child, usually the younger. The older child hears the
noise of cracking bones, and asks what is going on. Grandaunt
Tiger replies that she is eating something: variants of the story

have a wide variety of foodstuffs here, anything from peanuts to chicken bones. The child asks to be given some food also, and Grandaunt Tiger passes her a finger. As in the French tale, the child then asks to be allowed to go to the toilet. Grandaunt Tiger urges her to go in the bed, but she insists on being allowed outside. Again as in the French tale, Grandaunt Tiger ties a rope of some kind to the child – in one version of the story, it is made from the intestine of the younger child – which the child then ties to something else outside, typically a tree. Having extricated herself, the child climbs up the tree to hide. The tiger eventually realizes that something is wrong and comes looking for the child. The child calls down from the tree to ask Grandaunt Tiger to fetch some boiling liquid, either some oil or some water, usually making the excuse – rather transparent, one might think – that she has climbed the tree to catch birds and will cook them for the grandaunt. The child then pours the boiling liquid down the tiger's throat and kills her.

'Grandaunt Tiger' shares so many characteristics with the French 'Grandmother' tale, especially a number which immediately strike the reader as odd, that it must be sensible to regard it as cognate with the French tale. The best analysis of the story has been done by the sinologist and sociologist Professor Wolfram Eberhard, who collected more than two hundred versions of the story from a population of Chinese families living in Taiwan in the late 1960s.[2] Many of the conclusions that he was able to draw from this rich source of data shed light also on the French tale. In particular, he pointed out how the story is closely rooted in everyday, normal family patterns. In modern Taiwan, as in seventeenth-century rural France, it is not regarded as unusual for small children to sleep in the same bed as their close relatives of the same sex. In fact, it may well be regarded as a treat by the children themselves. This is reflected in the episode, found in a good proportion of versions of the Chinese tale, in which Grandaunt Tiger announces that only one child can sleep with her, and instigates a competition between the two, often by asking them to prove which of them can wash quickest. (In such versions, the elder child is suspicious, 'throws' the contest by not trying, and sleeps in another bed, only to be woken by the sounds of the tiger feeding.) Having won such a privileged situation, one of the child's chief fears may be that it will soil the bedclothes and annoy the elder relative, hence probably the origin of the urination/ defecation motif common to both French and Chinese versions. Professor Eberhard points out also that tying a string to a young child is very familiar to the Chinese. This is often done to prevent their infants getting into harm, and the same must have been true for seventeenth-century France. Modern toddler's harnesses are simply more elaborate and expensive versions of the same piece of basic childcare equipment.

All this is relevant in considering what meaning these 'grand-mother' tales may have had for their original audience. It is clear that the tales were regarded as educational by the adults who told them, with the specific idea often being mentioned by the Chinese parents that the story gave their young children a valuable warning to be careful in identifying strangers. By virtue of the fact that the little girl is out in the world on her own, without adult protection, the French werewolf tale conveys the additional idea that she must look out where she is going in such circum-stances. Some commentators have pounced on this aspect of the story, and read a great deal into the choice she must make at the crossroads, the choice between the Road of Pins and the Road of Needles. Bruno Bettelheim, who famously applied his psycho-analytical eye to this folk-tale, remarked in a footnote that another version of the tale makes clear the significance of the two roads.[3] It is easier to fasten things together with pins than sewing them with needles, the second version says; and so, Bettelheim concludes, by picking the Road of Pins, the little girl is doing something called 'electing the pleasure principle over the reality principle'. Disregarding for a moment the inconvenient detail that the little girl in the first version chooses the 'right' road, the Road of Needles, Bettelheim's theory fails to take account of the other variants of the story that have different names for the roads, in which the symbolism, if any, is even more obscure: the Roads of the Little Stones and of the Little Thorns in *langue d'oc*, for example, or the Roads of Roots and of Stones in the Tyrol. The storyteller's explanation of the choice between needles and pins sounds very much like an adult's tortuous attempt to impose some moral sense on what is, in fact, simply an absurd detail of the sort guaranteed to delight children.

If scholars are right in thinking that this folk-tale belongs to an oral tradition dating back to the seventeenth century in France and the Alps, then it followed on immediately from the height of the werewolf hysteria there. It demonstrates how quickly after adult belief in his existence had faded the werewolf was used as the bogey-man in a children's tale, and how little disguised was his cannibalistic nature. In fact, the story even goes so far as to have the werewolf trick the little girl into eating her own grandmother's flesh and drinking her blood, a gruesome parody of the Eucharist every bit as perverse as the witches' supposed overturning of the rituals of the mass at their sabbats. All this was too crude and unsophisticated for the French collector of tales or *contes*, Charles Perrault, who published a celebrated version of the tale in 1697, a literary rendition that was to have a profound and lasting influence.[4]

The first detail in which Perrault departs from the oral source is by individuating the little girl, who in the oral tradition is simply described as *une petite fille*, or some such term. In Perrault's version, she is said to be the prettiest girl ever seen, whose mother and grandmother both dote on her. Her grandmother has made her a little red hood, which is so attractive that everywhere she goes she is known as Little Red Riding Hood. Perrault may not necessarily have invented this name himself – there are plenty of examples of folk-tales where a particular variant of the story is known by some coloured article of clothing worn by the heroine, although in none of them does this article of clothing or its colour signify anything in particular. Howsoever she came by her name, Perrault's little girl sets out with a cake and a pot of butter to take to her sick grandmother. In the wood she meets old Father Wolf, who is too scared to eat her immediately because of the presence of some woodcutters nearby. He questions her, and gets out of her the exact location of her grandmother's house. He proposes to visit her grandmother as well, but suggests they take two different paths to see who gets there first. Little Red Riding Hood takes the longer path, and amuses herself on the way by picking wild flowers and nuts, and chasing after butterflies. The wolf meanwhile has gone on ahead, and by mimicking the grand-daughter's voice, gains admittance to the cottage. He kills and eats the old woman, and then puts on her nightgown and hides in her bed, waiting for Little Red Riding Hood to turn up. There is no happy ending in Perrault's version: after the well-known routine of questions and answers, the wolf simply gobbles her up.

The tale has attached to it a little moral in verse, which points the lesson, familiar from both French and Chinese oral tradition, that children should not listen to strangers. But Perrault goes on to spell out the particular significance of the wolf in his version of the tale:

> I say Wolf, for all wolves
> Are not of the same sort;
> There is one kind with an amenable disposition
> Neither noisy, nor hateful, nor angry,
> But tame, obliging and gentle,
> Following the young maids
> In the streets, even into their homes.
> Alas! who does not know that these gentle wolves
> Are of all such creatures the most dangerous!

This conception of the 'wolf' is still familiar today – a young man who chases after girls, probably 'wolf-whistling' at them as he goes – but it is clearly some distance from the cannibalistic werewolf of the sixteenth-century French stereotype. Although based on an oral story or stories, Perrault's version is evidently the work of a literary imagination. The nonsensical detail of the choice of roads, for example, has taken on moral colouring in his version. The rural setting, which is self-evident in the oral tradition and needs no explanation from the storyteller, is emphasized by Perrault's references to the forest, the woodcutters, and grandmother's cottage by the mill – all, no doubt, to heighten the contrast with the urban 'wolves' of which Perrault gives warning in the verse moral. There is throughout an ironic authorial detachment to the telling of the story which tips the wink to the adult audience that the story is to be understood metaphorically.

Although the figure of the wolf is a werewolf in the oral tradition, Perrault evidently conceives of the creature in a distinctly different way. Perrault's wolf has always the physical appearance of a real wolf, and must be careful not to be seen by the woodcutters talking to the little girl on that account. Perrault specifically states that the girl is not scared of him simply because she does not yet know better than to stop and talk to wolves. This is in contrast to the oral tradition, where it may easily be imagined that the werewolf is in human shape when he first meets the little girl. The horrific motif of the girl being tricked into cannibalism found in the oral tradition, and obviously related to earlier werewolf beliefs, is silently omitted by Perrault. When the wolf climbs into grandmother's bed in Perrault's version, he puts on her nightgown and pulls up the counterpane in an attempt to disguise himself; in oral tradition the werewolf has effectively abandoned all human disguise and is unclothed. Perrault's list of questions have a more than slightly prurient tone. 'What big arms you have!' Little Red Riding Hood exclaims; 'The better to embrace you with, my child!' the wolf replies. In contrast, the little girl's questions in the oral tradition draw attention to the wolf's body in general, and any sexuality implicit in them, or in the way the wolf makes the little girl undress, is only of the most juvenile sort. Perrault would have regarded the physical direct-ness implicit in these details as too crude for his ironic version.

Perrault's abrupt truncation of the story, with the wolf eating up the girl, means that all the motifs of the child asking to go to the toilet, being let out on a string, and ultimately triumphing over the wolf are necessarily omitted, and the resultant unhappy ending gives a very un-fairytale-like twist to the story. This was probably a deliberate literary decision on Perrault's part, al-though it may just possibly be that he had only heard an incomplete version of the folk-tale. This deficit was supplied a little over a century later by the celebrated German folklorists Jacob and Wilhelm Grimm, who included the story in the first volume of their famous *Kinder- und Hausmärchen* (1812), as 'Rotkäppchen', or 'Little Red Cap'. The opening movement of the Grimms' version follows Perrault fairly exactly, although the moral point of Little Red Cap's dallying in the woods is made even more explicit in Grimm by the mother warning her before-hand against straying from the path. The wolf – his Satanic nature to the fore – acts in the role of Tempter, pointing out to Little Red Cap the attractions of wandering off to pick flowers. The most obvious difference, however, is that the Grimms' plot continues past the point where Perrault leaves off. Having eaten Little Red Cap, the wolf goes to sleep, and his loud snores attract a passing huntsman. Suspecting that the wolf has eaten grandmother, the huntsman cuts the wolf open and pulls out both grandmother and Little Red Cap. Little Red Cap runs off to fetch large stones, with which they fill the wolf's belly. The wolf wakes up and tries to run off, but falls down under the weight of the stones and dies. Little Red Cap realizes that she has learnt a lesson: never stray from the path into the forest when your mother has forbidden it.

Unusually, the Grimms add a sequel to the tale in which Little Red Cap visits grandmother again, and is waylaid by another wolf. She is wiser after her close shave with the first wolf, and so goes straight on to grandmother's house. The wolf arrives at the door and calls to be let in, pretending to be Little Red Cap, but the little girl and her grandmother say nothing. The wolf climbs onto the roof, hoping to wait until Little Red Cap tries to go home, but the grandmother is too clever for him. She tells Little Red Cap to take a bucket of water in which she has boiled sausages and pour it into the trough. The wolf smells the sausages, and leans so far forward that he topples off the roof into the trough and drowns. This part of the story is intriguingly like the ending of Grandaunt Tiger. In both, the agency of death is a liquid. The Chinese storytellers were about equally divided in their choice of either oil or water, with the rationalization for the choice of oil being that hot water would not be enough to finish off a tiger. In the Grimm version, the liquid is a mixture of both, for water in which sausages have been boiled would be very greasy, and a rural peasant would have been hard put to it to find any liquid in everyday use which would be more likely to scald the skin.[5] Despite this concern with the greater efficacy of hot oil, it is possible to detect behind either version a hint of ancient werewolf beliefs, in which water played the key role in transformation: one thinks particularly of the Arcadian werewolves swimming back across their enchanted lake to retrieve their clothes, and Alphonse in *Guillaume de Palerne* being bathed by the queen. Here, however, post-Franche-Comté, the wolf must die.

The Grimm version is patently a more complete and satisfying story than Perrault's, and it has been praised by many writers for returning to oral tradition, but one or two caveats must be attached to the general acclamation. The most important of these is that, although the Grimms set out with the avowed intention of gathering authentic folk-tales from oral tradition, they themselves combined elements from different variants more or less to their own taste. As a result their printed story does not truly reflect any single traditional version. Although the Grimms were generally represented as collecting stories from German oral tradition, in the case of *Rotkäppchen* their chief source is known to have been partly French Huguenot, and not of peasant stock. Behind this version lies the French literary version of Perrault, with its treatment of the wolf as metaphorical seducer rather than as shape-shifting werewolf, its individuation of the heroine by her prettiness and her red head-dress, its aura of pubescent sexuality, and the complete absence of the twin traditional motifs of cannibalism and infantile bed-soiling.

It is worth re-emphasizing that the colour of the heroine's hood or cap cannot be traced back before Perrault, as many writers have made a good deal of it in their interpretations of this folk-tale. Red is, of course, an excellent choice for a motif in what is at bottom a werewolf story. Red is the colour of blood, and appears widely in nature as a danger signal (in the colouring of some poisonous fungi, for example); but it has given rise to many more intricate explanations than this. Various writers have seen in the little girl's head-dress the floral bonnet of the traditional Queen of May, the red liberty cap of the French Revolution, the flames of the Sun (swallowed up by Night, the wolf), a symbol of menstruation, of sexual attractiveness, and so on *ad infinitum*.[6] However convincing these interpretations may be, they can only be valid for the version of the story found in the literary tradition instigated by Perrault and propagated by the Brothers Grimm. On the interpretation of the cap as a symbol for menstruation, for example, it is clear that the tale as related in oral tradition both in France and the Alps, as well as in China, Korea, and Japan, has for its heroine a very young girl well before the onset of menstruation. If the story does embody any universal narrative of personal growth, it is surely the story of a girl passing from infanthood – a state in which she cannot safely distinguish those who impersonate even her closest relatives, has no control over her bodily functions, and must be tied up to prevent her coming to harm – to a childhood in which she has some control over all these aspects of herself, and therefore has significantly enhanced chances of self-preservation. The discreet hike in the girl's age in the Perrault–Grimm version actually undermines the traditional story's demonstration of the heroine's increased self-reliance: in Perrault the prettified pubescent simply fails to learn anything and is eaten; while in Grimm she is chiefly reliant on the aid of the huntsman – and, in the sequel, that of her grandmother – to outwit the wolf.

Whatever the virtues of the oral tradition, such is the power of the printed word that the Perrault–Grimm version has become the standard rendition of the story, known over a far wider geographical and social dispersal than the traditional version. In becoming so, it has carried forward the figure of the werewolf in a subtly altered way. Previously the wolf's associations with sexuality had chiefly been in the rather general area of fertility, and so too the werewolf. Perrault's sophisticated metaphor of the wolf as male seducer was to remain associated with the werewolf henceforward.

Nevertheless, this sophisticated conception remained just that throughout the eighteenth and nineteenth centuries, for the traditional conception of the werewolf remained surprisingly obdurate among rural communities, particularly in France. Ancient lycanthropic ideas, for example, quickly surfaced in the face of the depredations of the infamous *Bête de Gévaudan*. In 1764, in the southern French district of Gévaudan, high in the Massif Central, a ferocious wolf-like beast began a series of attacks on the local peasantry, the first incident being reported in June, near the little town of Langogne. Within five months it had killed eleven people, including two men. Everything about its behaviour seemed odd to the panic-stricken locals, for folk wisdom had come to recognize that, in the exceptional case of a wolf or wolves attacking humans, the victims were likely to be small children. Wolves were known to be surreptitious hunters, attempting to take human prey only when driven by desperate hunger in the dead of winter. This wolfish fiend was brazen in its defiance of these norms: in one horrific episode that autumn, it murdered an adult woman in her garden in broad daylight. The death toll rapidly mounted, until about fifty people were thought to have been killed by the *bête*.

Frenzied rumours soon began to fly, encouraged by a great eruption of printed broadsheets, featuring lurid woodcuts in which the *bête* took a variety of monstrous shapes. Local theories as to the beast's real identity were no less various: some said that it was a hyena escaped from a nearby fair, others that it was a large monkey. More distinct echoes of ancient fears can be traced: many said that it was the monstrous offspring of a bear and a wolf, which had loped over the Alps to torment them. The local bishop even claimed in his Christmas pastoral letter that it was an apocalyptic beast created by God to punish the Gévaudan. The orthodox God-fearing community shivered accordingly. But naturally the easiest conclusion for the majority of locals to reach was that the *bête* was a werewolf. Although trials of werewolves had ceased in France some two centuries earlier, the image was clearly alive in the popular heart, if only kept so by the oral tradition that produced the 'Grandmother' story and its cognates.

The self-appointed local beast-experts set about gathering a great deal of hearsay evidence emphasizing the *bête*'s semi-human qualities. 'You would laugh to hear all they say about it,' a wordly-wise local nobleman wrote to a friend. 'It takes tobacco, talks, becomes invisible, boasts in the evening about its exploits of the day, goes to the sabbath, does penance for its sins.' Despite his cynicism, others earnestly averred that they had seen the creature fording a stream on its hind legs, wading like a human. It was seen looking through the window of a house at Mazel-de-Grèzes where, the day before, it had killed a fourteen-year-old boy. The grieving father chased after it but could not catch it, and local villagers became taken with the idea that the *bête* spent its time looking into houses to see what the inhabitants were doing. One young boy said that he had been attacked by it, and escaped by wrestling with it (a tale reminiscent of Boguet's wolf's-ear-holding traveller, a folk-tale set in the adjacent Auvergne). The boy reported that its belly seemed to have buttons running up it, which many people took to be a waistcoat lycanthropically transformed. Another woman, going to mass in an area where the beast was roaming about, was accompanied on her way by a particularly hairy man, who suddenly vanished, an unremarkable event which was, however, taken to be a sure sign of his being the werewolf.[7]

The killings attributed to the *Bête de Gévaudan* were almost certainly the work of a group of wolves, rather than one single animal, and the persistence of werewolf beliefs in rural France through the nineteenth century is obviously related to the fact that wolves were still fairly numerous in that country, although perhaps it is significant that fear of wolves reached a peak during the years following the Revolution. Typical are the reports of

The 'Sorcerer of Trois Frères'. Belief in such shamanistic shape-shifting powers used to secure fertility lasted until at least the late seventeenth century in some parts of Europe.

Below left: Artemis/Diana, here in her later guise as Hecate, with three heads representing her dominion over air, earth, and underworld. The wolf's head (on the right) aligns her with the later gods and goddesses of death.

Below right: King Lykaon, transformed into a wolf by Zeus for his crimes. His story was told by both Pausanias and Pliny.

Above: A wall-painting from Çatal Hüyük, Anatolia, showing hunters wearing 'magic belts' of leopard skin, representative of the whole animal.

Left: A Cynocephalus, or Dog-Head, from an Armenian gospel book. Christians were quick to curse their rivals for the Holy Land as 'dogs'.

Below: The unfortunate Peter Stubb, the werewolf of Cologne, meets his fate in 1589.

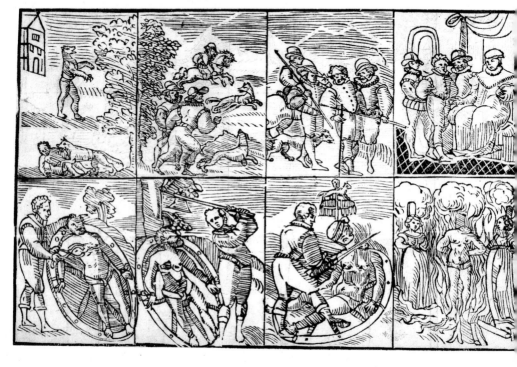

The great sceptic Johann
Weyer (1515–88), first
proponent of the
pharmacological theory
of werewolves.

VINCE TEIPSVM.

EFFIGIES IOANNIS WIERI ANNO
ÆTATIS LX. SALVTIS M.D.LXXVI.

Below left: Wagner the
depraved 'wehr-wolf'
interrupts a monk's funeral.
From G. W. M. Reynolds'
novel of 1857.

Below right: Kamala, one of
the wolf-girls of Orissa,
photographed in the 1920s.

SOCIALISM

PROSPERITY

THROTTLING THE COUNTRY

The werewolf makes it into party politics, in a Conservative Party poster of 1909. This is a visualization of the werewolf which has all but disappeared. Note, however, the pointed ears, the lupine heels, and the all-important stumpy tail, like Jean Grenier's in 1603.

The cinematic werewolf in action. This is Oliver Reed in *The Curse of the Werewolf* (Hammer Studios, 1961), but it might be any of the greats from Henry Hull onwards – the make-up remained virtually unchanged for thirty years. Note the inverted Dracula fangs jutting upwards from the lower jaw.

wolves devastating part of the country near Orléans and Chartres in 1796 and 1798, and the justice of the peace for the canton of Orgères who noted, in 1799, that terror and panic in the face of lupine depredations was universal. Over five thousand wolves were killed in 1797, according to an official estimate. Although this figure had dropped to under two thousand by 1806, wolves survived in some numbers throughout the nineteenth century in France, appearing in numerous memoirs of the period as feared predators. Sadly, since then the history of the wolf in France has been one of rapid depopulation, and its image in the superstitious imagination as the embodiment of ravening ferocity has contributed greatly to this decline. The wolfhunting *battues* have, in the long tradition including Charlemagne's *luporii* and the *louvetiers* of the Ancien Régime, finally done their work in France: the wolf is now extinct there, although occasional sightings of single animals are reported in isolated areas. In western Europe as a whole, the wolf only survives at the end of the twentieth century in small pockets in Spain, Portugal, Italy, and in northern parts of Scandinavia. Even where viable populations do remain, the numbers are small: in November 1977, for example, it was reported that only 100–150 wolves remained in the Italian Apennine mountains, surviving in scattered packs: in 1973 the numbers in Finland were reported to comprise a bedraggled dozen.[8] It is tempting to see some correlation between the geographical spread of the sixteenth-century witch-craze and its long aftermath, and the present-day extinction of the wolf – plot both areas on a map of western Europe, and note that they are remarkably congruent – although the spread of industrialization and modern farming techniques are the more orthodox explanations for the wolf's annihilation in north-western Europe.

By the nineteenth century it was clear that the image of the werewolf had splintered once more, and that the homogeneous concept which had prevailed among all classes in the sixteenth century was long gone. While peasants and the odd rural bishop might be prepared to believe in their existence, the intelligentsia were openly cynical about such creatures of peasant superstition. Even those folklorists like the Brothers Grimm, who raced to preserve folk-tales before their engulfment by the onrushing wave of industrial culture, could not help passing on the figure of the werewolf overlaid with metaphorical nuances largely alien to the ancient conception. This 'werewolf' was now a richly symbolic figure, ripe for appropriation by literature, psychoanalysis, and the other creative arts. Meanwhile, cases similar to those which had so plagued late sixteenth-century France still occurred, but their outcome was significantly altered. In 1824 a twenty-nine-year-old man named Antoine Léger was tried by the district court of Versailles. Earlier that year, he had left his father's house and gone to live in the woods. Thinking himself to be a wolf, he set up his lair in a cave, where he lured a little girl, killed her, and ate her.[9] Such people were now regarded as insane, diagnosed as such by 'alienists' (the contemporary term for psychiatrists), and treated accordingly. The diagnostic procedures which would in time lead to Monsieur X's treatment by the Bordeaux prison psychiatrists and the survey of lycanthropes at McLean Hospital in Boston were now firmly established.

In fact, even among the uneducated, the panic and fear aroused by werewolves had undergone a subtle change. The broadsheet popularity of the *Bête de Gévaudan*, and the many other monsters and prodigies of those times, suggests that these extraordinary stories were being enjoyed for their crude literary qualities. In the immediate local area where these beasts were said to roam, the fear probably outweighed the entertainment value of such stories, but their dispersal over wide areas meant that, for those people who read about them at a safe distance, they evoked the kind of *frisson* nowadays conveyed by horror films and books. As shown by the evidence of Chinese parents asserting that they particularly liked 'Grandaunt Tiger' for its educational content, parents were happy to keep more traditional stories of the *male bête* alive, as they felt they taught children valuable lessons about keeping guard against strangers and not dallying when sent out on errands. Parents may have felt happier now that the 'Grandmother' tale had been cleaned up by the removal of its infantile cannibalism and defecation motifs in the Perrault–Grimm literary version, although the contemporary invention of such pseudo-folktales as Dr Heinrich Hoffman's unpleasant *Struwwelpeter*, written in 1844, suggests that even highly literate European parents saw nothing wrong in inflicting a little psychological torment on their children in the name of moral improvement.

Judith Devlin, whose richly researched book, *The Superstitious Mind*, provides excellent background material for understanding the depth of belief in supernatural phenomena among the French peasantry during the nineteenth century, also points out that many apparently straightforward werewolf accusations, of the kind which once led people like Gilles Garnier to the pyre, seem in the nineteenth century to have acted merely as a vehicle for the expression of the accuser's personal likes and dislikes.[10] She quotes the story of a man named Bégou, from the village of Pontajou, whom she regards as having taken advantage of the contemporary panic engendered by the *Bête de Gévaudan*. One moonlit night, Bégou claimed to have come across a large, hairy man bathing in a stream. On seeing that he was observed, the hairy man transformed himself into a wolf and flung himself at the poor villager, but did not kill him or even inflict on him more than superficial wounds. Bégou told those who were willing to listen, and there were plenty among the panicky locals at the time, that his lycanthropic assailant was the generally disliked son of a corrupt local hunter. Bégou's story could hardly have been more conventional. It has standard elements which Petronius and Pliny would each have recognized, and it was just this type of accusation which had been ignored by the courts since the decline of the Franche-Comté stereotype. Almost certainly, this was precisely the reason why Bégou chose to make it. He knew that the story could never be proved – or disproved. In telling it, he was simply maligning a person known to him and to his audience without any great possibility of reprisal or even of further inquiry into his veracity. In such circumstances, it becomes clear why the story should be so conventional: it had simply to appeal to the prejudices of his audience. Any deviation from the outlines of the received werewolf narrative would have invited awkward questions and weakened the force of his calumny.

Nevertheless, storytellers had to be careful: several cases which featured accusations of lycanthropy or witchcraft ended up in the courts, with the alleged werewolves feeling it necessary to bring actions for slander to protect their reputations. In at least one incident in the Auvergne, for example, a man was accused of being a 'wolf leader'. This particular kind of werewolf was supposed to be a sorcerer in the pay of the devil who had donned a magical pelt and taken command of a real pack of thirty or so wolves. With his pack, the werewolf leader would roam the forests and valleys, waylaying travellers and extorting protection money from them. Once the victims had paid up, they were forced to accept an escort home from two wolves; if they should stumble and fall, they would be instantly devoured. This is obviously a recrudescence of the old idea of werewolf-as-outlaw, but an accusation of this kind could hardly be ignored. An author writing in 1857 noted that one such accusation, made about an inhabitant of St Gervais in the heat of a public disagreement in the market-place at Riom, ended up in court, with the slandered man issuing subpoenas to force witnesses to speak in his favour.[11]

Devlin cites several contemporary stories in which accusations of lycanthropy served some unspoken personal agenda. A farm servant in the village of Boin, near Beauvoir in the Vendée, was plagued by the daily visits of a horse which he suspected of being a sorcerer in lycanthropic disguise. He shot at the creature using bullets consecrated by a priest, and the *cheval mallet* collapsed, leaving behind a young girl whom the farm hand had previously courted but abandoned. This bizarre episode had the effect of reversing the existing moral *status quo* in their relationship. Previously the young man had been at fault for ending that relationship, but now that the girl had been found out resorting to sorcery he was, of course, fully justified in his actions. Another young man managed to pull back from the brink of marriage to a similar kind of shape-shifting fiancée. He set out with a friend one evening to visit her, but she was not at home. On the way back, the two young men saw a little goat, which they chased, and which turned out to be the girl transformed. Naturally the engagement was called off there and then. The fact that the young man had been astute enough to take along his friend as witness helped assuage any peer-group disapproval he might otherwise have suffered for breaking the engagement. The termination of any close friendship might be explained in the same way. A story was told of a young man from Arthex who was pestered by an animal whenever he approached a particular crossroads. At first the animal was a large dog, but one night it took the form of a goat, which put its forehooves up on his shoulders and prevented him from proceeding. Alarmed, the young man stabbed it, where-upon it was transformed into his best friend. His friend said: 'I have been trying for a long time to be wounded thus. Don't speak of this to anyone and we'll go and have a drink together!' But the young man refused this offer, saying that although he would keep the secret, he could never drink with that person again.

By now the werewolf had effectively gone underground, for the section of society in which these stories flourished was clearly distinct from those educated, literate, urban classes among whom such beliefs would have been ridiculed. A number of were-animal stories of the time express strong sanctions against those who would break with this self-regulatory code, just as the dog-goat urged his former friend to secrecy in the Arthex story. A man named Laburthe, for example, was attacked by a horse one night, and shot it. Immediately the animal was retransfigured to human shape, revealing himself as an acquaintance who told him that he had been under a spell, adding 'if you ever let slip a word of this, you're a dead man'. The former were-horse subsequently died, and one evening, when horror stories were being swapped over a glass or two, Laburthe decided it was safe to tell his secret. The next morning, he was found dead in his bed. Such dire warnings served as a reminder that accusations of lycanthropy presented a threat to social cohesion among the classes in which these beliefs persisted, while at the same time heightening the delicious sensation that these tall tales somehow preserved forbidden information.

Sometimes, however, such stories were told for no other reason than that they were entertaining. Their utterly conventional plots suggest that the werewolf was safely ensconced in an oral tradition in which the magical elements no longer represented a real threat of any kind. In 1880, for example, a villager from Thièvres told an elaborate werewolf story to a folklorist collecting stories in Picardy. A fellow villager of his had seen a neighbour transformed back from lupine to human form by rolling in a puddle. The werewolf explained that he was driven, against his will, to make the transformation at the time of the witch's sabbat. He could be rescued if the neighbour would come to the next sabbat. Once there, the neighbour should swing a sword around his head until he felt it hit the invisible werewolf, and then he would be able to grab him and take him away. The neighbour complied, and he subsequently relayed elaborate details of the fairies and witches he saw dining at the sabbat, as well as the rescue of the werewolf. The element of real fear, so characteristic of the werewolf in earlier French folklore, is almost entirely absent from this rather charming tale.

10

Feral Foundlings

... Come on, poor babe:
Some powerful spirit instruct the kites and ravens
To be thy nurses! Wolves and bears, they say,
Casting their savageness aside, have done
Like offices of pity.

SHAKESPEARE,
The Winter's Tale

In May 1972, Narsingh Bahadur Singh was bicycling home
through the forest of Musafirkhana, near Sultanpur, a town in the
northern Indian province of Uttar Pradesh, about 100 miles
south of the border with Nepal. According to the story he
subsequently circulated, Narsingh, a local *thakur*, or landowner,
was about to stumble upon living proof of one of the most ancient
motifs in the history of relations between man and wolf. A scuffle
of movement in the undergrowth caught his eye, and there he saw
four or five wolf cubs engaged in playful rough and tumble with
what appeared to be a human child about four years old. First
making sure that no she-wolf was in the immediate vicinity,
Narsingh dashed forward, scattering the terrified cubs, and
snatched the child into his arms. The boy struggled furiously,
scratching and biting his human captor, and Narsingh was forced
to wrap him up in a cotton towel to protect himself from the
child's wild violence. Eventually he succeeded in strapping the
bundle to his bicycle and set off for his home village, Narayanpur.

Narsingh took the boy into his household, and named him
Shamdeo. To Narsingh's eyes Shamdeo showed every sign of
having been reared by wolves. He moved only on all fours, and
the skin on his palms, elbows, and knees was calloused like the
pads of a wolf's paws. He had matted hair, uneven sharp teeth,

long claw-like nails, and curiously luminous eyes. He was incapable of human speech, and shunned human contact, preferring
to play with dogs. At night he had to be forcibly restrained from
joining the jackals howling outside the village. The most feral
characteristic of this latter-day Mowgli was his preference for raw
meat. On one memorable occasion he was seen by villagers to
attack a chicken, tearing its guts out with his teeth before eating
it whole.

His appearance and general demeanour aroused plenty of
debate within the village. Some were inclined to dismiss Narsingh's
story about the wolves, preferring to argue that the child had been
brought up by bears. This school of thought persisted in calling
him Baloo, like the bear in Kipling's *Jungle Book*. Others of a
more cynical bent questioned Narsingh's motives in rescuing the
child from the jungle at all. Narsingh had already rescued at least
one other abandoned child, an infant boy who been thrown, little
more than a foetus, into an open drain. This child, named
Ramdeo, had grown up an idiot and epileptic, but these cynics
pointed out that he could still usefully be employed as casual
labour on Narsingh's 30-*bigha* estate. Such reasoning gained
extra credence when rumours spread – indignantly denied by
Narsingh – that he had been charging people money to see the
famous wolf-boy.

Shamdeo made only limited progress in Narsingh's care. He
never learnt to speak, but used sign language to express simple
needs. Constant massage of his limbs with mustard oil did
succeed in straightening them and he was eventually able to walk
upright more like a normal human being. Within three years he
was doing odd jobs like taking straw out to Narsingh's cows. He
accepted modification to his feral diet only slowly, moving at first
from raw meat to eating dirt and earth. Eventually, however, he
was persuaded to switch to normal food. Accounts vary as to his
history after this point, although it is certain that he was eventually taken in by nuns who came across him in 1978. He was taken
to Prem Nivas, Mother Theresa's Home for the Destitute and
Dying in Lucknow, where he was to remain for the last seven
years of his life. The nuns renamed him Pascal, and attempted a
more rigorous programme of education. His first friendship at
the Home, however, was with a dog, and he was never to be
trusted with other children, as he was liable to attack them at any

moment, clawing at their eyes with his fingers. But he learnt a few simple things, like the Indian greeting *namaste*, in which the palms are pressed together, and he was fond of travelling round the garden in the back of a bicycle rickshaw. He died at the Home in February 1985 after an untreatable attack of cramps. Photographs show him to have been in an advanced state of emaciation.[1]

It is naturally tempting to take the side of the village sceptics, and come to the conclusion that Shamdeo's case had little to do with wolves and everything to do with some undiagnosed mental aberration which caused him to behave in the bizarre way he did. But there is one persuasive reason not to do so: Shamdeo's behaviour is very far from unique. Numerous historical cases tell of children succoured by wolves, and in some cases by other animals, before being rescued by man. The majority of modern cases, like Shamdeo's, come from the Indian sub-continent, and in practically every instance the behaviour of these so-called feral children is the same: they are found naked, they cannot talk, they walk on all fours (and have callouses which suggest they have done so for some time), their appearance is animalistic, and they eat raw food. Because such children are usually discovered and raised by people whose education does not permit them to make observations accurate enough for western scientific opinion to accept, attention in the west has naturally focused on those cases where the body of evidence is felt to be capable of scientific verification. The paradigm of such cases is the famous history of Kamala and Amala, the wolf-girls of Orissa.

These children were discovered in October 1920 in an isolated part of the jungles of Bengal, some 400 miles south-east of Shamdeo's home territory, in an area chiefly the domain of a traditional non-Hindu people called the Santals. A visiting Christian missionary, the Reverend J. A. L. Singh, was told by the Santals of *bhuts*, or ghosts, living in the jungle close to their village. The villagers spoke of them as *manush-bagha*, man-beasts with human form and the head of a devilish animal. His curiosity and hostility to such primitive superstitions aroused, Singh eventually tracked down the lair of these man-beasts to a vast white-ant mound which had been abandoned by insects and taken over by wolves, who had hollowed out the base for use as their own den. Singh kept watch over the wolves' comings and

goings, and soon realized that the wild-looking creatures he saw
running along on all fours with the wolf-pack were not *manush-
bagha* but human children. A plan was made to capture both
them and the she-wolf who had presumably nurtured them, but
the plan misfired and the mother wolf was killed by Singh's
assistants as she fought to protect her brood. Unmolested now,
the diggers soon cut open the termite mound, revealing in its
scrupulously clean hollowed-out lair two wolf cubs and two
human children entwined together in a protective ball. The
children were taken back by Singh to the orphanage he ran at
Midnapore, and christened Kamala (a Bengali name meaning
'lotus') and Amala ('bright yellow flower').

The girls were certainly not twins, and they appeared not even
to have been related by blood, but the circumstances of their
being allegedly brought up by a wolf (and even the coincidence
of their barely differentiated names) is an obvious echo of the
story of Romulus and Remus. In the legendary version of that
story, the two infants had been placed in a trough and thrown into
the Tiber by their wicked granduncle, Amulius, who had usurped
the throne of Alba from their grandfather. The trough came to
ground in the marsh which was later to be the site of Rome. There
the babes were suckled by a she-wolf and fed by a woodpecker
before being found by shepherds. The story appears to have been
imported to Rome from Cretan legend,[2] and the essential pattern
of this myth is very far from being specifically Roman, or even
Mediterranean. Similar stories are told in such a wide variety of
cultures that they can be regarded as archetypal. The key motif
of abandonment of the child to the whims of nature is found in
stories as early as those told about Sargon the Elder, a historical
Babylonian king of the third millennium BC. His mother put him
in a basket of reeds which floated away, and he was found and
raised by an irrigator. The parallel with both Romulus and
Remus afloat on the Tiber and the well-known biblical account
of Moses' early life is striking. There are no animals in this or
Moses' story; instead the river represents Nature in all her
unpredictability.

The animal motif is present in the Chinese legend of Hou Chi,
a human ancestor of the Chou dynasty, who was reckoned to have
lived in the first half of the eleventh century BC. He was abandoned by his parents in a country lane, where he was saved by

cows and sheep. Hou Chi was even unluckier than most abandoned heroes: having saved him once, his bestial guardians then
managed to leave him behind in the woods, where he was found
by some woodcutters. The woodcutters too proved indifferent
parents, and left him out on the ice to die, but he was saved by a
bird bringing him food. In this story the emphasis by repetition
of the pattern of abandonment to wild nature, which, however,
proves capable of nurturing the helpless infant, is utterly appropriate for a culture hero like Hou Chi, who lived to raise crops,
found sacrifices, and eventually become an agrarian divinity.

These stories were not confined to quasi-legendary figures. A
Chinese chronicler whose writings were included in annals
compiled by Confucius in the fifth century BC gave a version of
the early life of Tseu Ouen, prime minister of Tch'ou province,
dating the events to 604 BC. According to this chronicler, Tseu
Ouen's father seduced the daughter of the Prince of Iun. The
child's grandmother, the prince's wife, had the infant Tseu Ouen
exposed, but a tigress nourished him. The prince witnessed this
miracle, brought the child back to court, and gave him the
nickname *Teou jeou ou t'ou*, 'Teou who was reared by a tigress'.
Another fifth-century chronicler, recording the events of the later
Han dynasty (AD 20–220), told a similar story about the King of
Fu Yü's difficult childhood. His mother, a serving woman in the
royal court, was impregnated by a cloud. The child was abandoned in a pigpen on the king's orders, but the pigs breathed on
the child, which kept him alive. He was then exposed in a horse
enclosure, but these animals also protected him. The king
realized that these were marks of divine favour, and raised the
child as his own son and heir.

Similar stories of foundlings reared by animals were told all
over the world, and like the tale of Romulus and Remus, they
were often myths of tribal foundation. A Turkish legend told how
the ancestors of the Turks had all been slaughtered in battle,
leaving only one survivor, a small boy who was thrown into a
marsh. A she-wolf brought him food and fought off a soldier sent
to kill him. He grew stronger under her care, and eventually had
intercourse with her. She gave birth to ten sons, one of whom was
Assena, who became King of the Turks (in Turkestan) and used
a wolf's head as his emblem. The sexual relationship between
man and animal in this story is unusual, but, as the fourteenth-

century version of the Welsh tale of *Arthur and Gorlagon* demonstrates, not unique in wolf-lore. In Persia, too, foundling legends
were common. Zal, a traditional early ruler of that land, was
exposed on the side of a particular mountain, home to a giant
mythical bird. The bird swooped down on the infant and carried
him off to feed to her chicks, but ended up nurturing the child
instead. The Persian religious leader Zoroaster was exposed in
his infancy before cattle, horses, and wolves, who all spared him.
Perhaps the most elaborate Persian tale of this kind is that told
about the childhood of Cyrus the Great (d. 529 BC) by the Greek
historian Herodotus.[3]

As Herodotus tells it, Cyrus was born at a time when the
Persians were ruled over by the Medes. Astyages was the Median
king of Asia, an old man with no son to succeed him. His only
child was a daughter called Mandane. One night the old king
dreamt that his daughter passed so much water that the whole of
Asia was flooded. He was alarmed by this dream and, when the
time came, he chose to marry her off to a Persian rather than a
socially superior Mede. But again he dreamt of Mandane, this
time that a vine grew out of her vagina and spread over Asia. He
asked his priests to interpret the dreams, and they told him that
he would be usurped by his daughter's child. As Mandane was
now pregnant, he called for her to visit him. He also sent for
Harpagos, his trusted steward, and told him to take away and kill
Mandane's child as soon as it was born. But Harpagos was
worried what would happen if Mandane were to succeed to the
throne and avenge her loss on him. Accordingly he entrusted the
job to a herdsman called Mitradates, who was married to another
of the king's slaves, Spaco (a word which means 'bitch' in the
Median language, Herodotus explains, giving a Greek equivalent
– Kyno – to make the point clearer). These two slaves lived in a
high, mountainous, thickly wooded part of the country, where
wild beasts roamed. Harpagos told Mitradates that this would be
the ideal place to expose the baby.

Spaco, however, had just been delivered of a still-born baby,
and when she saw the royal baby in her husband's arms she
pleaded with him to expose their dead baby instead. Mitradates
gave in, and the couple brought up the child as their own. When
he was ten years old, Cyrus was playing a game of 'kings' with
other boys in the street, and taking his turn as king, he savagely

whipped the son of a distinguished Mede. As a lowly herdsman's son daring to attack his social superior, he was brought in front of the old king to be punished. The boy answered the accusations against him with a natural nobility, and the king realized who he was. Mitradates soon confessed the truth, and the king turned his rage on his steward. Harpagos too told the truth, that he had entrusted Mitradates with the task, and had himself been deceived. The king pretended to be pleased that all had ended well, but secretly he blamed his steward. As a gruesome punishment, he arranged for Harpagos' own son to be murdered and pieces of his flesh to be served up at dinner. Cyrus was sent back to his father's palace, and later led the Persians in revolt against Astyages. The old king made the unaccountable mistake of appointing Harpagos as his commander-in-chief to quash Cyrus' rebellion, and Harpagos, remembering the insult of that revolting supper, deliberately threw away the battle. Thus Cyrus became ruler over all of Asia, and Harpagos became his much-feared lieutenant.

This is the well-known variant of the foundling legend that Shakespeare had in mind when writing his play, *The Winter's Tale*. There are two familiar ideas expressed in it. First is the notion that a simple pun may give rise to an animalistic legend, remarkably similar to Livy's explanation that the surrogate mother of Romulus and Remus was not a real she-wolf, but a *lupa*, a whore. Herodotus prefers this kind of thinking: he says that it was Spaco's canine name that gave Cyrus' parents the idea of creating a legend among the Persians about the miraculous preservation of their son, and that it was they who spread the story that a bitch had found the infant Cyrus abandoned in the mountains and had suckled him. It seems much more likely that the process happened the other way round, that the earlier mythical version on the traditional foundling pattern had been rationalized by the time of Herodotus' history. Herodotus admits that he could have chosen any one of four different accounts of Cyrus' life, and that he followed the Persian account that seemed to him the least mythopoeic. The second familiar element is the appearance in this story of the cannibalistic feast – the king having his steward's child killed, cooked, and served up to him at dinner – a feature distinctly reminiscent of the Lykaon myth. And indeed, like Lykaon, Harpagos *is* transformed, from faithful steward to predatory lieutenant. His name means 'the rapacious', a quality the Greeks would certainly have associated with the wolf, as well as with that other half-human, half-animal creature of myth, the Harpy, whose name has the same etymological root. Once again, behind the allegedly historical account lies the mythical pattern of the werewolf legend.

The foundling-saved-by-animals motif found in so many biographies of national or cultural heroes reveals a basic urge to dramatize the significance of such men's lives. When eulogists came to write their hero's history, they often had little by way of early biographical detail to work on, and the natural instinct was to dramatize the way in which divine favour had shown itself. These heroes needed to be shown as something out of the ordinary, even as helpless infants. Narrative tension was created by emphasizing how near to non-existence the hero had come. There is an obvious reversal of the natural order in wild animals nurturing human infants, a reversal made even more striking when the animal is, like the wolf, usually regarded as so fundamentally vicious, a simple point which may explain why the wolf is the most commonly featured animal in such stories. By the time these legends came to be retold by sophisticates such as Herodotus an inevitable rationalization had taken place, which removed or at least disguised the more overtly miraculous and animalistic elements.

Nevertheless, the nexus of ideas persisted. The Christian story of the birth of Jesus, for example, shares many characteristics with the basic pattern. Like the King of Fu Yü, his mother is impregnated by miraculous means. He is born in a stable, and in the crib-scenes of Christian tradition is always shown there in the company of an ox and an ass (for which there is only Luke's mention of a manger as slight biblical precedent), attended by herdsmen. His human father is a shadowy figure, and the role of angry king/father-figure in the story is played by Herod, who slaughters the first born of Israel in his anger at the birth of a new culture hero. Illustrations of the flight into Egypt, one of the most commonly depicted scenes in medieval Christian art, always included the donkey that carried the infant to safety. Popular hymns and legends grew up about this animal's humble yet essential part in the story, reaching a peculiar culmination in the *festum asinorum* held in many churches during the Middle Ages.

In the cathedral of Beauvais, a donkey was actually led up to the altar by a girl playing the role of Mary, and a high mass was then celebrated, during which the congregation brayed.

Lesser figures in the Christian tradition were also suitable for conformity to the foundling archetype. Saint Albeus, who was supposed to have been archbishop of Emly in Ireland around the end of the fifth century, was said to have been exposed as a baby. A she-wolf came across him, but while she was away looking for food to feed the infant, a man named Lochanus found him and gave him to some Britons, who reared him. He was converted to the Christian faith, visited Rome, and returned to perform miracles in his native land. One day the same she-wolf who had attempted to nourish him in his infancy came to him seeking protection from a wolf hunt. He offered her sanctuary, and thereafter her cubs ate at his archbishop's residence every day. Another Irish saint, Saint Bairre, bishop of Cork in the sixth century, had origins made possible by the aid of a wolf. His grandfather, a count in Connaught, drunkenly committed incest on his daughter, who gave birth to two sons. The count had one thrown in the river, and the other, Amargenus, exposed. A she-wolf suckled the child, and some wandering swine-herds found him. They brought him before the count, who recognized his son. Amargenus subsequently married a woman of remarkable beauty, who gave birth to the miraculous child Saint Bairre. These saint's legends, which so easily reconciled Roman mythology with the local Celtic substratum, were written down in Latin at roughly the same time as the Anglo-Norman werewolf romances, and both contribute to an understanding of how widespread was the contemporary belief in the possibility of such things. In England it was regarded as a point of honour to claim descent from a wild animal: Siward, Earl of Northumberland in the reign of Edward the Confessor, claimed that his grandmother had been ravaged by a bear, and as late as the eighteenth century the Devonshire family of Sucpitches explained their unusual name by a story that their ancestor had been found, Cyrus-like, in the Prussian woods being suckled by a bitch.[4]

As Charles Dunn points out in his book *The Foundling and the Werwolf*, the twelfth-century poem *Guillaume de Palerne* combines the two separate yet closely related figures of the foundling and the werewolf into one narrative: like Romulus and Remus and their counterparts in other classic foundling stories, the royal lovers Guillaume and Melior are cast into the wilderness, where they are succoured, not by a real wolf, but by Alphonse the werewolf, who brings them food and helps them evade their pursuers.[5] *Guillaume* has probably most in common with the Cyrus legend: like Cyrus, the animal-nurtured Guillaume himself is eventually recognized on account of the natural kingliness of his bearing – the old story that 'blood will out'. Yet all these stories of children suckled by wolves have a more direct relation to the werewolf legend than *Guillaume*'s relatively simple juxtaposition of the two motifs. If children were occasionally found who really had been raised by wolves and who subsequently exhibited wolfish characteristics, such unusual and dramatic events would explain the persistence of the belief that men could in some way become wolves.

Interest in this theme was not confined to societies in the classical era, for although the ancient fears that had made possible the sixteenth-century judicial burnings of werewolves subsided considerably with the gradual ascendancy of the rationalist over the religious world view, the categorization and separation of man and animal was still a matter of infinite weight to thinkers from the Renaissance onwards. The borderline between man and animal, which marked the division between the godliness to which man aspired and the bestiality which he feared, was guarded with great care. According to the great humanist Erasmus, differentiation between human and animal behaviour was vital even in the comparatively small matter of good table manners. To smack one's lips was behaviour appropriate only for a horse, Erasmus warned in his *De civilitate morum puerilium*. Similarly, one ought not to swallow meat without chewing, like a stork; gnaw the bones, like a dog; or lick the dish, like a cat. Erasmus also spoke out against animalistic traits in general comportment, warning his young readers not to shake their heads, like a colt; nor neigh when laughing, like a horse; show their teeth, like a dog; move the whole body when speaking, like a wagtail; nor speak through the nose: 'It is the property of crows and elephants.'[6]

It was clear to moralists that man's rationality did not automatically prevent him descending to the levels of the animals, indeed that in such traits as drunkenness, lying, motiveless violence, or waging war against his own species, man could far outdo the worst excesses of beasts. Thomas Tryon, writing in 1683, was typical of this pessimistic line of thought when he pointed out that lions and tigers are 'not more savage and cruel, geese and asses not half so stupid, foxes and donkeys less knavish and ridiculous, wolves not more ravenous, nor goats more lascivious than abundance of those grave, bearded animals that pride themselves with the empty title of rational souls'.

Such moralistic themes took on new urgency in the eighteenth century under the pressure of materialist ideas like those of the French theologian-turned-physician and philosopher La Mettrie, who thought of the body in purely organic terms, seeing the soul only as the thinking part of the body, coexistent with it and so not continuing past death. Death for him was the moment of acknowledgement that life's black comedy is played out (*la farce est jouée*). On the subject of the division between man and animal, La Mettrie alarmed his contemporaries by arguing that animal intelligence was different from human only in scale: 'From animals to men the transition is not violent,' he wrote. Such ideas, which with hindsight can be seen as preparing the way for theories of evolution, were put into stark form by the great Swedish naturalist Linnaeus, who in his *Systema naturae* (1735) took the revolutionary step of categorizing men and primates in the same order. The eccentric Scottish philosopher Lord Monboddo further muddied the waters in 1774 by reasserting the popular idea that orang-utans (whose Malay name means 'wild man of the forest') were members of a primitive race of men that had not yet learned to speak. This was disturbing, as speech was regarded as probably the only uniquely defining characteristic of mankind, and, according to Monboddo, the orang-utan might soon be able to bridge that final gap. The discovery that the larynx of the orang-utan is constructed in such a way that it could never speak, no matter how much it learnt, was greeted with considerable relief, although the effort to teach primates to communicate with man continues into our day with the chimpanzee and gorilla.

To such rationalists the ancient motif of the foundling raised by wolves was of no interest had it been purely legendary. Like Dickens's Mr Gradgrind, they wanted nothing but Facts, and investigation of the plausibility of these cases was taken up by such rationalist thinkers as the historian Bernard Connor at the end of the seventeenth century, and the naturalist Buffon and the philosopher Condillac in the eighteenth.[7] One important authority to be persuaded of the reality of feral children was Linnaeus, who subdivided his order of humans to include *Homo ferus*. In later editions of his *Systema naturae*, he discussed feral children at length. In 1755 the philosopher Rousseau, whose enthusiasm for the 'noble savage' was set to be a crucial influence on the Romantic movement, cited five examples of feral children in his *Discours sur l'Origine de l'Inégalité*: the wolf child of Hesse, discovered in 1344; the bear child of Lithuania, 1694; two children found in the Pyrenees in 1719; and the wild child, Peter of Hanover, discovered in 1724.[8] Another famous eighteenth-century case he might have mentioned was that of the 'girl of Sogny', Mademoiselle LeBlanc, who spent some years in the wild near Châlons with a companion. She was exceptional among feral children in that she did later acquire language, although there was no suggestion of her being nurtured by animals. With so much attention focused on the subject, it was virtually inevitable that the next feral child to be discovered in western Europe would be subject to greater scrutiny than ever before.

The feral child the Enlightenment philosophers were awaiting was to be christened the 'Wild Boy of Aveyron', from the French *département* in which he was discovered. The boy had first been sighted in 1797, running naked through the woods in the mountainous region of Lacaune, in the south-central part of the country. The following year he was captured and exhibited for a time as a fairground freak, but he eventually escaped. Over the next fifteen months he was seen several times by locals living wild in the forest, and numerous places were said to be his lair, including a sheltered hollow lined with leaves and moss. In 1799 he was captured again by hunters, who gave him into the care of an old widow. His preferred diet at this time was most peculiar, comprising raw acorns, chestnuts, walnuts, and potatoes: he would at first eat no meat, either cooked or raw.

The wild boy did not stay long with the widow, escaping into the wilds once more, but this time he shunned the forest for the nearby mountains. He climbed up to the broad plateau between Lacaune and Roquecézière, in the department of Aveyron, and spent a particularly cold winter there, wandering around naked and occasionally entering isolated farmhouses in search of food. When the occupants took pity on him and gave him potatoes to eat, he would throw them in the hearth as if to cook, but he retrieved and ate them only a few minutes later. During the day he could be seen swimming and drinking in streams, climbing trees, running at great speed on all fours, digging for roots and bulbs in the fields, and laughing uproariously at the wind. In January 1800 he was captured for the final time, and taken to a local orphanage. At this time he appeared to be between twelve and fifteen years old. He was completely mute on entering the orphanage, but within a fortnight was uttering various unintelligible cries. He refused to wear any clothes, tearing them off in fury, and it was almost as difficult to get him to accept food, which he would always smell suspiciously before putting in his mouth. His appearance caused some excitement, and when he was shown before crowds of people, he became extremely agitated, biting people foolish enough to come too near.[9]

Naturally his case caused great excitement among those whose appetite for feral children had been whetted by the writings of Condillac, Rousseau, Linnaeus, *et al.* One such was a young physician named Jean Itard who had trained under the great proto-psychiatrist Philippe Pinel, and who was subsequently taken on as resident physician by the celebrated director of the National Institute for Deaf-Mutes, Abbé Sicard. The infant science of psychiatry, as represented in the person of Pinel, was not particularly interested in the wild boy: he was carefully examined by a distinguished committee whose report, written by Pinel, reached the firm conclusion that he was a congenital idiot. Itard was not so certain. He was buoyed up in his optimism by recent successes in the education of deaf-mutes at Sicard's Institute, which, founded only shortly before the turbulent years of the French Revolution, was itself a revolutionary institution, for until this enlightened age deaf-mutes had traditionally been treated as if they were insane. Aristotle had called them irremediably ignorant, the Romans had taken away their civil rights, and La Mettrie had regarded them as harder to teach than orangutans. Even Condillac argued that they demonstrably lacked the faculty of memory and hence the power of reasoning. When it was shown that, if allowed to use a language appropriate to their particular needs, a language which was to evolve into the sign language in use among deaf people throughout the world today, a deaf-mute could communicate as well as any other human, the repercussions within the educational world were profound.

Fired with enthusiasm, Itard volunteered to take the wild boy, whom he christened Victor, and try on him a new system of education based on that given to deaf-mutes at the Institute. He realized almost immediately that Victor was not deaf, but the wild boy did have a large horizontal scar across his throat, which was generally considered to have been inflicted on him by whoever abandoned him in the woods in the first place. Itard established that his larynx had not been critically damaged in this attack, and that Victor was theoretically able to speak. The story of Victor's education has been told many times, in novels, films, and, more recently, in a detailed book by Harlan Lane,[10] a psychologist specializing in the study of language, speech, and learning, but the plain upshot is that, despite Itard's best efforts, Victor never learnt to speak. Frustrated by lack of tangible development, the French government withdrew funding for the project in 1806 and sent Victor to live with Itard's former housekeeper near the Institute. The naturalist Virey visited him there in 1815 and lamented that he remained 'fearful, half-wild, and unable to learn to speak, despite all the efforts that were made'. The case was ostensibly closed in 1828 with Victor's death. From this sad tale it might be assumed that Victor was, after all, simply an idiot who had never been able to speak and had been abandoned on that account: Harlan Lane, however, is more inclined to point to a number of significant technical failings in Itard's programme of education at that time. Itard's later successes with deaf-mute patients came about after he himself made significant improvements to his teaching methods, some apparently based on lessons learnt from the failure of Victor's education.

Lane believes that Victor was not an idiot, but that his abandonment in the woods at an early age crucially damaged his development of language, that his continuing to live in isolation for many years further suppressed whatever linguistic ability he originally had, and that Itard's programme was then sufficiently flawed for Victor's recovery of language to be impossible. Although there is no suggestion that Victor was nurtured by wild animals, he shares a number of features with the other feral children, including the Indian wolf children, Shamdeo, Kamala and Amala. The implication is that a human raised in isolation from society, although provided with adequate nourishment by an animal surrogate-parent, will be permanently damaged by the experience, and will become a human with noticeably feral characteristics.

After Victor of Aveyron, by far the best-documented case of feral children is that of Kamala and Amala. Their story has recently been re-investigated by Charles Maclean, in his book *The Wolf Children*,[11] basing his account on the detailed diary of the girls' development kept by the Reverend Mr Singh. In several respects their case prefigures that of Shamdeo half a century later. Like him, they fought furiously to avoid capture, scratching and biting the men who dug them out of the ant-mound. Once returned to the orphanage, bathed and shaved, they looked more human than they had first appeared to Singh in the jungle half-light, with the broad-nosed, dark-skinned features of the aboriginals of that part of India, but they proved unable or unwilling to stand upright, and even when lifted appeared unable to straighten their lower limbs. They would accept only milk to drink, until one day the younger girl, Amala, broke away from her new guardian and wrestled a bone from the orphanage dogs, retreating to a corner of the yard to gnaw at it greedily, occasionally rubbing it along the ground to separate the meat from the bone. From then on their apparent preference for raw meat continued to shock the rather strait-laced missionary. He recorded in his diary that the wolf children refused all other food, including cooked meat.

Another feature of their diet which appeared to be feral in character was their habit of swallowing earth and pebbles after eating or before defecating. Singh was intrigued by this odd behaviour, and discussed the habit with the orphanage's local doctor. Some companions of his with whom he went hunting told him that they had observed sand-eating among a number of different carnivores. Whether this is specifically a lupine habit is unclear: animal behaviourists[12] note that all wolves eat grass, and that as the cellulose in the grass is never digested, hypothesize that this is to scour the digestive tract and remove worms. Presumably sand and pebbles would perform the same function.

Kamala and Amala also showed disrupted sleep patterns, dozing fitfully and lightly, waking after midnight to prowl around the place, occasionally howling with a cry not quite wolf-like yet hardly human. They had no notion of personal hygiene, urinating or defecating whenever the mood took them, and sometimes dragging their bottoms along the ground as dogs will, as if in irritation at worms rather than in an attempt to get clean. They were impervious to cold, and shunned human company, showing interest only in the orphanage dogs and the wolf cubs. These latter had been brought back by Singh, but they were only rarely allowed to fraternize with their former den-mates for fear of retarding their return to normal human development.

This proved frustratingly slow, however. At the date of their capture Kamala was perhaps five or six years old, Amala about three, but neither had language, and all their interests seemed to be purely animal. Given toys, they chewed them up. Approached by other children, they snarled, bit, and scratched. Left by an open gate, they dashed for freedom on all fours. Any signs that some improvement might be being made came from the younger wolf child. Some six months after her capture, Mrs Singh noticed, Amala would utter a sound as she approached water to drink, and soon came to make the same sound when she wanted something to drink. After a long programme of attempting to instil in the uninterested wolf-girls the names of certain foods, Amala seemed to give some sign of reaction when Mrs Singh happened to mention them in another context. But this promise was wiped out when Amala died of a kidney infection in September 1921.

Left alone, Kamala struck up relationships with the orphanage kids, with a cat, with a hyena cub the Reverend Mr Singh had bought for her in the bazaar, with anything, it seemed, but a human. A programme of massage and stretching exercises taught her to kneel and stretch up, but this and the other small improvements always revolved around food. One day, walking with Mr Singh in the field behind the orphanage, Kamala spotted a dead cow, surrounded by vultures. She headed for the carcass on all fours, chased the vultures away, and tore into the raw meat with her teeth before she was pulled off by the padre. A few days later she was discovered to have dragged the carcass into the garden, where she sat contentedly gnawing at it. Any educational project the Singhs attempted with her had always to involve food as an incentive, and when Kamala finally stood upright, unsupported, in June 1923, it was with lumps of raw meat that the Reverend Mr Singh tempted her to her feet.

Kamala did not live enough for any cast-iron conclusions to be drawn from her case. Like her fellow wolf-girl, Amala, she died young of kidney failure, and she never shook free of her bouts of feral behaviour, drinking raw blood and eating dirt and pebbles even in her final illness. Although it is impossible to be sure, and the doctor who attended cannot be expected to have diagnosed such a cause of death, it is tantalizing to question whether the extreme carnivorousness of her diet had anything to do with it; wolves supplement their food with copious draughts of water to prevent uremic poisoning from the high production of urea associated with a meat diet. Unlike Victor, Kamala succeeded in overcoming mutism, had picked up a small vocabulary, and was constructing small sentences shortly before her death (Maclean quotes 'Ma, the little one hurts' and 'Parul, I will ease myself so take me out of the room').

Naturally the publication of Singh's account of this sad wolf child threatened to overturn a number of widely held orthodoxies, especially his insistence on several wolf-like physical peculiarities he noted in both girls. The most controversial of these observations was made during a period when the girls were ill, and sat together in the corner of the darkened sickroom, shunning light: 'On such occasions when we used to approach them in the room,' Singh wrote, 'we noticed that as soon as they turned towards us, the shape of the bodies used to disappear showing only two faint blue lights in proportion to the strength of the light then emitting.' For many commentators, this detail proved how far Singh had strayed from scientific accuracy, for, unlike the eyes of many mammals, the human eye lacks a tapetum, or reflective membrane, which would have made such a phenomenon possible. Not even the most ardent supporter of the reality of feral children would argue that an upbringing with wolves could bring about any physical rather than behavioural change. Furthermore, without further witnesses, the whole story depended on Singh's testimony as to the killing of the she-wolf and capture of the children. In 1952, doubt was cast on even this element of the story with the publication of *On the Trail of the Wolf-Children* by William Ogburn, an American sociologist, and Nirmal K. Bose, an Indian anthropologist. They had set out to find the village in the jungle near where Singh claimed to have captured the children. There, they felt, they might be able to find witnesses to the capture of the children, as well as someone who had seen them at the orphanage and could describe any truly feral aspects of their behaviour. Failing to find any of these things, including even the village itself, Ogburn and Bose concluded that Singh's account of the discovery of the children in a wolf's den was a fiction.

A picture had now been built up in which Singh's evidence could be largely discounted. It was becoming widely accepted among the scientific and medical community that Singh had been influenced – either knowingly or unknowingly, according to taste – by the powerful and universal motif of foundlings succoured by wild nature. As the owner of an orphanage, it was natural that these children would have been brought to him, probably by villagers telling superstitious tales of their having been raised by wolves. He could not explain the strange behaviour of these two children, and so was happy to believe the villagers' version of events. What was, according to this account, his crucial lie – that he had personally supervised the digging out of the wolves' den – was attributed to a natural wish to have himself starring in the story he subsequently spread to the outside world. And the purpose of that story, it was reasoned by those who wished to see some good in what would otherwise be an unmitigated catalogue of fraudulent misrepresentation, was to attract publicity and funding for his small orphanage.

What this version of events failed to explain was the strange behaviour of Kamala and Amala. Not even Ogburn and Bose denied that there had been two such children at the orphanage, and that they had behaved noticeably oddly. An explanation for their behaviour was needed, and to be truly satisfying it had to be an explanation that would also account for the remarkable correspondence between the descriptions of the behaviour of all the historically attested feral children. Following hard on the heels of Ogburn and Bose's scepticism, such an all-encompassing account was put forward by the American child psychologist Bruno Bettelheim.[13] According to him, the answer was simple: Kamala and Amala, and indeed many of the other so-called feral children, were suffering from childhood autism.

This explanation, or diagnosis, was profoundly satisfying for a number of reasons. The condition of autism had only recently been described, in independent publications by Leo Kanner, who worked in Baltimore, in 1943, and by Hans Asperger, working in Vienna, in 1944. If the condition had only recently been distinguished from a whole range of other mental disorders by such experts as Kanner and Asperger, how could an amateur such as the Reverend Mr Singh be expected to recognize it some twenty years earlier? The chief characteristic of the autistic child is his extreme aloneness, an inability to relate in the ordinary way with other human beings. Autistic children do not make eye contact in the normal way, do not use the full human capacity for facial expression and physical communicative gestures, and their use of language is always at best unnatural. They learn extremely slowly, although they often have isolated areas of interest in which they can achieve startling feats, notably of memory. This is the classic textbook description of autism, but Bettelheim felt that many of the so-called animalistic symptoms described by Singh were autistic features which only someone like himself with considerable firsthand clinical experience of autistic children would recognize. For example, he pointed out that their fearsome appearance – naked, haggard, and with their hair a 'hideous ball of matted hair' – did not prove that Kamala and Amala had been lost for any length of time. In his own clinic, he had plenty of experience of autistic children who were capable of reaching such a dishevelled state within hours of being unsupervised. He also pointed out that autistic children have an almost incredible capacity to elude their guardians, so that someone keeping a careful eye over them may suddenly lose them even in a modern city street, let alone the jungles of northern India. Bettelheim found persuasive analogies in the behaviour of autistic children for several of the supposedly animalistic characteristics of the feral children, such as incontinence, inappropriate behaviour, imperviousness to cold, peculiar gait, the ability to find their way around in poor light, and inability to laugh.

In his book *The Empty Fortress*, Bettelheim's discussion of feral children is placed within the context of his humane plea for the better treatment of autistic children. To simplify greatly what is an elaborate and closely argued theory, Bettelheim believed that autism is caused by a breakdown in the essential steps towards growth of the self. Because of faulty development, self and non-self are never adequately distinguished, and the autistic child erects strong, almost impenetrable defences around a self which, paradoxically, is not formed – hence the 'empty fortress' of the title. Bettelheim believed that this failure comes about in the earliest years of development, and that it is susceptible to treatment using techniques based on psychoanalytical theory. In some parts of the work he shies away from apportioning blame for the creation of the original problem, but in other places he is very clear that autistic children are 'utterly unacceptable to their parents for one reason or another. This characterizes the background of all autistic children.'[14] Thus, it is the failure of the parents to offer enough love and positive nurturing at the crucial early stage of development which creates autism.

Bettelheim's new perspective on the issue of feral children has some interesting results. For instance, he regarded the foundling-raised-by-animals motif not as an expression of a wish that the childhoods of culture heroes should be dramatically different from those of mere mortals, but as a projection of guilt for the habit of exposing children. Exposure of children is a practice known to most cultures, he argued. Parents who cannot bring themselves to murder their children expose them instead, and cling desperately to the possibility of the child having somehow survived. The modern equivalent of these guilty ancients is the parent of the autistic child who, constrained by the circumstances of modern civilization, 'exposes' the child by withdrawing the parental affection necessary for the child to develop adequately, and so creates an autistic child. Unable to acknowledge the existence of such children, Bettelheim argued, these people prefer to believe that such deformities of the human self have been created by an animal upbringing.

This is an intriguing reassessment of the foundling myth, although if the myth really does have its roots in guilt and a denial of despicable human behaviour, it seems incongruous that it should so often be applied to culture heroes or to themselves by people wishing to glamorize their own ancestry. But there is a more significant question in regard to feral children which Bettelheim never quite gets to grips with. Assuming that he is right about the causes of autism, surely Kamala and Amala's abandonment in the jungle at an early age would almost inevitably lead to faulty development of the self, thence possibly to autism. A wolf might be able to protect and feed the two children, and so perform the same kind of minimal role as an unloving human parent, but it would always be by nature incapable of supplying the full range of a human child's emotional requirements. So, is it possible that a wolf could mistake an abandoned human child for a wolf cub and bring it up as its own, even if only for a short time? Bettelheim does not adequately deal with the likelihood of what is, after all, the central question raised by the story, merely implying that it is impossible that a wolf should have nurtured the two children, despite his own admission that he knows nothing whatever about the behaviour of wolves. He even throws doubt on the circumstance of Kamala and Amala having been rescued from a wolf's lair inside a hollowed-out white-ant mound, apparently unaware that such mounds can reach ten or more feet in height and circumference, and that the versatile Indian wolf, smaller and more fox-like than its northern cousin, will often den in the deserted lairs of other animals. His argument is resolutely circular (ironically, a criticism he is quick to level against other writers on this subject): starting from his preconception that Kamala and Amala were autistic, he then insists from his own clinical experience that autistic children could never have survived in the company of wolves, *ergo* Kamala and Amala could not have been raised by a wolf. But if they *had* been raised by a wolf, surely it is possible, according to Bettelheim's theory of the aetiology of the condition, that such an unusually deprived upbringing could have sent their unformed personalities scrambling back to the empty fortress that is autism.

It turns out, however, that Bettelheim was plain wrong about the causes of autism. The disorder occurs in all kinds of families and cultures, whether or not there is a disposition on the part of the parents to disengage from the child, and there is no evidence of any weight to sustain his theories as to its origin. Bettelheim's explanations of the causes of autism now look as outdated as similarly psychogenic theories about once-mysterious conditions such as Down's syndrome, which was recognized early in the twentieth century as being caused purely by chromosomal abnormalities. Of course Bettelheim's only purpose in following his psychoanalytical approach was to find ways of curing or alleviating the sad effects of autism, yet one cannot help reflecting on the pain and distress felt by the many loving parents of autistic children who read that this terrible condition was essentially their fault. It is for this reason that modern approaches to autism go to such lengths to emphasize that the condition is nobody's fault: one recent example offers a typical case history of an autistic boy which begins, 'Peter is the much-wanted and much-loved son of a well-adjusted and well-to-do family.'[15] Current work towards understanding the causes of autism is directed at the organic factors which are undoubtedly responsible for the disorder (and probably have biological roots well before birth) rather than any psychogenic cause.

Even so, just because Bettelheim's theories on autism are now known to be unsatisfactory does not mean that his extensive clinical experience of the behaviour of autistic children can be dismissed. His diagnosis of Kamala and Amala's behaviour as suggestive of autism still stands as a plausible explanation. There is, however, one area in which his argument is a little weak. To a great extent, he relied on Ogburn and Bose, whom he thought had disproved the essentials of Singh's story. In fact, many of Ogburn and Bose's most important discoveries had been entirely negative: they had failed to find the village in the jungle near where Singh claimed the children were found, and they had failed to find any witnesses to the opening out of the white-ant mound and capture of the children. This does not disprove Singh's story; it only proves that Ogburn and Bose could not confirm it. For such negative evidence to carry any weight, it must be shown that the best possible efforts had been made to trace the village and witnesses. Twenty-two years after Ogburn and Bose, Charles Maclean retraced their steps to Calcutta University and on to Midnapore, the site of Singh's orphanage. There he uncovered a number of possible factors suggesting that Ogburn and Bose's investigation had not been as thorough as might be wished. The chief author of the investigation, the American Professor Ogburn, had been simultaneously engaged on another project at Calcutta University. An old man who found it difficult travelling to Midnapore in the hot weather and asking questions of numerous villagers unable to speak English, he had not been able to give the wolf children as much of his attention as he would have liked. He could not finish the research, and before returning to America, he persuaded Nirmal K. Bose to continue the work. According to Maclean's informant, Bose had not been particularly interested in the wolf children, but had known the Midnapore district and was famous in his own right as a follower of Gandhi and freedom fighter against the British (a man unlikely to have been sympathetic to Singh, who had been a keen admirer of the Empire). Maclean's informant at the University suggested that the legwork on the project had actually been done by Bose's students, and that the information was written up at second-hand by the two nominal authors. Buoyed up by this information, Maclean set off into Orissa, where he succeeded in tracing the Santal village nearest to the site of Kamala and Amala's capture, and securing the testimony of one old man who had taken part in the hunt as a boy and was able to corroborate Singh's description of events.[16]

It must be concluded that the jury is still out on the question of whether Kamala and Amala were truly nurtured by a wolf. The evidence in its favour is slight, ultimately relying on the word of only two men: Singh, now long dead, and Maclean's Santal villager. What is fundamentally lacking from all discussion of the truth behind the feral children legend is firm evidence that any wolf has ever nurtured any human being, or indeed that such a scenario is at all possible. None of the feral children allegedly brought up by wolves presents overwhelmingly strong proof, and as a few have been shown to be hoaxes, sceptics feel vindicated in their belief that such a thing is impossible. Animal behaviourists have done work on instinctual bonding between infant and parent in a number of species, and have shown that in certain cases disruption to the bonding process can result in the parent of one species nurturing the young of another: the greylag goose which thought Konrad Lorenz was its mother is one well-known example, and some species, like the cuckoo, rely on bonding confusion for their very survival. No one, however, has yet demonstrated such an effect occurring spontaneously in the higher species. Bettelheim is right to point to the existence of an ancient mythic pattern in which a child abandoned to nature is nurtured by savage beasts, and to emphasize that this myth may well provide a framework by which all puzzling and mysterious behaviour in abandoned children can be interpreted, although, of course, some might argue that the myth could have arisen from an original incident in which a child was actually seen to have been nurtured by a wild animal.

Whatever the truth about feral children, they have joined the rich complex of mythic and legendary ideas accumulated around the figure of the werewolf. The circulation of details of the wolf

child of Hesse in the mid fourteenth century or of the late
seventeenth-century Lithuanian bear child confirmed for many
Europeans that the relationship between man and beast was
ambiguous and very often surprising. The notion of the wolf as
the embodiment of evil allowed a telling moral inversion to be
made, by which the occasional kindness of this ravening beast
could be contrasted with the inhumanity of unkind human
parents. As the case of Shamdeo shows, the legend is still alive
today in the Indian sub-continent, and new cases appear each
year in the Indian press. What is fascinating is the degree to which
the descriptions of feral children tally, so that clear similarities
can be seen between the behaviour of Victor of Aveyron, Kamala
and Amala, and Shamdeo. Only one of the classic werewolf cases
shows signs of belonging to this series. After his condemnation in
1603, the young French werewolf Jean Grenier was confined to
the monastery of the Franciscan Cordeliers at Bordeaux. Judge
De Lancre visited him there in 1610 and found him in a sorry
state, extremely withdrawn, unwilling to look anybody in the eye,
and unable to comprehend even the simplest things. His keepers
told De Lancre that the boy had at first run around the monastery
grounds on all fours, and that he had eaten raw meat. In answer
to patient questioning, Jean insisted that he had been a werewolf,
and that he would still like to eat children if he could. He died later
that year, aged about twenty.[17]

II

Doctoring the Myth

Pray thee, what's his disease?
A very pestilential disease, my lord;
They call it lycanthropia.

WEBSTER,
The Duchess of Malfi

In the 1960s the science of psychiatry had reached a low point in its brief history. Its past achievements were being scrutinized closely, its underlying theories subjected to intensive criticism and reassessment, and its future as a branch of medicine brought into question. An 'anti-psychiatry' movement, which denied the very existence of mental illness, had gained many supporters: among its leading proponents and theorists were Michel Foucault in France, R. D. Laing in Britain, and Thomas S. Szasz in the USA. Dr Szasz wrote a sequence of books outlining his objections to the prevailing idea of 'madness', in which he argued that the concept of mental illness was erroneous and misleading, and that the enforced incarceration of patients diagnosed as suffering from 'mental illness' was both immoral and counterproductive. In one of those books, *The Manufacture of Madness*,[1] provocatively subtitled 'A Comparative Study of the Inquisition and the Mental Health Movement', Szasz hit upon an astonishing metaphor for the abuses which he felt psychiatrists inflicted on their patients: the modern institutional psychiatrist was simply the equivalent of the medieval witchfinder. Just as the medieval witchfinder had used contemporary belief in the reality of witchcraft in order to wield power over the witch, employing as the tools of his trade the rack, the ducking-stool, and the pyre, so the modern institutional psychiatrist used contemporary belief in the reality of mental illness to wield power over the mental patient, employing as the tools of his trade the strait-jacket, the hypodermic, and electroconvulsive therapy.

Szasz's polemic contained enough shreds of truth to contribute to a period of fierce debate and critical self-examination within the psychiatric community. Although the central tenet of the anti-psychiatric movement – that mental illness does not exist other than as a cultural construct useful for marginalizing non-conformist members of society – is now generally discredited, conscientious psychiatrists have heeded Szasz's warnings against any abuse of the power the physician inevitably wields over his or her patient. But in making the direct comparison between witch-hunter and physician, Szasz had homed in on an area of particular interest to the werewolf myth. The implications of Szasz's analogy are especially apt for the later period of the continental witch-craze, as it was at this point that the essential role of diagnosing who was a 'witch' or a 'werewolf' began to pass from the jurist to the physician. The process is clearly marked at the end of the era of werewolf trials in sixteenth-century France: Jacques Roulet, who confessed to a court in 1598 that he had killed and eaten a child, apparently while in the shape of a wolf, was not burnt as a werewolf, but sent to an insane asylum on the advice of doctors; Jean Grenier, who had done his utmost in three trials during 1603 to incriminate himself as a werewolf, was examined by doctors, pronounced to be malnourished and an idiot, and ultimately sentenced not to death but to incarceration in a monastery, presumably the closest approximation in that part of France to a lunatic asylum. A generation earlier both these alleged werewolves would have been tried by jurists confident in their own ability to diagnose diabolic possession, who neither felt the need for medical intervention nor sought the help of the local physician in the matter.

To the modern mind, it is clear that a doctor would be better placed to examine such people than a religion-raddled judge with his mind full of nonsense from the *Malleus Maleficarum*, but in fact it is noticeable that the two kinds of authority were not so easily distinguishable, at least in the diagnostic terms they used. Judge Boguet, for example, was quite capable of introducing discussion of the four humours into his treatise on lycanthropy, while the reported diagnoses of the doctors in the Roulet and Grenier cases suggest that they shared many of the assumptions

of Boguet and his kind as to the devil's role in lycanthropy, yet
reached different conclusions as to what should be done about it.
One popular way of explaining this similarity in the terms of
reference used by physician and witch-hunter is to say that
doctors felt obliged to couch their diagnoses in the language of
current orthodoxy in order to ease the way for their new radical
approach. By this line of reasoning, Grenier's doctors' explanation, that the child suffered the illusion of being a werewolf
because demons had affected his judgement, is regarded as an
instance of purely metaphorical speech: the doctors did not
believe in the demons, any more than a writer in the twentieth
century referring to someone with psychological problems as
'tormented by personal demons' believes in the physical actuality
of such beings. Yet there is always the danger of anachronism in
regarding doctors of the sixteenth and seventeenth centuries as
such angels of enlightenment and reason, divorced utterly from
their own social and cultural context.

One of the most interesting figures to walk this ambiguous line
between witch-hunting and modern medicine was the physician
Johann Weyer (or, in its Dutch form, Wier), author of *De
praestigiis daemonum*, first published in 1563. Weyer has been
hailed as a father-figure of modern psychiatry, as well as being
one of the very few sixteenth-century sceptics to write a treatise
on witchcraft from that point of view. One of the few fellow-
sceptics writing in that era was the English author Reginald Scot,
but his reasons for doing so seem to have been at least superfi-
cially very different from Weyer's. Scot's *Discoverie of Witchcraft*
of 1584 exhibits a distinctively Protestant line of argument on the
great question of the era, although he was himself no theologian.
The age of miracles has passed, Scot argues, ending with the
death of the last apostle. Since God no longer works miracles in
the world, he would never allow the devil to continue to conjure
up such marvels as turning a witch into an animal or allowing
women to fly through the air on broomsticks. *Ergo*, those who
confess to witchcraft and lycanthropy are either lying or deluded.
Scot was isolated from the continental debate, and that the man
who was to become his monarch, James VI of Scotland and I of
England, could argue the exact opposite from a Calvinist position
shows that such theological points were at best inconclusive in
solving these riddles. Nor were Scot's arguments unique to his

treatise: they appear in a number of contemporary continental demonologies, where they support a great variety of conclusions, including those of such as Boguet who were diametrically opposed to Scot and believed vehemently in the existence of witches and werewolves.

Weyer, however, was a physician, and according to the view which sees doctors in this era as the harbingers of rationality and science, could argue his case on different and intrinsically better grounds than those of the demonologists. Throughout the medieval era doctors and jurists had tended to share a particular view of the world, as the church kept a tight grip on medical qualifications, passing on the teachings of Hippocrates, Galen, and his Arabic commentators only in the medical schools at Salerno, Montpellier, Bologna, Paris, Padua, and Oxford. The elite grade of physicians in medieval western Europe were predominantly clergymen who had been trained at one of these schools, although there were lesser grades of doctor, ranging from surgeons (who actually undertook operations on their patients, unlike the school-trained physicians, and who gradually gained in status during the medieval era), through the illiterate barber-surgeons and apothecaries, down to the lowest level of unlicensed and nonprofessional doctors who mainly served rural communities, and of whom a significant proportion, something like 15 to 20 per cent to judge from English evidence, were women.[2] Although this hierarchical structure persisted until the Renaissance, medicine could not remain isolated from the new ideas beginning to be disseminated in intellectual circles all over Europe. Weyer's education seems to have come under the influence, either directly or indirectly, of new humanist teachings in the Low Countries, his place of birth. His progressiveness was further compounded by his studying under Cornelius Agrippa, an important early scientist who mixed mystical beliefs with scepticism, and who was widely reputed a black magician; Weyer seems to have distrusted his master's mystical leanings, and retained from his education under him chiefly the mental discipline of scepticism. After this significant apprenticeship, Weyer took his medical degree at Paris, and in 1550, aged about forty-five, took up the most important appointment of his life, that of personal physician to Duke Wilhelm V of Cleve, Jülich, and Berg, in the lower area of the Rhine. The duke was a ruler of tolerant views, who was to provide the shield behind which Weyer could begin his innovative investigations into the nature of contemporary witch-craft.

Happily, Weyer has now been well served by the first transla-tion into English of his great work, *De praestigiis daemonum*,[3] an event that will almost certainly lead over the next few years to a deeper understanding of his work in English-speaking circles. A reading of its 584 pages reveals that Weyer's attitude to witch-craft, and in particular to the central question of how much power the devil was able to wield in the world, is not always easy for the modern reader to interpret. Weyer does not consistently exhibit all the attitudes of a modern sceptic: the first of the six books into which his work is subdivided deals solely with 'The devil, his origin, aims, and power', ostensibly admitting the existence of Satan and the possibility of his interfering in the world, although Weyer goes to such lengths only in order to demonstrate the narrow limits of the devil's power. As the historian Stuart Clark has pointed out, Scot had a much more rigorous attitude to this question, arguing that all demonic agents were entirely nonphysical, and so could have no power at all in human affairs.[4] Weyer has been called inconsistent for his lack of intellectual stringency and for his acceptance of the literal truth of some obviously legendary material,[5] but his chief felicity in modern eyes is that he was clearly aware of many psychological phenom-ena that would have to wait another three hundred years or so for psychiatrists to rediscover – in particular, psychosomatic illness, the power of suggestion, the placebo effect, and other similar manifestations of mental suggestibility which, Weyer demon-strated, allowed unscrupulous clerics and doctors to attribute illnesses to demonic causes and to administer quack remedies. What is perhaps his most famous case illustrates this facet of his thinking perfectly. While travelling through Duke Wilhelm's territories, Weyer came across a ten-year-old girl from Unna, named Barbara Kremers, who was supposed to have lived for a year without eating or drinking, although she remained in good health. Her case had been taken for a miracle in the locality, pamphlets had been written in her honour, and the city council had presented her with an elaborate certificate testifying to the truth of her wondrous condition. Intrigued, Weyer visited the girl and offered to take her back to his home in Cleve in order to study her condition more closely. The family was reluctant, but eventually agreed, and Barbara's older sister Elsa was sent with her as chaperone. Once the two girls were installed at Weyer's house it soon became clear that Elsa was surreptitiously feeding Barbara at night. Weyer and his wife did not challenge Barbara directly, but lavished care and consideration on her, and soon she was sitting up at table, eating with the rest of her temporary family. Weyer diagnosed her case as one of unconscious malingering, done to gain attention within her immediate social circle, and managed to get the Duke to agree to send Barbara home without punishment, although he burnt the ridiculous pamphlets written about her before she left.

Weyer's demonstration and understanding of the power of unconscious psychological forces was particularly impressive to the neurologists of the late nineteenth century who were keenly interested in the phenomenon of 'hysteria'. The most important of these was Sigmund Freud, who developed the theory that hysteria was a delayed emotional reaction to sexual abuse inflicted on the hysteric in childhood, but then, in a crucial redevelopment of his theory in 1897, added the all-important gloss that the sexual abuse had never actually taken place, that it had been imagined by the patient who had experienced unconscious sexual fantasies in infancy. For better or for worse (Freud's theory allowed him to ignore cases in which sexual abuse clearly *had* taken place), this formulation was to become the foundation stone of twentieth-century psychoanalytic theory. It has been suggested that one of the key influences on Freud's thinking on the subject of hysteria was Weyer, a French translation of whose great work was reprinted at Paris in 1885, at the same time as Freud was studying there under Charcot. In 1906, Freud stated that, if asked to list the 'ten most significant books' ever published, he would nominate 'such scientific achievements as those of Copernicus, the old physician Johann Weier [*sic*] on the belief of witches, Darwin's *Descent of Man*, and others'.[6]

Weyer's influence was not something Freud chose to acknowledge publicly again, very likely for the reason that it would hardly have looked impressive to reveal that one of the guiding lights behind the new twentieth-century science was an obscure sixteenth-century demonologist, but in the 1930s one of Freud's followers, Gregory Zilboorg, took up the challenge of analysing

Weyer's writings for their psychological import.[7] His conclusions
were that Weyer's approach to witches, werewolves, and the rest
was resolutely 'medical', in that he trusted only to observation
and clinical experience. Zilboorg went further, implying that this
medical approach sufficed as a method of interpreting the entire
phenomenon of medieval and Renaissance witchcraft, and that
Weyer was its pioneer. According to Zilboorg, 'From the very
outset Weyer proceeded to look upon the demoniacal world
around him as an enormous clinic teeming with sick people.' He
noted that Weyer divided the general category of 'witch' into two.
The first group comprised poisoners, those who deliberately
administered toxic substances to others; their actions needed no
recourse to theories of the supernatural to explain them, and they
could be punished under the usual laws laid down for such
crimes. The other category comprised all those who were, to a
greater or lesser extent, mentally ill.

Reading Zilboorg's thesis, one senses his enthusiasm for the
new practices of psychoanalysis and psychotherapy, and his
desire to read into Weyer's humane work the first stirrings of a
movement towards such a science. Undoubtedly he overdoes it,
for Weyer did not by any means regard all people accused of
diabolical crimes as suffering mental psychosis. A good example
of how Weyer presented a medical explanation is his treatment
of werewolves. Weyer did not write a great deal about alleged
lycanthropes, probably because he wrote at a time when the brief
flurry of werewolf trials was still in the future, and he had no
firsthand experience of them. His main treatment of the subject
occupies chapter twenty-three of his fourth book, 'Concerning
the disease of lycanthropy, in which men believe themselves to be
turned into wolves'. The title alone seems to bear out Zilboorg's
thesis that Weyer regarded all manifestations of the supernatural
as a delusory illness, and Weyer launches into the standard
medical explanation for lycanthropy familiar from Paulus Aegineta
and other early sources: the so-called werewolves are actually
suffering from a disorder of their melancholic humour, Weyer
says, with much sootiness of their black bile.

They therefore go out of their houses, especially by night,
imitating wolves or dogs in their every action. They are pale,
and their eyes are sunken and dry. They see but dimly and have

a dry tongue and a great thirst, while their mouth lacks saliva. Their legs are so covered in sores that they cannot be healed – because of frequent injuries and dog bites.

Like any good doctor, Weyer proceeds to prescribe remedies for these poor deluded lycanthropes:

These individuals are cured by the letting of blood (even to the point of losing consciousness), and also by good juicy foods, fresh water baths, buttermilk, the 'sacred antidote' of Rufus or Archigenes or Justus (made from colocynth [a drug extracted from a type of cucumber]), and all the other remedies useful against melancholia. Before the accession of the illness their heads are rinsed with sleep-inducing agents and their nostrils are rubbed with opium. Sometimes, too, a soporific must be taken by mouth.

None of this is original or surprising for the date; indeed much the same kind of diagnosis had been given over a thousand years earlier.

Yet when it comes to reporting a recent case of alleged lycanthropy, Weyer does not utilize the classic medical diagnosis of 'melancholic lycanthropia'. The case he chooses to deal with in depth is that of the Poligny werewolves, Pierre Bourgot and Michel Verdung.[8] These two had confessed in 1521 to vowing allegiance to Satan, using ointment to transform themselves into wolves, killing and eating children, and copulating with real wolves. Weyer's main drift is that these men were not suffering from a mental illness, but were simply deluded. The devil promised them money and protection for their cattle from wolves, Weyer points out, but neither actually materialized. Pierre said that over the years succeeding his pact with the devil he would occasionally spot wolves who did not harm his cattle, but Weyer explains this by saying that the devil 'was only making a rather clever attempt to frighten and deceive Pierre and keep him in his service by means of wolf-images (which he could pour forth at will).'

Once again, Weyer's portrait of 'the devil' is ambiguous. Zilboorg might have argued that he uses the term metaphorically, and that what Weyer really means to convey is that Pierre was mentally ill and suffering hallucinations, but this seems like a modern misreading: Weyer is not nearly so consistent. A few lines later, he argues that the wolves might have been real, driven there by Satan for the purpose of bending Pierre to his will. Ironically, considering the dichotomy which is sometimes proposed between jurist and doctor, Weyer's line of argument is recognizably legalistic. He is happy to use a scatter-gun approach, like the defence lawyer who argues that his client did not commit the murder as he was out of town at the time, that although he was at the scene of the crime he did not have a gun, that it was not he but his girlfriend who pulled the trigger, that he only intended to fire a warning shot over the victim's head, and that in any case he was not in control of his mental faculties at the time he shot the victim through the heart. More or less the lone voice of reason in a troubled century, Weyer found it necessary to argue in much the same way, utilizing every possible argument in the defence of his thesis, which, in this chapter at least, is not that all werewolves are mentally ill, but that the devil has no real power over mankind.

This leaves, of course, the great question as to why Pierre and Michel should have confessed what they did. Here Weyer proposes a solution which was to have great influence over future theories about the cause of werewolf delusions: according to him, the secret lay in the constituents of the ointment with which Pierre and Michel allegedly smeared themselves before achieving their lycanthropic transformation. Although Weyer does not say so, magical ointments, unguents, and powders had by this stage become a regular feature of witchcraft trials, and yet they were not a common feature of the werewolf legend. In the ancient Greek story of the Antheus family, for example, the transforming agent for turning men into wolves had been plain water, and the motif of water had recurred as recently as the twelfth-century werewolf romances, including *Guillaume de Palerne*, which had last been printed at Lyon in 1552, only eleven years before the first edition of Weyer's book. The alternative tradition suggested that it was necessary to use a magical wolf-skin or, as in the cases of the Norse 'wolf-coats' and Cologne's Peter Stubb, a simple girdle or belt representative of the whole pelt.

These two agents, water and the wolf-skin, were the basic choices for any would-be werewolf, and their persistence in folk-

belief as late as the nineteenth century suggests that they be-
longed to a relatively uniform and fundamental set of folk
werewolf beliefs. Powders and ointments seem to have been
much more of an imposition on popular beliefs by judges and
inquisitors of all eras. Horace, for example, wishing to please his
emperor by denigrating Roman witchcraft practices, had portrayed Canidia and her cronies cutting up a young boy's liver for
use in a potion. His contemporary, Virgil, giving the earliest
recorded portrayal of the werewolf-as-magician, had specified
Moeris' occult herbs grown in Thessaly as his means of transforming himself. In the fourteenth century, lepers and Jews
blamed for the outbreaks of plague had been accused of poisoning wells with all manner of pestilential powders and potions, and
similar accusations were soon levelled at witches. The ingredients of these magical concoctions rarely varied much from the
stereotypical list of occult herbs, human and animal hair and
bones, blood, excrement, urine, and ground-up consecrated
hosts. A great favourite in the fifteenth and sixteenth centuries
was the addition of matter prepared from the bones or fat of
unbaptized children.

The appearance of such substances in witch-trials probably
reflects the fact that a good proportion of the alleged witches were
practitioners of folk medicine, in which art great play would have
been made of the occult substances going into the medicinal pot.
A love-potion gone wrong, accidentally poisoning the folk-
doctor's client, might easily spark off an accusation of witchcraft.
Richard Kieckhefer, who has written on the imposition of learned
notions on popular beliefs in the witch-trials, has pointed out that
it was usually the inquisitors who developed fantasies about the
ingredients of these liquids. In the records of the Innsbruck trials
of 1485, for example, Kieckhefer remarks that it is the commen-
tary of Institoris, principal architect of the *Malleus*, rather than
the testimony of the witnesses, that reveals a fascination to know
more about unguents prepared from the corpses of unbaptized
children.[9] Weyer, of course, has no such prurient interest, for he
is sure that there is something in these potions and ointments
susceptible to rational, scientific analysis. 'The liniment with
which they anointed themselves when about to take on the form
of wolves was no doubt a sleep-producing agent,' he avers,

because it achieved its effects when it was spread upon the exposed parts of the body and then activated by the body's innate heat . . . [T]he other liniment with which they anointed themselves when they wanted to return to human form was either imaginary (and they were asleep when they thought they were using it), or else it might have been effective against the harmful effects of the sleep-producing ointment; or it might even have done nothing at all, save that by means of it the demon deceived his clients – as though it had some special powers with regard to the metamorphosis.[10]

Thus Weyer diagnoses the lycanthropy of the Poligny werewolves as a drug-induced illusion. At various other points in his book, Weyer explains that Pierre and Michel's ointment, and others like it, contained powerful pharmaceuticals capable of inducing sleep, hallucinations, and the illusion of transformation into an animal. The werewolf would apply this ointment on the wrists or at the temples, where the ingredients would be most readily activated, and fall into a drugged slumber in which he imagined that he took on a wolf's shape and committed terrible crimes (even including bestiality). This is a remarkable, even brilliant, suggestion, which, if true, would provide an elegant resolution to many difficult questions about the reliability of the testimonies of shape-changing werewolves and broomstick-flying witches alike. A plethora of writers on werewolves and witches since Weyer have fastened onto it, and all manner of substances have been identified which might have given the sought-for soporific and hallucinatory effect. The idea is not original to Weyer. In book three, chapter seventeen, he quotes at length a passage from book two of Giovanni Battista Della Porta's *Natural Magic or Natural Miracles*, first published at Antwerp three years before Weyer's book.[11] Like Weyer, Della Porta was of a scientific cast of mind, and he had investigated the matter of ointments carefully, interviewing a number of reputed witches himself. He states that they revealed to him the ingredients of their ointments, and he prints a few of these recipes. Mingled with the innocuous (chicken stock, water parsnip, wild celery) and the theatrical (bat's blood) are plants like aconite and deadly nightshade with well-known toxic properties. Della Porta then relates the story of his encounter with a witch, who voluntarily offered to bring him back messages from beyond. She asked to be left alone, and Della Porta and his fellow witnesses went out of the room, but watched her through cracks in the door. She stripped naked, rubbed herself all over with the ointment, and soon collapsed to the floor – overwhelmed by the force of the soporific drugs in her ointment, Della Porta explains. The observers entered the room but could not wake the woman from her deep sleep, even by striking her with some force, and so they went out again to wait for the effects of her ointment to wear off. 'Awaking from sleep, she began a long raving story of crossing seas and mountains, and she brought forth false responses. We denied her story, but she insisted upon it. We showed her the black-and-blue marks, but she became all the more stubborn.'[12]

Della Porta's story has a number of remarkable features. The first is that the episode appears to be exceptionally good evidence for what might be called the Ginzburg theory of witchcraft, that the activities of the medieval and Renaissance witches were really those of people practising ancient shamanistic rites. The woman in the story is clearly fulfilling a shamanistic function: she offers to 'bring back responses' for Della Porta, that is, to relay messages from the spirit world, and she emerges from her trance with stories of distant flight. That she should not be believed by a Renaissance scientist compiling a book on magic at the height of the continent-wide witch-craze is hardly surprising. There is, however, another and puzzling facet to the story. The whole episode is presented as one which Della Porta has personally witnessed, and yet at a formal level the story bears a striking resemblance to the famous episode of Lucius witnessing the transformation of Pamphile. In particular, it shares that story's motifs of the nakedness of the woman, the vigorous application of ointment, and silent observers peering through a gap in the door. The resemblance is heightened by Della Porta's aside that these women are called *Striges*, because of their likeness to the *strix* or nocturnal screech-owl, the same bird into which Pamphile was transformed. This may all be the merest coincidence, or it may be that Della Porta was signalling to his educated readership that the witch's activities were to be compared to the episode in Apuleius' comic novel, perhaps with the implication that they were not to be taken too seriously. A third possibility, not at all creditable to Della Porta, was that he had not in fact witnessed the episode at first hand, and that he added colour to someone else's account (or even invented the episode wholesale) from one of the few literary descriptions of a witch's transformation he is likely to have read. It is impossible to judge purely from the text which is the correct interpretation, and further evidence in Della Porta's writings is not forthcoming. His book caused great controversy, being attacked by Jean Bodin for its alleged necromantic content, and Della Porta silently omitted this passage from all subsequent editions – probably because it gave what amounted to step-by-step instructions for preparing what Bodin and his like thought of as a devil's brew.

Whether Weyer and Della Porta were right in attributing shape-shifting and other magical phenomena to the action of narcotic agents in the witch's salves is a question that has been vigorously debated. As a theory it has an obvious appeal to the rational twentieth-century mind. It does not require belief in the idea that every alleged werewolf or witch brought to trial during the continental witch-craze must have been forced to confess to deeds of shape-shifting or night-flight which he or she knew to be impossible. Nor does it require any reliance on ideas of surviving shamanistic and ecstatic religious beliefs, concepts which cause some unease in many rationalist circles. And there is no doubt that some of the alleged ingredients of witches' unguents have potentially impressive effects. There are four good candidates for narcotics with mind-altering properties powerful enough to induce the requisite kinds of delusions: the alkaloids aconitine, hyoscyamine, scopolamine, and atropine, drugs which can be got with little difficulty from plants like wolf's-bane, henbane, and deadly nightshade. These plants were regularly featured among the ingredients of witch-ointments, and their toxic effects had been well-known for centuries: wolf's-bane, for instance, probably got its name not from any perceived connection with werewolves, but because the deadly poison extracted from it was used to tip the arrows of ancient wolf-hunters. Non-lethal doses of these drugs produce a wide range of symptoms – visual and auditory hallucinations, vertigo, mental confusion, irregular heart-beat, impairment of normal physical movement, even convulsions – which later enthusiasts of the pharmacological theory of witchcraft have interpreted as explaining illusory effects of flying and physical transmutation among witches and werewolves.

There are, however, some major problems with attributing all lycanthropic belief to the ointments. The first is that there is some considerable doubt as to whether rubbing these drugs on the skin would lead to them being absorbed into the bloodstream in sufficient quantities to produce the required hallucinatory effect.[13] Equally important is that in the witch-trials and the demonological literature of the earlier period, from 1300 to 1500 (a period in which werewolves do not feature), the main accusation was that witches smeared magical ointment not on their bodies, but on their broomsticks, or any other implement they allegedly used to ride out at night, thus reducing almost to zero the chance that any narcotic ingredients in the ointment induced their visions.[14] It is reasonably certain that the presence of magical ointments and unguents in sixteenth-century werewolf trials is a late arrival, imported from earlier witch-trials where the learned demonologists had succeeded in grafting the idea onto popular beliefs. It is noticeable that many of the confessions in later werewolf trials, such as those of Peter Stubb and Jean Grenier, combine an ointment with the more traditional wolf's pelt or girdle, a symptomatic over-egging of the pudding by the accused. The ultimate problem with pharmacological explanations such as Weyer's is that they ignore the mythological background to werewolf beliefs. They fail to see that even the ointment has been assimilated into an irrational set of beliefs, part learned, part popular, and that the mentions of ointment in werewolf confessions are as stereotypical as accounts of pacts with the devil, eating the flesh of children, and all the rest. Ironically, in chasing his rational medical explanation, Weyer distorts what are likely to have been the true facts of the Poligny case. In his account, he makes it clear that he is aware that Michel and Pierre had very probably been tortured, and that their testimony is therefore sure to be riddled with ideas put there by their inquisitors, but in his eagerness to apply his new scientific analysis, he does not pause to consider whether the ointment was also an idea similarly introduced. In pushing forward his pharmacological theory at the expense of his usual empathy with the accused, he demonstrates very clearly that Renaissance doctors had no less of a predetermined cultural agenda than the demonologists.

Although the likelihood of hallucinogenic constituents of

witch-ointments having caused werewolf delusions is small, other equally 'pharmacological' explanations have been put forward with increasing regularity. One of the most fashionable of these in recent years has been that the medieval and Renaissance werewolves were suffering from ergot poisoning. This rare condition is caused by eating bread made from rye infected by the *Claviceps purpurea* fungus. The parasitic growth, which forms a hard purplish-black object called the sclerotium between the grains on the ear of the plant, is found chiefly on rye, and was therefore more prevalent during the medieval and Renaissance era in the north, where rye's greater hardiness meant that it took the place of wheat as the principal bread corn. Rye produces far less gluten than wheat, is harder to work as dough, and cannot be refined to such light colours: its most characteristic use today is in the traditional dark and black breads of northern Europe. The *Claviceps purpurea* fungus thrives on rye particularly in wet summers and autumns, generating a number of ergot-related alkaloids with varying degrees of toxicity. Ergot has a benign side – in its most common form it was used in medieval times as a medicine to hasten childbirth, and it is known to alleviate migraine, epilepsy, and hypertension – but under certain rare conditions it can mutate into related alkaloids of extreme and powerful effect, including one, ergonovine, very closely akin to the hallucinogenic drug lysergic acid diethylamide, commonly known from its Swiss name Lyserg-Saure-Diethylamide as LSD. Under certain rare conditions, people who ingested rye bread infected with ergot alkaloids were, to all intents and purposes, receiving a massive overdose of LSD.

LSD was first synthesized in Swiss laboratories in the 1940s, and reached a zenith of popularity in Europe and the USA as a recreational drug in the 1960s, when the effects of ingesting infinitesimally small amounts of the potent chemical were advertised by such self-appointed gurus as Dr Timothy Leary. Perhaps by reason of its modishness, especially among contemporary academics aware of the effects of hallucinogen usage among their students and colleagues, an increasing number of articles on werewolves and lycanthropy from this time onwards began to include references to the possibility that the medieval and Renaissance werewolves may have been suffering from ergot poisoning. The theory was that ergot poisoning would have caused them to suffer hallucinations during which they believed themselves to be werewolves or other were-animals, and that their convolutions while under the influence of the drug could have been misinterpreted by contemporary observers as animalistic behaviour. Surawicz and Banta's publication in 1975 of their case history of Mr H, who had first suffered the delusion of becoming a werewolf under the influence of LSD, lent weight to this argument. More or less equal prominence was given in some circles to the idea that the general populace in medieval times suffered periodically from ergotism, during which they may have hallucinated that other people were werewolves, or indeed witches, for the new theory was pleasingly malleable and could be applied to anything from werewolves to the Salem witch-trials. The crucial question, however, remained: how closely did the symptoms of mass ergotism compare with what were believed to be those of lycanthropy?

The effects of ergot poisoning were far from unknown in the Middle Ages, although its precise cause was not to be guessed at until the latter part of the sixteenth century and only gradually circulated in medical writings thereafter. The *Dictionnaire Encyclopédie de Science Médecine* of 1887 refers to epidemics after 1600 in Silesia, Prussia, Bohemia, Sweden, and in some provinces in central France, particularly Sologne, and notes particularly severe epidemics in Württemberg in 1735, Gatinais in 1674, and Switzerland in the same general period.[15] The earlier epidemics are less clearly documented, although occasional outbreaks occurred throughout the medieval and early modern era all over Europe, but particularly in the north. Medieval observers had no doubt that they were in the presence of a very particular condition, the characteristic symptoms of which were 'tingling and burning of the hands and feet, and then a frightful heartburn. Fingers and toes are bent nearly double and clamped; the mouth is full of foam. Often the tongue is lacerated by the strength of the convulsions. There is a severe secretion of spittle. The sick utter that they are being destroyed by a burning fire. They feel great giddiness, and some of them become blind; the intellectual capacities are polluted, a fog comes over and destroys the mind.'[16] The 'burning fire' experienced by sufferers was felt to be so characteristic of the condition that it formed part of its medieval name, St Anthony's Fire, the first element reflecting the popular belief that only prayer to St Anthony, the patron saint of hopeless causes, could alleviate the symptoms.

Thus far ergotism reveals no werewolves, nor any symptoms related to them, although foaming at the mouth is vaguely animalistic. Nevertheless, ergot poisoning could take many surprising public forms. The dancing manias of medieval Germany, for example, perhaps had ergot as their root cause. The most serious outbreak of this curious phenomenon started at Aix-la-Chapelle in July 1374, when sufferers began to dance uncontrollably in the streets, screaming and foaming at the mouth. Some cried out that they were drowning in a sea of blood, others had more pleasant visions in which the heavens opened to reveal Christ enthroned with the Virgin Mary. All this sounds very like ergotism, but the outbreak eventually inspired something different, a kind of mass hysteria in which people who appear to have been free of ergot poisoning began imitating the dancers' frenzied movements. Thousands were drawn into the dance, and the craze swept through the Low Countries, moved along the Rhine, and appeared throughout Germany. By this time the dancers had become a populist anti-clerical movement which threatened the cities of Cologne, Mainz, and Strasbourg, taking over monastic houses and demanding the removal of the hated Prince-Bishops. In the later phases of the craze it was noted that the dancers appeared to be entirely insensible to pain or other external stimuli, which is a symptom equally of hysteria and of certain phases of ergotism, but which is likely to have been entirely hysterical by that stage.

The medieval era was characterized by a number of similar epidemics of mass hysteria, including the flagellant movement, in which participants whipped themselves to atone for the sins of the world. Like the dancing mania, the flagellant movement quickly degenerated to an unruly mob attacking priests and Jews, and had ultimately to be suppressed by the pope. There was a seventeenth-century outbreak of something apparently similar in France, in Luc in the parish of Béarn, at the furthest south-west corner of the country, where men began barking like dogs.[17] Unlike the dancing craze, this has some superficial connection with lycanthropy, or kynanthropy at least, but it is fairly clear that it had nothing to do with ergot. The barking men were soon cured by having put around their necks the *Agnus castus* plant[18] – which suggests that the origin of the epidemic was purely hysterical, as there is no such sudden cure for ergotism – and the geographical position of the outbreak is some way to the south of the historically attested areas of St Anthony's Fire.

Luckily for students of ergot poisoning, and very unluckily for its inhabitants, the small French town of Pont-Saint-Esprit, in the Rhône valley, suffered an outbreak of ergot poisoning in 1951, in which the exact nature of their delusions could be studied more closely according to modern precepts.[19] Although improved methods of agriculture and grain-storage have virtually eliminated ergot from modern Europe, by some unfortunate chance a small amount of flour made from ergot-infected rye was added to the bread flour of that town, and in the subsequent outbreak eight people died and several hundred were infected with the most extraordinary madness. The symptoms of the sufferers matched those of the medieval and early modern descriptions of St Anthony's Fire with unerring accuracy, including the characteristic agonizing delusion that their limbs were being consumed by fire. Many of the Pont-Saint-Esprit victims hallucinated that they were being attacked by animals, some – like tigers, lions, and snakes – frightening enough in reality, others mythological and fantastic. However, not one of them is recorded as having hallucinated being attacked by wolves, or as thinking that their friends or neighbours were werewolves; nor did one of them suffer the delusion that he or she was a werewolf. This might be partially explained by the absence of wolves in that area in the middle of the twentieth century, but then tigers and lions are not common in those parts either.

One of the most ingenious connections proposed between the symptoms of the ergot poisoning at Pont-Saint-Esprit and historical lycanthropy is advanced by the English folklorists W. M. S. and C. Russell.[20] They note that one of the patients in the Pont-Saint-Esprit outbreak shouted out to the ambulance workers trying to take him to hospital, 'Please, sirs, cut my skin. Cut my skin! I'll feel better. Get me a bicycle and cut my skin!'[21] They compare this with a similar reference to cutting the victim's skin made by the lycanthropic Duke in John Webster's tragedy *The Duchess of Malfi*. The relevant passage from the play is worth quoting in full:

Pray thee, what's his disease?
A very pestilential disease, my lord;
They call it lycanthropia.
                         What's that?
I need a dictionary to it.
                         I'll tell you:
In those that are possessed with it, there o'erflows
Such melancholy humour, they imagine
Themselves to be transformed into wolves,
Steal forth to church yards in the dead of night,
And dig dead bodies up. As two nights since
One met the duke, 'bout midnight, in a lane
Behind St Mark's church, with the leg of a man
Upon his shoulder; and he howled fearfully;
Said he was a wolf; only the difference
Was, a wolf's skin was hairy on the outside,
His on the inside. Bade them take their swords,
Rip up his flesh, and try.

Webster's play was published in 1614, at a time when the melancholic anti-hero, of which Hamlet is the most celebrated example, was a stock type in English drama. With contemporary physicians so clearly agreed that excess of melancholy was the prime cause of lycanthropy, it is hardly surprising that at least one instance of the werewolf should have turned up on the melancholy-obsessed English stage, especially in a play such as Webster's, with its exotic Italian setting and themes of murder, poisoning, and vengeance (although it is noticeable that his audience are not expected to know what lycanthropy is, the English werewolf tradition being long dormant by 1614).

The surprising notion of the werewolf's fur growing on the inside Webster has clearly taken from one particular well-known Italian case, told by both Job Fincelius[22] and Weyer in works published in the second half of the sixteenth century. In 1541 a farmer had been arrested near Padua, having allegedly killed a number of people in the surrounding fields. The man declared that he was a wolf but that his fur grew on the inside, and the investigators, with a fine display of Renaissance anatomical curiosity, promptly cut off his arms and legs to see if this were true. The farmer was thus exonerated of the dreadful charge of lycanthropy, but died a few days later of loss of blood and shock. It is just possible that this farmer had become deranged through ergot poisoning and had committed his crimes under that influence, but it does not seem from either Job Fincelius' or Weyer's account that he asked his captors to cut his skin, rather that they took it into their own heads to do so in order to test his unusual claim. For all W. M. S. and C. Russell's ingenuity, there is a considerable discontinuity between this poor man's plight at the hands of his captors, the dramatist's reworking of the episode into the melancholic Duke's almost arrogant challenge in *The Duchess of Malfi*, and the pleas of the agonized Frenchman in 1951, which, if anything at all can be construed from the cries of a deranged man, seem to refer to the terrible burning pains experienced by the victims of St Anthony's Fire.

Carlo Ginzburg prefers to approach the ergot-lycanthropy hypothesis from a very different angle, looking for some possible connection between the two themes in folklore and etymology.[23] He notes a number of mid-nineteenth-century rural German folk-tales, apparently intended to scare children away from the rye-fields, featuring the 'rye mother' (*Roggenmutter*), a ghastly creature whose iron breasts are the purplish-black sclerotia of *Claviceps purpurea* which she offers to children to suck, thus poisoning them. Her partner in terror is the 'rye wolf' or 'rye dog' (*Roggenwolf, Roggenhund*), with which, according to Ginzburg, the werewolf was then associated: he quotes a German saying, 'The werewolf sits amid the grain.' Insignificant though it may seem, this is in many ways the best piece of evidence for any connection at all between ergotism and lycanthropy. Ginzburg argues that the properties of ergot were well-known in folk medicine from their use in inducing labour, and that the fungus was probably also eaten deliberately to induce ecstatic states such as those in which Theiss and his fellow 'dogs of God' fought for the fertility of the fields. If he is right, it would have been an extremely dangerous procedure, requiring only some small chemical mutation in the ergot to release the alkaloid derivative which would lead to madness and possible death. It is worth emphasizing the potential power of the ergot-derivative responsible for St Anthony's Fire: at Pont-Saint-Esprit one woman ate only one slice of infected bread no bigger than her little finger, the bread itself having contained about one part in twenty of rye flour, in which ergot was present at the usually insignificant rate of one unit per thousand. In spite of such a minute intake of the drug, this woman experienced complete insomnia for a month, and was still suffering exhaustion some three months later. In the first experimental dosages of LSD, deep psychic disturbances and hallucinatory delirium could be induced in laboratory volunteers with approximately one two-millionth of a pound of the drug, which has been expressed as the rough equivalent of a single drop of rain stirred into a swimming pool.[24]

With this in mind, it may be possible to see the nineteenth-century German *Roggenmutter* stories as a simple warning to children of the potentially fatal danger hidden in the insignificant-looking fungus. The wolf would be an appropriate animal to use in such a story, especially in the Germanic world, for its ancient associations with death. However, there are other similar wolf figures in European folklore – the 'Green Wolf', 'Grass Wolf', 'Corn Wolf', 'Pea Wolf', and 'Bean Wolf' – whose connection with rye is less specific and who may be related to the old Germanic concept of the werewolf-outlaw, who might well have spent time hiding in the fields.[25] The *Roggenmutter* stories are in any case late, and are unconvincing evidence for the content of practices which were stamped out centuries earlier. Ginzburg also adduces the fact that the black fungal excrescence produced by ergot was known in Germany as 'wolf's tooth' (*Wolfzahn*), or merely *Wolf*, but these terms may have arisen purely from the appearance of the protruding sclerotium. It has occurred to several authorities that there could be some etymological connection between the Germanic combined term for werewolf and outlaw (German *warg*, Old Norse *vargr*) and the word 'ergot', but such a connection cannot be demonstrated. The Oxford English Dictionary states that the word 'ergot' derives from Old French *argot*, meaning the spur of a cock, which is a similative description of the physical appearance of the curved, protruding sclerotium just as apt as the German 'wolf's tooth'. The comparison with a cock's spur is widespread: ergotized rye is known as 'spurred rye' in England, and *ergoté* means both spurred and blighted by ergot in modern French.

Ginzburg's hypothesis that the fungus may have been deliberately used by individuals or small groups to induce ecstasy at least has the advantage that it gets away from the completely untenable idea that medieval and Renaissance werewolves could have been victims of large-scale epidemics of ergotism. Outbreaks of ergotism were always associated with the consumption of bread made with rye flour: indeed, it may have been the actual processes of milling, kneading, and baking which were responsible for the unravelling of the potentially lethal alkaloids from the comparatively benign ergot-base. This ensured that ergot-poisoning was characteristically suffered by groups of people rather than individuals. The milling of flour was one of the earliest 'industrialized' processes, the owner of the mill taking in raw materials from many sources, and producing from those materials a more or less uniform manufactured product. In some cases the supplier of the grain might insist on having his flour milled only from his own grain, but in the majority of cases, to save two trips to the mill as much as anything else, the grain supplier would accept someone else's flour that had already been milled. For those who did not grow their own grain, flour was simply purchased from the miller's surplus for cash or for other goods in kind. Given this processing and distribution system, it was inevitable that the effects of ergotized rye very rarely stayed confined to one family, let alone one individual, and that outbreaks of St Anthony's Fire should mostly be characterized as epidemics. The picture is very different with lycanthropy. Everything known about early-modern werewolves suggests that they were seen as individuals, as *loups-garoux*, solitary recluses, or as *vargr*, outlaws. Even the ancient Greek werewolf legends suggested that it was only one or two at any one time who were fated to wander in wolf-shape. Although some later traditions, particularly the Livonian tales, describe werewolves roaming abroad in their hundreds, these seem to be related to Germanic folk-beliefs in the Wild Hunt. Nor did the inquisitors of western Europe ever succeed in bringing to trial more than a few sad individuals: Boguet's three Gandillons represent one of the biggest recorded hauls.

In addition to this, many of the comparisons made between the behaviour of the ergot victims and that of werewolves are more than somewhat strained. The screams of ergot victims could possibly have been interpreted as wolfish howls, but there is little else to connect the two, in particular no suggestion of any physical resemblance of the victims to wolves. Any educated man aware of the classic medical description of 'melancholic lycanthropia' would never have confused the two conditions, as one of the characteristic symptoms of ergot-poisoning is excessive salivation leading to frothing at the mouth, whereas the melancholic lycanthrope is a dry-mouthed fellow, unable to produce saliva at all. Nor is there any record of such a confusion between ergotism and lycanthropy having been made by contemporary observers. Several sources mention that bystanders during outbreaks of St Anthony's Fire believed the sufferers to have been possessed by demons, but this was an idea constantly advanced to explain any or all forms of mental disturbances from the earliest times. It does not appear to have been shared by the victims themselves. In the Pont-Saint-Esprit outbreak, sufferers experienced lucid phases during which they were well able to recognize that they had been undergoing delusory states. Even if one of them had thought him- or herself a werewolf at the time (and it is worth repeating that none of them did), the delusion would not have persisted after the hallucinatory state had passed.

Similar objections apply to other diseases which have been advanced as leading to belief in werewolves. One such with a superficial likeness to lycanthropy is rabies, the terrible viral disease transmitted by the saliva of a rabid animal or human. In humans the symptoms of an attack of rabies include a feeling of apprehension, sensations of burning or tingling at the site of the bite, followed by periods of mania and convulsions. Although the rate of infection among persons bitten by a rabid animal is only about 40–50 per cent, once the symptoms have begun to show themselves, death is practically inevitable. It is the nature of the convulsions of a rabid patient that has attracted the werewolf theorists: these include muscular spasms, causing the jaws to snap open and shut and the head to jerk rapidly. The patient's voice may become hoarse, and he may emit strange noises during his spasms. As with ergot poisoning, foaming at the mouth is reported. The classic route for infection of humans is via the bite of a rabid dog, but the virus can produce disease in any warm-blooded animal, although degrees of susceptibility to it are known to vary among different animals; the opossum is one animal said to have a high degree of resistance. By contrast, the wolf seems to share the domestic canine's high rate of susceptibility. A rabid wolf is an especially fearsome creature, as its superior strength allows it to inflict great damage during its manic state: a single wolf has been recorded as biting twenty-nine people in one rampage.[26] There is also some evidence that wolf-bites lead to a higher rate of human mortality than dog-bites, with the rate going up as high as 60 per cent, probably because the wolf so often bites at the face or neck, thus depositing the virus nearer the brain than a bite on the limbs would do. One authority, writing in 1953, remarked that although wolves were responsible for only 0.1 per cent of rabid animal bites, they accounted for 6.8 per cent of human deaths.[27]

Nevertheless, those who point to such connections have to face one telling fact: rabies is a swift and certain killer. Once the symptoms have started to manifest themselves, although some patients might howl and snap their jaws in a faintly wolfish manner, death is no more than a few days away, and anybody who had seen a neighbour or family member suffering the final throes of the disease would know that. There is no such element of sudden fatality in the werewolf legend: in fact, one of its chief features is that the situation continues over many years and can only be extirpated by magical remedies. The werewolf does not die from his condition, but must be cured or killed by an outside agent, whether a Gascon peasant armed with a blood-rusted key or a Jura demonologist with the Bible in one hand and burning faggots in the other. Furthermore, rabies was not in any way mysterious or esoteric: as Robert Burton wrote in his *Anatomy of Melancholy*, published in 1624, 'Hydrophobia [rabies] is a kind of madness well known in every village, which comes by the biting of a mad dog.' Preventative measures against rabies had been written into the Babylonian legal code by about 2300 BC, and most physicians from the earliest times onwards described the disease in clear and relatively knowledgeable detail. It is a safe assumption that any medieval or early-modern European, no matter how ill-educated or ignorant, would have known what the result of a bite from a foam-flecked dog's jaws was likely to be, and would not have confused that swiftly fatal result with lycanthropy.

One popular theory which avoids associating lycanthropy with a common and well-understood disease was first advanced by the British neurologist Dr L. Illis.[28] Dr Illis speculated that some alleged werewolves may have been suffering from the rare genetic disorder, congenital porphyria. Congenital porphyria involves a failure of the bone marrow to function properly. Its visible manifestations include a reddish-brown pigmentation of the patient's urine and, sometimes, teeth, and dramatic discoloration of the patient's skin. The discoloration of the skin is related to the porphyric's severe sensitivity to light, as a result of which lesions form on the skin, sometimes accompanied by hypertrichosis (excess hair), leading eventually to ulcers which may attack the sufferer's cartilage and bone. Left untreated, this ulceration will eventually mutilate the porphyric, eating away at the extremities such as the nose, ears, eyelids, or fingers, ultimately giving the poor sufferer a gruesome appearance. Dr Illis adduces a number of interesting features of the disease, including the fact that it is particularly prevalent in a number of mountainous areas in Switzerland and Sweden. He also notes that the porphyric's skin pigmentation and hypertrichosis resulting from exposure to sunlight will be especially noticeable in such mountainous regions, and remarks that the nervous manifestations of the condition include a wide range of mental disorders. He asks what impression such a person – red-toothed, passing red urine, mutilated in hands and face, perhaps wandering about at night to avoid the sunlight, exhibiting more or less deranged behaviour – may have had on a superstitious rural population in an isolated mountainous region.

Dr Illis's ingenious theory is hampered by the lack of anything lupine about it. His porphyrics do not really look like wolves, although they may have some patches of excess facial hair, nor do they behave like wolves. While the presence in the community of such 'monsters' could certainly strengthen ideas relating to lycanthropy, it cannot be said to account for their origins, for it does not follow that the progressive slow deterioration of a porphyric would necessarily lead to the invention of a legend in which a man was periodically transformed into a wolf. Equally the presence in the community of all manner of 'hairy people' reinforced, but did not give rise to, werewolf beliefs. One boy suffering quite remarkable hypertrichosis, known as Jo Jo, the Russian Dog Face Boy, was a famous attraction at Barnum's circus in the late nineteenth century. In the summer of 1991 the English tabloid press worked up a story out of the case of two hypertrichotic Mexicans, Larri and Danni Ramos-Gomez, who had been refused work permits to appear at a Blackpool circus, where they were billed as the Werewolf Kids, on the grounds that their acrobatic act constituted a 'freak show'.[29] In both these cases, the public already knew the basic shape of the werewolf legend and paid out good money to see whimsical confirmation of its 'truth'.

One tangential issue arising from the werewolf legend which has received some scientific attention is the question of the influence of the full moon on human behaviour. The belief that the phases of the moon have such an influence is ancient, enshrined not only in the werewolf legend but also in long-held views of the nature of mental illness, or 'lunacy'. Until 1808, the infamous Bedlam Hospital in London had programmes for beating patients at certain phases of the lunar cycle in order to prevent violent episodes. Other illnesses were also attributed to the moon: the Italian word for influence is supposed to have given rise to the naming of 'influenza', from the supposition that incidence of flu epidemics had something to do with the moon. The notion that the moon might have some influence over human behaviour is not as far-fetched as these examples may make it seem. The earth has a powerful geomagnetic field which the moon modulates during its monthly twenty-nine-and-a-half day cycle, with the effect reaching its greatest intensity at full moon, and this geomagnetic field could conceivably act upon the human biological system and influence its functions. Lunar influence has been demonstrated in many biological systems – in plants, fish, rodents and other animals, and in some aspects of human biology, including post-operative haemorrhaging.

Nevertheless, it has proved much harder to demonstrate lunar influence on wider aspects of human behaviour. One study, made in 1965, used psychiatric hospital admissions and ward behaviour statistics as a picture of extremes of human behaviour, correlating them against a range of geophysical parameters, and found no evidence at all of correlation between lunar cycles and these measures of human behaviour. In 1985 the psychologists Rotton and Kelly published an overview of recent lunar research, 'Much ado about the full moon',[30] in which they argued vigorously that none of the various pieces of research could reliably posit any connection between the phases of the moon and incidences of psychiatric disturbance. Undaunted, some diehard supporters of the lunar hypothesis have pointed out that the effect

of the full moon on the earth's geomagnetic field varies considerably according to its celestial latitude, and that as most statistics
thus far gathered have paid no attention to this factor, there may
be better work to come on this subject.[31] Nevertheless, it is clear
that even if the moon's influence over human behaviour were
eventually to be demonstrated, the effect would prove to be an
extremely subtle one, certainly too subtle to be observed even by
the most careful human doctor using only his clinical experience.
The ancient association of mental disturbance with the phases of
the moon could not therefore have been based on empirical
observation, but was more likely based on the mythical associations between the moon-goddess and the animalistic ecstasies of
the hunter.

In the process begun by Weyer in the sixteenth century and
continued by many medical writers to the present day, the doctor
has come to assume some of the traditional functions of the
witch-hunter. It is by no means necessary to take the same
jaundiced view of this victory as Thomas Szasz did in the 1960s,
for in acquiring the witch-hunter's mantle, the modern doctor
has substituted the desire to cure through diagnosis and allevia-
tion of pain in this world for the demonologists' desire to 'cure'
the patient by dispatching him to the next, a change which can
only be seen as an improvement. Nowadays, in the West at least,
anybody who insists that he or she is a werewolf is examined by
a doctor, and will with luck find themselves treated by the learned
and compassionate doctors of such institutions as McLean
Hospital. But, in terms of modern understanding of the historical
phenomenon that is the werewolf, a certain price has been paid
for the gain. The attempts to give retrospective pharmacological
and medical explanations for werewolf beliefs generally betray a
crucial disregard for the mythical and religious beliefs of the time.
On the one hand, pharmacological-medical theories give the
medieval and early-modern peasant credit for not holding 'superstitious' beliefs, and place the blame squarely on the witch-
hunters for imposing the idea of lycanthropy on mentally-sick or
narcotic-deranged members of the community. Yet, on the
other, such theories imply that the average member of that
community was so ill-educated and unworldly that practically all
manifestations of derangement, even those with such a well-
known aetiology as rabies, were attributed to the mythical

process of lycanthropy. Yet it is plain that the werewolf legend has ancient roots of such richness and complexity that it is unnecessary, even misleading, to refer to this or that mental or physical condition to explain it. The conditions suggested in the pharmacological or medical theories examined here may have *reinforced* pre-existent belief, but each condition is, by itself, inadequate to explain the legend's origins.

12

Howling All the Way to the Bank

I used to be a werewolf, but I'm better
now-ooooooooooooow!
Very old joke

In 1941 Universal Studios, the undisputed kings of Gothic
horror since such box-office smashes as *Dracula* and *Frankenstein*
(both 1931) and many successful sequels, released their second
attempt to bring the legend of the werewolf to the cinema screen.
Six years earlier, the same studio's *Werewolf of London* had been
a commercial but not an artistic success, and now one of
Universal's prolific screenwriters, Curt Siodmak, thought that he
had some new ideas that might elevate the basic story of a man
changing into a wolf from a simple essay in trick photography
to the status of modern myth. The new movie was not to be the
most expensive horror film ever made, nor the best designed or
acted, but it largely achieved its aims: *The Wolf Man* became
the definitive cinematic treatment of the werewolf legend. That
in doing so it introduced a great number of new elements
completely alien to the folkloric and historical tradition was,
of course, of not the slightest concern to anyone associated with
it.

The star of the film was a lumbering hulk of a man, born
Creighton Chaney. Creighton's father was Lon Chaney, the
leading light of silent horror, whose innovative make-up techniques and willingness to suffer pain for his art were legendary.
One of his favourite techniques was to imitate an amputee by
binding his calves up against the backs of his thighs and hobbling
around on his knees. For his Quasimodo in *The Hunchback of
Notre Dame*, he strapped himself into a harness and rubber hump

weighing some seventy pounds, which prevented him walking upright. For *The Phantom of the Opera*, he inserted wires into his nose to flare the nostrils and pull back the tip, wire springs up under the bony ridges of his eyesockets to pull the lids back from his eyeballs, and prongs inside his mouth to stretch the corners. The final effect was that of a hideously grinning skull, one of the most memorable images of the silent cinema. Lon had always attempted to dissuade Creighton from taking film work, and Creighton made a slow start in his chosen career after his father's death in 1930. Things picked up after the expiry of his RKO contract in 1935, when he took the name Lon Chaney Junior, evoking the glorious memories of his father's impressively masochistic career in horror films.

Lon Chaney Junior's particular qualities, the combination of a brutish physical appearance with his mild, boyish nature, were to be crucial in the establishment of the cinematic werewolf, for Siodmak understood that a werewolf had to be human first and lupine a distant second. In an unwitting revival of the twelfth-century werewolf romances, the lycanthrope was about to become sympathetic once more. *The Wolf Man* tells the story of Larry, played by Chaney, who returns to the family home in Wales after many years spent in America (thus giving an alibi for Chaney's gruff Americanisms), to take up his responsibilities as the only remaining son of Sir John Talbot (played by Claude Rains). Larry takes a fancy to a local girl, Gwen, who works in an antique shop in the village. Mooching around the shop in the hope of meeting her, Larry finds an ornate walking stick with an unusual design on its silver top, a wolf's head carved inside a five-sided star. Gwen explains that the pentagram is the sign of the werewolf, and Larry buys the cane as a curiosity. He also gets Gwen to agree to come on a date with him to the gypsy fair that evening, despite the fact that she is engaged to be married to Frank, the son of Sir John's gamekeeper. Gwen brings along her friend Jennie as chaperone, and the three set off for an evening's entertainment.

At the fair Jennie visits a gypsy fortune-teller played by Bela Lugosi (the character's name is also Bela, one of those self-referential jokes the horror film has always favoured), who sees the dreaded pentagram in her palm and warns her to escape. Jennie foolishly ignores the warning and is attacked by a wolf – an

Alsatian dog, actually, but the audience knows what is meant. Larry steps forward with his silver-topped cane to beat off the 'wolf', but is bitten himself in the scuffle. The next day, Larry awakes to find a pentagram marked on his chest. His father tells him that Bela's dead body has been discovered with the silver-topped cane near him. All this seems to affect Larry badly: he can't concentrate on anything or enunciate his confused feelings, and when he tries a little recreational shooting at the fair he is alarmed to see that the target is a wolf. Eventually he seeks out the help of gypsy Queen Malvena, who elucidates the details of what for Larry (but not for the audience) has been dim and murky thus far: her son Bela was a werewolf, and now that he has bitten Larry, Larry is fated to become one too. She supplies him with an apotropaic against this terrible destiny, a pendant with the sign of a pentagram, but he, like the good-natured dimwit that he is, gives it to Gwen. That night, undressing for bed, Larry is transformed for the first time, perhaps surprisingly not into an Alsatian like Bela, but into a Wolf Man, a two-legged monster with yak-hair creeping down his forehead and cheeks, fangs jutting up from his lower jaw, and hairy paws.

The pace is fast and furious as the Wolf Man rampages around Hollywood's idea of Wales for the next two nights. At one stage he is caught in a trap but manages to escape with Malvena's help. During the day he visits his beloved Gwen, who makes it fairly clear that she is still planning to marry Frank. Larry sees a pentagram in her hand, and remembers that Bela had seen the pentagram in Jennie's hand just before attacking her. With a terrible sense of foreboding, Larry returns to the castle and pleads with his father to lock him up for the night. Sir John refuses, but does agree to take from him the wolf-headed, silver-topped walking stick.

The finale comes in a fog-shrouded forest at night. Sir John has joined the wolf-hunters, Larry is after Gwen, and Gwen, despite a fairly explicit warning from Malvena, just happens to decide to take a little stroll in the woods. Obviously torn between human scruples and bestial desires, Larry lumbers hesitantly through the mist towards Gwen, who faints in his arms. Before his rubber fangs can tear into her soft, delicate flesh, Sir John enters and draws himself to his full height (still about twelve inches shorter than Larry) and clubs him to death with the silver-topped walking stick. As the life force ebbs away, Larry's human features reform. Malvena appears from nowhere, and cradles the dying boy in her arms, whispering gypsy consolations in his ear. Sir John, distraught at having killed his own son, is led off into the billowing dry ice, while the police inspector delivers the official verdict on the case: Larry is a hero, killed by a wolf when he tried to rescue Gwen from its attack.

The Wolf Man is in essence the key generating text for the modern figure of the werewolf, making the werewolf almost unique among the classic figures of horror film in having a purely cinematic rather than literary pedigree. The other big two of Universal horror, Dracula and Frankenstein's monster, could each trace their literary origins back to that famous evening at the Villa Diodati on the shores of Lake Geneva in June 1816 which saw the genesis of Mary Shelley's *Frankenstein* (1818) and Polidori's *The Vampyre* (1819), while the figure of the vampire received further and definitive literary treatment in Bram Stoker's *Dracula* (1897). By contrast, the werewolf was sadly shortchanged by the nineteenth-century Gothic novelists, who appeared to have regarded shape-shifting as suitable only for minor characters, such as the lycanthrope in Charles Maturin's *The Albigenses* (1824).

The earliest attempt to buck this trend was George W. M. Reynolds' *Wagner, the Wehr-Wolf*, of 1857, in which for the first time the eponymous hero is a werewolf. The attempt is a failure for a number of reasons, not least for the fact that Reynolds constructed a plot of such immense variety (not complexity) that Wagner keeps disappearing from the scene while the rest of the characters are put through their paces. After his first wolfish episode, for example, Wagner is falsely accused of murder and thrown into gaol. Then follow forty-three closely printed pages in double column in which Reynolds luxuriates in a lurid sub-plot describing a subterranean convent full of bare-breasted nuns whipping each other, without a word about Wagner. On the occasions when Wagner does come to the fore, Reynolds does not have anything particularly interesting for his werewolf to do. Wagner has been inflicted with this dread condition through a Faustian bargain with the devil, for the date of the story is 1520, and this Wagner is the former servant of that famous Faust who sold his soul to the devil. Although historical accuracy is no great recommendation in horror fiction, Reynolds has homed in on more or less the right period for the Renaissance werewolf-craze, and the pact with the devil is appropriate enough for the story. As a reward for acting as Faust's servant for the last eighteen months of the wicked Doctor's life, Wagner, in reality a ninety-year-old man, has been granted youth, good looks, and great wealth, but each month he must rage around in the shape of a wolf. Reynolds seems loath to have his hero do anything so disgusting as eat or even bite people, so the 'wehrwolf' simply runs and runs and runs, knocking down anybody in his way. Admittedly this causes some satisfactorily gory havoc, especially in his first rampage when he barges into a funeral cortege of monks, dashing out the brains of one of them against a gravestone, and spilling the corpse from the coffin, but the excitement generated by this brief lycanthropic episode quickly fades. In the longest section of the book, Wagner is shipwrecked on an uninhabited island with his buxom lover Nisida, who does not know his terrible secret. Reynolds explains that, in order to keep her in the dark, each month Wagner climbs over the mountains in the middle of island (something he can only do in human form, apparently) and rages harmlessly on the other side. The lack of excitement stems from the fact that, in his wolf guise, Wagner is never brought into close contact with anyone who matters to him.

Reynolds also seems uneasy with other aspects of the legend. He has understood that the change is supposed to take place monthly, but instead of the traditional and ominous full moon acting as the natural signal for the transformation, he has Wagner become a werewolf on the last day of each month. When the action has moved to the island, where it is unclear how Wagner could have kept any kind of calendar without consulting the moon, Reynolds explains that Nisida did not notice that Wagner's trips over the mountains were taking place on a regular basis, evidently serenely unaware that a woman would be more than likely to recognize something running to a monthly timetable. In fact, the whole novel operates on an unnatural time scheme, blind to anything but the calendars and clocks of the industrial-ized nineteenth century. Even though the action is supposed to take place in the early sixteenth century, many of the characters are continually glancing at the clock (a water clock, Reynolds explains, careful to commit no outright anachronism).

Wagner's lycanthropic curse is eventually lifted by the bizarre combination of having resisted the devil three times and visiting the founder of the Rosicrucian order (don't ask), who tells him that the spell 'shall be broken only on that day and in that hour when thine eyes shall behold the bleached skeletons of two innocent victims suspended to the same beam'. It is a mark of Reynolds' lack of interest in Wagner's transformation from man to wolf that the eradication of his curse should have nothing to do with the lupine motif. Wagner sees the bleached skeletons (the product of another sub-plot), ages rapidly to his true hundred years or more, and expires on the floor, more Dorian Gray than Wolf Man, leaving Reynolds and the reader to plod through another eighteen pages of concluding plot without another mention of werewolves.

Although his book is not very interesting, the nature of Reynolds' failure is instructive. First, he did not succeed in establishing many ingredients that could be universally applied to other werewolf stories, either by stage melodramas or by the cinema. In particular, the idea that the curse of the werewolf could be lifted by seeing two skeletons swinging from a beam was solely related to the plotline of that individual novel. This is no good to the seeker after the horrific and the sublime, who always wants only some slight variation within an unchanging framework of established 'myth'. In the cases of Dracula and Frankenstein's monster, for instance, the cinema took its stories and motifs not directly from the literary originals, but from the melodramas adapted from them which were so successful on the nineteenth-century stage. The key to these melodramatic reconstructions was that they simplified and codified the complex and contradictory folkloric and literary material. Unlike the messy confusion of alternative remedies which de Tournefort had come across on eighteenth-century Mykonos, for example, the melodramas established that from now on a vampire would always turn into a bat (which was easier to simulate on stage than a wolf – a flash of smoke, a trapdoor for the actor, and a bit of black paper fluttering on invisible wire did the trick), would always shy away from garlic and the Cross, and would only die when staked through the heart.

It was exactly this kind of element that Curt Siodmak's screenplay for *The Wolf Man* succeeded in establishing for the first time in the werewolf legend. The gypsy lore of the film, for example, is entirely his invention, notably the famous quatrain:

> Even a man who's pure at heart
> And says his prayers at night
> May become a wolf when the wolfbane blooms
> And the autumn moon is bright.

Siodmak's contrivances were so successful that they are often quoted as authentic gypsy lore, and they became standard fare in werewolf movies – in *I was a Teenage Werewolf* (1957), for example, which in all other respects does without the mythic paraphenalia, the immigrant office-cleaner at the police precinct who recognizes the signs of a werewolf is from the Carpathian mountains. Historically, gypsies did believe in werewolves, but then so did most Europeans. In narrowing the origin of the belief down to them alone, Siodmak was playing up to the popular preconception of the gypsies as a race still in touch with ancient magical traditions. (He was also following the earlier *Werewolf of London*, in which the hero's nemesis is a lycanthropic doctor from the University of Carpathia.) It is less clear why the film should be set in Wales. One likes to think that Siodmak was aware of the fourteenth-century Welsh tale of *Arthur and Gorlagon*, but it's a fond hope.

The function of the sign of the pentagram, another of Siodmak's inventions, is more complex. The pentagram has nothing at all to do with the werewolf of legend: it is a symbol traditionally inscribed inside their magic circles by practitioners of the occult arts. Siodmak was not worried by that, however. His purpose in introducing it to *The Wolf Man* was twofold. He needed some unique apotropaic, both for Gwen to wear for protection, and to imbue the silver-headed walking stick with extra magical power against the werewolf – the pentagram is the equivalent of the garlic and the sign of the Cross in the Dracula cinematic tradition. But the pentagram appearing in the hands of potential victims, or on the chest of the future werewolf, also acts as a forewarning, a kind of mute Greek chorus prophesying doom. Again a comparison can be found in the Dracula myth, where the same function is performed by the ominous neck-punctures and pallid faces of the young ladies of the house. Without such signs of impending catastrophe there can be no tension, and without tension there would be no horror movie.

The mingling of tension and pathos aroused by *The Wolf Man* and its descendants depends finally on the cinematic convention that the bite of another werewolf inevitably inflicts the dread curse. This was not Siodmak's invention; *The Werewolf of London* had already established the idea. In the 1935 film the hero, played by Henry Hull, is Dr Glendon, who visits Tibet in search of the *Mariphasa lupino lumino* plant, a rare and strange (and entirely fictitious) flower that blooms in moonlight: a prick of its pollen thorn is the antidote to lycanthropy. On his trail is the gypsy doctor Yogami, who is himself a werewolf and wants the plant to sort out his own problem. In Tibet Yogami switches to werewolf mode and bites the good doctor, thereby inflicting the curse on him, although Glendon seems to be safe because he is able to take a cutting of the plant back to England and grow it in his laboratory. But Yogami follows him back and steals the plant, a foolish thing to do, it transpires, as Glendon then transforms into a werewolf and kills Yogami.

The idea that lycanthropy is like an infectious disease, transmitted from werewolf to innocent person, is essential to the cinematic conception of the werewolf. In *Wagner*, Reynolds had already tried the ancient idea that the werewolf brought the curse upon himself, and it hadn't worked. Much of the blame for this probably lies in his choice of the old witch-hunters' cliché of the pact with the devil. Great art can be made from the Faustian theme, but Reynolds was not up to the standards of Marlowe, Goethe, or Thomas Mann, nor did the Universal screenwriters feel drawn in this direction. If treated seriously, such a theme must inevitably leave the audience out of sympathy with the main character, or at least fully understanding why he remains damned. In the cinematic werewolf legend, on the other hand, the pathos comes from the fact that the character suffers out of all proportion to any wrongdoing, or, as Malvena puts it so much more lyrically to Larry in *The Wolf Man*, 'The way you walk is thorny through no fault of your own, but as the rain enters the soil, the river enters the sea, so tears run to a predestined end.' The werewolf has found himself in the wrong place at the wrong time, and when he does finally die, he is not damned, but released from his suffering.

However, Siodmak's greatest contribution to the cinematic

werewolf was to realize his true age, for his werewolf-hero is not a hundred-year-old man like Wagner, nor an adult doctor like Hull's Glendon. Although at the age of thirty-five Chaney may not look like it, Larry is the archetypal teenager. He is the younger son suddenly come into his inheritance, and unsure about it. He is having trouble fitting in to his new milieu – 'I can work only with my hands', he warns his father, who evidently resents having to go to the trouble of making Larry face the adult responsibilities of running the family castle. His chief interest is that of any red-blooded American male adolescent – girls – and his troubles really arise when he sets his cap at a girl he can't have, someone else's fiancée. Of course, all horror cinema is adolescent: its target audience is adolescent and its founding texts were products of the adolescent imagination (Mary Shelley was nineteen when she wrote *Frankenstein*). As a result, the more successful horror archetypes explore themes of particular interest to the intended audience. For example, at one level Dracula works as a fable of sexual initiation: the girls must learn to resist their sexual feelings for the father-figure of Dracula (feelings which, if acted upon, will lead to bad blood in every sense), transferring them to their proper boyfriends, and accepting in Dracula's place the appropriately non-sexual father represented by Van Helsing; the boys must use their best endeavours, and any stakes that happen to be lying around, to ensure that this transference is made successfully. Frankenstein's subtext is the attempt by a young male to evade his adult responsibilities by attempting to reproduce non-sexually: the doctor, usually played in the early Universal series by a youthful Colin Clive, is forever spurning his wife's attempts to get him to abandon his laboratory, where he is having too much fun attempting to do with electricity and a boxful of spare parts from the local graveyard what Elizabeth is quite capable of doing naturally, if only he would come out of the lab and spend a quiet evening alone with her.

In *The Wolf Man*, Larry's problems with the trials of adolescence seem to arise from what a social worker would call his dysfunctional family. Larry has neither a surviving elder brother nor, we assume, since she is never mentioned in the film, a mother. Instead he has a surrogate mother in Malvena, who calls him 'my son' at every opportunity, commiserates with him on his sad fate, and saves his life when his leg is caught in the wolf-trap, and a surrogate brother in Malvena's real son, Bela, who, instead of teaching Larry how to behave with girls and other things a big brother ought to do, inducts him into the ancient fraternity of werewolves with his bite. Siodmak's Wolfman is the original mixed-up kid, the eternal male adolescent, with only a single familial male role model in Sir John, who is distant and patrician to a fault. From this angle, Larry's outbreaks of lycanthropy can be seen as a product of his male-dominated family. His are natural but excessive masculine drives, inappropriately directed and dangerously overpowering.

This is an interpretation of the werewolf to which the cinema has returned over and over again, never more enticingly expressed than in the title of *I was a Teenage Werewolf*. The hero of that film, Tony (played by teen heart-throb Michael Landon), has the same kind of minimal family as Larry's, except that his widower-father is blue collar, works nights, and so cannot give him the attention he needs ('I should have married again,' Tony's father tells the concerned policeman). As this is the 1950s, Tony expresses his alienation by fighting and going to bongo parties. Although his lycanthropic transformation is actually wrought by an ill-advised course of treatment from a wonderful mad scientist, who babbles about recapturing the primitive and injects Tony with scopolamine (the pharmacological theory of lycanthropy returns here), the film repeatedly signals the real cause of Tony's lycanthropy from the beginning with a number of not-so-subtle forewarnings: Tony loses his temper a lot, likes his hamburgers raw, and so on. The point is bludgeoned home when Tony's final transformation is triggered by seeing a nubile young beauty in a leotard bending over backwards from a piece of equipment in the school gym.

This interpretation of the werewolf legend was taken probably as far as it can go in *Teen Wolf* (1985), where the changes of lycanthropy – strange body hair, growling voice, greater physical strength, urges towards sexuality and irresponsible behaviour – are used solely as a metaphor for the changes of puberty. The traditional elements have almost disappeared, apart from one or two playful references to eating chickens and the obligatory shot of the full moon. The hero Scott (played by another teen heart-throb, Michael J. Fox) once again has only a father for family, although, as this is a comedy, Dad is the kind of gosh-darn-I'm-so-understanding father every teenager is supposed to want. Dad also happens to be a werewolf himself, for in this film there is no need for the bite of another werewolf, or a pact with the devil – the change is hereditary and just happens at a certain age. 'Why didn't you prepare me for this?' Scott wails to his dad, upset to see from his reflection in the mirror that, instead of teenage pimples, he has broken out in yak hair. 'I wasn't sure it would happen to you; sometimes it skips a generation,' his dad murmurs in self-exculpation. Puberty has transformed Scott into a 'wolf', and he has to learn to regulate his new powers, including his new-found prowess at basketball. (Why a wolf should be good at basketball is anyone's guess.) He is able to control his transformation once he has faced his adult responsibilities, resisted his best friend's entrepreneurial desire to make a fast buck out of Teen Wolf T-shirts, stopped surfing on the roof of his van, chosen the right girl, and so on. *Teen Wolf Too* (1986) is practically a carbon-copy of the first film, with the hero now at college, notable only for the fact that instead of basketball the featured sport is boxing, obviously a reference to the ancient Arcadian legend of Damarchus.

Having located the werewolf in eternal puberty, *The Wolf Man* also established how each of these *angst*-ridden teenagers should look. It goes without saying that the cinematic werewolf does not look very much like a wolf. The use of a real wolf had been tried by the Canadian director Henry McRae in his 1913 short *The Werewolf*, in which Watuma, a white-hating half-caste Navajo, was transformed via a simple dissolve into a timber wolf, but the real animal was neither scary nor unsympathetic enough for the purposes of later film-makers. Seen close to, the wolf has an appealing demeanour, especially when it is making the classic wolf-gesture of appeasement, with gracefully lowered head and sidelong glances, to its animal-handler just off camera. Even in a film like *The Company of Wolves* (UK, 1984), which used packs of 'wolves' running through a moonlit forest, their eyes flashing with reflected light, the effect was alluring rather than horrific. The idea that a werewolf should not look like a real wolf has been by no means confined to twentieth-century film-makers. By the sixteenth century, it had become popular to describe werewolves as differing in some way from real wolves: the most common distinguishing mark was said to be that a werewolf has no tail. The reason for this is obvious: when a wolf was alleged to be a man supernaturally transformed, there was no better way of 'proving' that it was really a werewolf than by insisting on some mark of its oddity. One adolescent girl testifying against Jean Grenier corroborated her own evidence by saying that the wolf she saw had no tail, and its hair was red, like Jean's. Taillessness performed the same function as the more traditional sympathetic wound: what else was one to say if the alleged werewolf had no wounds when he was arrested?

Jack Pierce's Wolfman make-up for Lon Chaney Junior has caused some hilarity among sophisticated viewers, yet most of the werewolf films over the next three decades followed it very closely. (Incidentally, the make-up introduced another layer of myth to the cinematic werewolf, in which ludicrous anecdotes about the pain Chaney endured during the filming of his trans-formation scenes were circulated, including one in which it was alleged that Chaney's hands had to be nailed to the table to keep him absolutely motionless for the stop-action sequences – suspi-ciously reminiscent of tales of his famous father's masochism.) *Après* Pierce, the cinematic werewolf usually has fangs protruding up from his lower jaw (although Michael Landon was a snaggle-toothed exception to the rule), a great deal of facial hair, and furry, clawed hands. He walks upright on two feet, with an odd, crouching gait which has more of the ape about it than the wolf. He is always fully clothed, even though, as in *The Wolf Man*, he might have been half undressed when the transformation over-came him. It was only in the 1980s, when make-up artists Rick Baker and Rob Bottin used pneumatically operated masks to give the illusion of a wolf's maw bursting out through the human face, that cinematic werewolves began to look anything like wolves, and even then, in *The Howling* (1981) at least, they seem to prefer to move around on two legs. The first film since the earliest days of cinema to have the werewolf-hero dropping to all fours was *An American Werewolf in London* (1979), although a single shot of the beast as seen from the top of a London Underground escalator reveals it to be more monstrous than natural wolf. (The same film makes a further and welcome return to the folkloric core by having the hero tear his clothes off, so that, for once, the werewolf is naked. The resurrection of this motif has a further comic benefit when the hero wakes up after an evening's flesh-rending in the wolf-house of London Zoo and has to find a way to get back home across London without clothes.)

For some idea why the cinematic werewolf looks as he does, consider the facial make-up of Henry Hull for the title role in *The Werewolf of London*, Jack Pierce's first attempt at the job. Hull's werewolf has much less facial hair than Chaney's Wolfman. His sideburns are a little excessive perhaps, and a deep widow's peak extends down his forehead almost to the line of his eyebrows, but the rest of his face is clean-shaven. His ears are not furry, but pointed and bent out at the top. From the state of his putty nose, one would guess he puts in some heavy sparring now and then. Two large eye-teeth extend upwards from his jutting lower jaw. Some comparisons immediately spring to mind: the first with Dracula, who shares the widow's peak and twin fangs, the main difference being that Hull's werewolf has the fangs in upside down; the second with Fredric March's Hyde in the 1932 *Dr Jekyll and Mr Hyde*.

The connection with Hyde is not purely fortuitous, since one reason that no literary text in the nineteenth century was wholly successful in portraying the figure of the werewolf may have been that Robert Louis Stevenson had hit on an almost perfect re-rendering of the ancient myth in *The Strange Case of Dr Jekyll and Mr Hyde* (1886), which seemed suddenly to make the werewolf-as-morality-tale redundant. There were, of course, many werewolf stories published both before and after Stevenson's alternative version, but many of the nineteenth-century efforts, even the better attempts like Clemence Housman's *The Were-Wolf* (1896), laid on the pseudo-historical colouring with a trowel and so kept the whole subject distanced from the reader.[1]

Stevenson's fable brought the werewolf into the nineteenth century, and put the psychological implications of the legend to the fore – the recognition of the beast within us all, the difficulty of reconciling primitive urges with civilized notions of propriety, the dangers of unleashing repressed desires. In order to plunge his hero into the accursed role of shape-shifter, Stevenson revived the Faustian theme of the man seeking forbidden knowledge, but sensibly kept the supernatural figure of Satan out of it, giving the story a serious moral force which has eluded most makers of werewolf films. Hyde as he appears in the story is the perfect half man, half animal for the modern age. He is undoubtedly bestial

– in one fine image, Jekyll speaks of 'the animal within me licking the chops of memory' – but not so bestial that he cannot move unmolested through a modern city. Jekyll often refers to his *alter ego* as 'ape-like', but Hyde is clearly human: 'He is not easy to describe,' one witness says. 'There is something wrong with his appearance; something displeasing, something downright detestable. I never saw a man I so disliked, and yet I scarce know why. He must be deformed somewhere; he gives a strong feeling of deformity, although I couldn't specify the point. He's an extraordinary-looking man, and yet I really can name nothing out of the way.' Interestingly, Hyde is younger and physically smaller than Jekyll in the book, almost Jekyll as he was as an adolescent, a point which is nearly always lost in filmed versions of the Jekyll and Hyde tale but which found an echo in the teenage cinematic werewolf.

Jekyll and Hyde was the most frequently filmed story in the early years of the cinema. It offered unrivalled opportunities for fine actors like John Barrymore, whose 1920 Hyde was an oddly spiderish *tour de force*, and for inventive directors like Rouben Mamoulian, whose 1932 version was the first talking Jekyll and Hyde and still remains a classic of the genre. Something like a dozen versions of the story were made in the first two decades of the century, and in all but one of them a single actor was used to portray the two sides of Jekyll's personality. The most effective scene in nearly all these films is the climactic moment when, thanks to trick photography displaying varying degrees of technical expertise, the face of the dying Hyde returns to that of the good doctor. Given such a well-established and popular motif, it was inevitable that every werewolf film made from *The Werewolf of London* onwards should follow in Jekyll and Hyde's well-worn footsteps and show the human features of the hero returning in death.

The reciprocal influence between the cinematic werewolf and Jekyll and Hyde is shown in many other ways. For obvious reasons, Stevenson's description of the evanescent quality of Hyde's unpleasant physical appearance could not be reproduced on screen, and most Jekyll and Hyde transformations were unsubtle affairs, involving liberal use of make-up and prosthetic devices. (When, in 1941, Spencer Tracy attempted a Hyde without the use of anything of that sort he was greeted with derisive reviews and Somerset Maugham's overheard query while visiting the set, 'Which is he now, Jekyll or Hyde?') It was generally preferred to have Hyde as ostentatiously repulsive as possible, and a strong visual expression of his bestiality was the obvious road to go down, Barrymore settling for a tarantula, while March picked up the 'ape-like' hints from the text to produce a noticeably simian Hyde. But the cinematic werewolf offered another possible template, and lupine Hydes appear in a number of later movies, such as *Abbott and Costello Meet Dr Jekyll and Mr Hyde* (1953), *Daughter of Dr Jekyll* (1957), and, as the title makes plain, the Spanish *Dr Jekyll and the Werewolf* (1971). Conversely, Henry Hull's Dr Glendon is clearly Dr Jekyll by another name: he even has the same mad scientist's laboratory at the back of his London townhouse.

Perhaps the most curious of such cross-fertilizations is the motif of the walking stick, the fatal weapon in *The Wolf Man*. As with the Dracula and Frankenstein films, filmed accounts of Stevenson's novella relied largely on popular melodramas derived from the book rather than on the original version itself, which in this case meant Thomas Sullivan's 1887 stage version. In the book Jekyll has no family, but for the stage Sullivan expanded the shadowy figure of Sir Danvers Carew into a full-blown father-in-law, whose lovely daughter is engaged to Jekyll. A favourite scene in many of the early Jekyll and Hyde films was Hyde brutally clubbing to death the irritating old man with his walking stick. This was presumably where Siodmak found the idea of the walking stick as fatal weapon, although in *The Wolf Man* the roles are reversed and it is the father who clubs the monstrous son to death. (The Freudian implications of this phallic violence are best left unanalysed.) The fact that its head should be made of silver is quite natural for a walking stick, but also has symbolic overtones, silver being an emblem of purity.

Curiously, the celebrated motif of the silver bullet, the most famous of all the generally recognized features of the cinematic werewolf, did not occur until the third Universal film in which Chaney's Wolfman appears, *House of Frankenstein* (1944), where again it is a gypsy, Larry's new girlfriend Iloka, who is wheeled on to authenticate the spurious folklore: a werewolf can only be killed, Iloka tells him, 'by a silver bullet fired from a gun in the hand of a woman who loves him'. Guess how Larry dies in that one. Such is the public awareness of the silver bullet motif that most modern werewolf films have fun subverting these expectations. When David, the American werewolf in London in the film of that name, sitting in a sex cinema in Piccadilly Circus surrounded by his undead victims, suggests using a silver bullet to kill himself, he gets a withering 'Oh be serious, would you?' from one of them – although the same film re-uses Siodmak's pentagram symbol without apparent irony. In *The Howling*, the werewolf-hunters manage to buy a full box of silver rifle-bullets from the cynical owner of an occult bookstore who had them made for one of his wackier clients and now can't get rid of them.

Once all the well-known aspects of the Wolfman had been brought together from their diverse sources, there was little for the studio to do but sit back and count the box-office receipts as Larry growled and lurched his way through a number of films in the company of varying combinations of the other Universal monsters, including Abbott and Costello. In these films, which are usually seen as a sad falling-off from a splendid beginning, Larry is alternately pathetic and heroic. He escapes a tragic death in only one of them, *House of Dracula* (1945; not written by Siodmak), where his lycanthropy is cured by a quick brain operation before the mad doctor's lab goes up in smoke, but he is back in wolfish guise in time for the next. The Wolfman was now a cinematic archetype, ripe for exploitation by anyone who could think of an unusual twist – a female werewolf in *Cry of the Werewolf* (1944); a mummified werewolf in *La Casa del Terror* (Mexico 1959: retitled *Face of the Screaming Werewolf* for the American market); a lycanthropic motorcycle gang in *Werewolves on Wheels* (1971) – and by some, like the makers of the dire *Lycanthropus* (Italy/Austria 1961: retitled *Werewolf in a Girl's Dormitory* for the US, and *I Married a Werewolf* in Britain), who couldn't.

An obvious response to a well-established convention is parody, and the cinematic werewolf has been parodied as much as any other horror monster. In the enjoyable *Werewolf of Washington* (1973), for example, the journalist-hero (Dean Stockwell) is bitten on a trip to Hungary and returns to the United States to mount a series of attacks in the nation's capital, including one on the President. Of course, most werewolf films are parodic to some degree, and even 1980s American werewolf films tended to be riddled with knowing references to the Wolfman archetype, undercutting the genuine horror built up by their technical expertise. Visual and musical puns abound in these films: *The Howling* has pictures of the young Lon Chaney Junior on the wall, Allen Ginsberg's *Howl* on the table, and the cartoon wolf in Disney's *Three Little Pigs* on television; *An American Werewolf in London* has a soundtrack consisting entirely of songs with 'moon' in the title. The unusual thriller *Wolfen* (1980) takes a different course towards subversion of the cinematic myth. The film starts out like an orthodox werewolf shocker. Bloody murders are being committed in a rundown modern city, and a policeman (played by Albert Finney) is told to investigate. Everything points to the involvement of werewolves. Some native Americans are obvious suspects. They taunt the Finney-character with boasts of their culturally inherited talent for shape-shifting. There is a superb scene in which Finney follows one of them to the shore, where the young man strips naked, and dances in the silvery light of the full moon, falling down on all fours to lick the reflection of the moon in a puddle. But the transformation never takes place. The murders are being committed not by werewolves, but by 'wolfen', mutant-descendants of wolves whose natural habitat has been destroyed and who lead a feral existence in the belly of the rotting city, feeding on the human flotsam ignored by a heartless social system.

The British have appeared much more willing than the Americans to play the werewolf straight, attempting in their film versions to return to the genuine folklore behind the legend. Probably the most successful effort in this direction is Hammer Studio's *Curse of the Werewolf* (UK, 1961). With the literariness that has always been at once the chief virtue and the besetting fault of the British film industry, Hammer's screenwriter Anthony Hinds (credited as John Elder) returned for his inspiration to the one modern werewolf text of any literary quality at all, Guy Endore's *Werewolf of Paris* (1933). But, in order to heighten the atmosphere of Catholic religiosity, his screenplay relocated the story from France to rural Spain, an unfortunate move from the point of view of authenticity, in that it leaves behind the *locus classicus* of the early-modern werewolf for one of the few countries in Europe with virtually no indigenous werewolf-lore. Nevertheless, the film has undoubted merits. Its chief concern is with the hereditary causes of lycanthropy. Probably no werewolf was ever more ill-omened than Oliver Reed's Leon, conceived through a rape inflicted on a deaf-mute serving wench by a crazed old beggar driven feral by prolonged isolation, and born on Christmas Day. To make matters worse, his mother dies shortly after giving birth to him (although she was given a curious new lease of life in the publicity stills for the film, in which she is shown being ravaged by her own werewolf-son, presumably because hers is by some way the biggest bosom in the cast), and Leon grows up with his eyebrows meeting in the middle. Naturally enough he's soon banging away at the bars on his bedroom window thoughtfully provided by his foster-parents, although they love him so much that his lycanthropic fits are kept to a minimum in childhood. His real troubles begin, as usual, when he sets out on the rocky path to adulthood, leaving home, getting a dead-end job in a winery, and, like Larry, falling in love with the wrong girl. The film is one of Hammer's best, straddling the unrelated demands of reasonably authentic folklore and box-office pull with some success, although many viewers probably felt slightly cheated by the fact that Reed's werewolf is only on the screen for the last five or so of the ninety-one minutes of the film. Curiously, thirteen years later the same screenwriter managed to concoct one of the dullest werewolf films ever made – *Legend of the Werewolf* (UK, 1974) – in which the only feature of any interest at all is that the hero becomes a werewolf because he was brought up by wolves.

Both these Hammer films have disappointingly traditional cinematic werewolves who walk upright and wear big white shirts. They have furry cheeks, but are clean-shaven around their putty noses, and their inverted Dracula fangs are basically no different from Henry Hull's in 1935. Technical improvements led to a later British werewolf film, *The Company of Wolves*, being able to try out a far greater range of special effects, with startling images galore – a man ripping off his own skin and turning into a flayed wolf; a wolf's head thrown into a bucket of milk floating to the surface as a human head; a wolf, fur and all, bursting out through a human mouth; a wolf's forepaw turning out to be a human hand. (This last ancient folk-motif seems to have been popular with 1980s film-makers: *The Howling* features a particularly gory visualization of it.) The whole script, adapted from

Angela Carter's story of the same title, is a folklorist's dream, dripping with wolf and werewolf lore. Here is Little Red Riding Hood being warned not to stray from the path, here is the Perrault–Grimm werewolf as seducer of pubescent girls, here is the young boy being given werewolf-ointment by the devil (played by Terence Stamp, driving up in a Rolls-Royce), here is the apposite biblical quotation, Isaiah 11:6, 'the wolf also shall dwell with the lamb, and the leopard shall lie down with the kid', and the old knowledge that a werewolf's eyebrows meet in the middle, that he is born feet first, that his fur grows on the inside. That all the elements do not quite cohere is probably due to the intricate construction of the dream-like screenplay, in which stories are placed inside stories and inside other stories again. Nevertheless, the film is an impressive and allusive footnote to the tradition of the cinematic werewolf.

13

The Tail of the Wolf

The pass was steep and rugged,
The wolves they howled and whined;
But he ran like a whirlwind up the pass,
And he left the wolves behind.

MACAULAY,
The Battle of Lake Regillus

And so in the end, despite the best efforts of the earnest British cinema, the werewolf has become something of a joke. The few 'facts' the general public knows about the figure were mostly invented by a Hollywood screenwriter churning out horror films for a teenage audience, and the image of the werewolf, or Wolfman, as visualized by Jack Pierce is available for comic manipulation in a variety of media: in circus entertainments, in advertising, on television.

The alternative folkloric tradition lies dormant, but it is still available for those who wish to seek it out. Its earliest discernible traces can be found amid the hunters and scavengers of the Palaeolithic age, when the natural skills and strengths of the wolf were mimicked by humans desperate to confirm their new ecological niche among the predatory animals. The lunar hunting deities first worshipped at that time, mysteriously beautiful yet quick to punish man's presumptuous nature, were remembered long after the monthly ritual of hunting for meat had been superseded by the less urgent patterns of the agricultural lifestyle, and the power of such goddesses as Ishtar and Artemis to transform men into animals inspired awe and fear among later poets and audience alike. The complex of imagery surrounding the figure of the werewolf was already rich by classical times, containing within it the disparate notions of the wolf as image of death and the shamanistic theme of the wolf as bringer of fertility. But this latter idea tended to become obscured as first Graeco-Roman and then Christian culture placed man firmly at the centre of the cosmos, yet increasingly denied him the possibility of operating personally in the spiritual sphere except through the intercession of divine beings – angels and saints in the Christian tradition. The werewolf threatened to destroy this neat hierarchy of (in ascending order) animal–human–angel–God by blurring the boundaries between them, and evidence that werewolf rituals had survived in such places as Arcadia was either disbelieved or, as Pausanias chose to do, nervously skirted around. As Christian self-confidence increased, however, the survival of the werewolf to the end of the first Christian millennium among the northern pagans, for example, was suppressed with little apparent difficulty, and tales of this strange mythical creature could safely be told in medieval fairytale-like romances and sagas, even by avowedly Christian authors.

If this were the whole history of the werewolf, there would be little left to say and precious few interested parties to say it to. The werewolf would be trapped in a quiet byway of cultural history, the subject of the occasional academic thesis, nothing more. The key to the werewolf's continuing interest lies in the part it was forced to play in the great upheaval of ignorance, intolerance, and fear that was the European witch-craze. In part, the werewolf owed its place in the witch-craze to apparently unrelated ecological pressures, such as the reforestation of Europe after the initial onslaught of the Black Death and the increasing numbers of sheep being farmed – as fear of the natural wolf returned, so too did fear of the werewolf. But it was the perceived monstrosity of the werewolf that sealed its fate, associating it forever with the Satanic rabble of demonic agents, witches, and warlocks who were believed to be engaged in a dreadful apocalyptic conspiracy to subvert the victory of Christ. If Carlo Ginzburg is right, the werewolf of early-modern Europe was something much more interesting: only one among a number of representatives of the survival of shamanistic ideas that were, however, destined to be entirely misunderstood in the then prevailing western culture and so persecuted mercilessly. The scars inflicted on western culture by this lengthy episode of untrammelled paranoia are still visible today. Whenever someone speaks out against the childish pleasures of Halloween as 'dabbling in the occult', for example, they are bringing back to life the wilder imaginings of the Inquisitorial witch-burners, acting in their ignorance as the mouthpiece of such unlamented opponents of human freedom and diversity as Henri Boguet. Thankfully such people remain in the minority, as perhaps they have been ever since the decline of the European witch-craze and the return of the werewolf to the realms of fairytale and fantasy.

And yet it is almost entirely due to the part it played in the witch-craze, however peripheral, that the werewolf is still a widely known figure. Its fearsome aspect as seen by the inquisitors was picked up by Hollywood screenwriters looking to imbue their teen melodramas with a *frisson* of terror. Ultimately they could not resist adding a layer of humorous distancing that is also detectable even in the dry case-studies of modern psychiatric journals. Like its close anthropoid cousins, the Himalayan Yeti and the North American Sasquatch or Bigfoot, the werewolf lives today most vividly in the pages of the tabloid press, where its potent blend of wonder, fear, and comedy can be guaranteed to while away a few idle minutes at the supermarket check-out. Even in more serious reporting, the werewolf always lacks true terror. While this book was being written, two cases were reported in the British press which used the werewolf as a hook to catch the public imagination, but applied it in a way that was almost purely ironic. In July 1990, a sex attacker was gaoled for seventeen years after a series of rapes across south-east England.[1] He was known as the 'werewolf rapist', because many of his attacks took place at the time of a new moon (itself a rather forced analogy with the legend). There was nothing else wolfish about him – one of his victims described him as 'very nervous and pathetic' – but the werewolf tag stuck, despite other unrelated but unusual aspects of the case which might have been used to individuate it, such as the fact that he was trapped by his extreme dislike of chocolate, a dislike noted by one of his victims and confirmed by the policeman who interviewed him. A year later, another rapist managed to escape from the high security Broadmoor hospital and spent a couple of days on the run in south-west England. He was known as the Wolfman, ostensibly because of the resourceful way he had managed to live off the land during the three-week manhunt that led to his original arrest. The

English newspapers had a field-day with lurid headlines about 'the Wolfman' and his eventual recapture outside a pub in Devon.

It is interesting to note that both these werewolf-criminals were rapists, and that the tag 'werewolf' should not have been applied by the press to a serial killer like Jeffrey Dahmer, the Milwaukee Strangler, whose anti-social habits and horrendous acts of murder and cannibalism fit much better the older idea of the murderous *loups-garoux* of the sixteenth-century werewolf trials. It seems that the werewolf no longer has the power to frighten, at least not enough to convey the bloody enormity of Dahmer's perversions. Probably because of its descent into comedy in the twentieth-century cinematic tradition, the werewolf is an appropriate label to apply to lesser criminals whom society wishes to diminish by ridicule. The pathetic chocolate-hating rapist would like to be a 'wolf', and he has his wish mockingly granted; the Wolfman living on the moors scares a few locals but is quickly rounded up by an unarmed British bobby. The fear they cause is contained, and the terrible spectre of the rebirth of the werewolf once again fails to materialize.

A Werewolf Chronology

(All early dates are approximate)

75,000 BC	Earliest human altars, including evidence of prehistoric bear-cult
10,000 BC	Domestication of dog
6000 BC	Çatal Hüyük cave-drawings depict leopard men hunting
2000 BC	*Epic of Gilgamesh* written down (first literary evidence of werewolves)
850 BC	*Odyssey* written down (includes many traces of werewolf beliefs)
500 BC	Scythians recorded as believing the Neuri to be werewolves
400 BC	Damarchus, Arcadian werewolf, said to have won boxing medal at Olympics
100–75 BC	Virgil's eight *eclogue* (first voluntary transformation of werewolf)
55 AD	Petronius, *Satyricon* composed (first fully-fledged werewolf story)
150 AD	Apuleius, *Metamorphosis* composed
170 AD	Pausanias visits Arcadia and hears of Lykaian werewolf rites
432 AD	St Patrick arrives in Ireland
600 AD	Saint Albeus (Irish) said to have been suckled by wolves
617 AD	Wolves said to have attacked heretical monks
650 AD	Paulus Aegineta describes 'melancholic lycanthropia'
900 AD	*Hrafnsmál* mentions 'wolf-coats' among the

Norwegian army
Canon Episcopi condemns belief in reality of
witches as heretical
1020   First use of the word 'werewulf' recorded in
        English
1101   Death of Prince Vseslav of Polock, alleged
        Ukrainian werewolf
1182-3 Giraldus claims to have discovered Irish werewolf
        couple
1194-7 *Guillaume de Palerne* composed
1198   Marie de France composes *Bisclavret*
1250   *Lai de Melion* composed
1275-1300 *Völsungasaga*, Germanic werewolf saga, written
        down
1344   Wolf child of Hesse discovered
1347-51 First major outbreak of Black Death
1407   Werewolves mentioned during witchcraft trial at
        Basel
1450   Else of Meerburg accused of riding a wolf
1494   Swiss woman tried for riding a wolf
1495   Woman tried for riding a wolf at Lucerne
1486   *Malleus Maleficarum* published
1521   Werewolves of Poligny burnt
1541   Paduan werewolf dies after having arms and legs
        cut off
1550   Witekind interviews self-confessed werewolf at
        Riga
        Johann Weyer takes up post of doctor at Cleve
1552   Modern French version of *Guillaume* published at
        Lyon
1555   Olaus Magnus records strange behaviour of Baltic
        werewolves
1560   First publication of Della Porta, *Magiae naturalis*
1563   First publication of Weyer, *De praestigiis
        daemonum*
1572   St Bartholomew's Day Massacre; intensification of
        French civil war
1573   Gilles Garnier burnt as werewolf
1575   Trials of the *benandanti* begin in the Friuli (and
        will continue for a century)

1580	Rebellion at Romans with cannibalistic overtones
1584	Reginald Scot's *Discoverie of Witchcraft* published
1588	Alleged date of Auvergne female werewolf (Boguet)
1589	Peter Stubb executed as werewolf at Cologne
1598	Roulet tried as werewolf; his sentence commuted 'Werewolf of Châlons' executed at Paris Gandillon family burnt as werewolves in the Jura
1602	2nd edition of Boguet, *Discours des sorciers*
1603	Jean Grenier tried as werewolf; sentenced to life imprisonment
1610	Two women condemned as werewolves at Liège; Jean Grenier dies
1614	Webster's *Duchess of Malfi* published
1637	Famine in Franche-Comté: cannibalism reported
1652	Cromwellian law forbids export of Irish wolfhounds
1692	The Livonian werewolf Theiss interrogated
1697	Perrault's *Contes* include 'Little Red Riding Hood'
1701	De Tournefort sees vampire exhumation
1764	*Bête de Gévaudon* starts werewolf scare in the Auvergne
1796–9	Widespread fear of wolves reported in France
1797	Victor of Aveyron first seen
1806	French wolf population falls below 2000
1812	Grimm Brothers publish their version of Little Red Riding Hood
1824	Antoine Léger tried for werewolf crimes; sentenced to lunatic asylum Charles Maturin, *The Albigenses* (first werewolf in Gothic fiction)
1828	Death of Victor of Aveyron
1830	Sioux warriors reported hunting in wolfskins
1857	Accusation of being 'wolf leader' ends in court in St Gervais G. W. M. Reynolds, *Wagner the Wehr-Wolf* published
1880	Folklorist collects werewolf tale in Picardy
1885	Johann Weyer's book reprinted at Paris
1886	Robert Louis Stevenson, *Dr Jekyll and Mr Hyde*

	published
1906	Freud lists Weyer's book as among ten most significant ever published
1913	*The Werewolf* (film) using real wolf in transformation scene
1914	Freud publishes 'Wolf Man' paper
1920	Kamala and Amala, the Orissa wolf children, discovered
	Right-wing terror group 'Operation Werwolf' established in Germany
1932	*Jekyll & Hyde* (film) starring Frederic March
1935	*Werewolf of London* (film)
1941	*Wolf Man* (film) starring Lon Chaney Jr
1943–4	Childhood autism first described; LSD discovered
1944	*House of Frankenstein* (film) includes first mention of silver bullet
1951	Outbreak of ergotism at Pont-Saint-Esprit
1952	Ogburn & Bose, *On the trail of the Wolf-Children* published
1957	*I was a Teenage Werewolf* (film)
1972	Shamdeo discovered living among wolves in India
1975	Surawicz & Banta publish first two modern cases of lycanthropy
1979	*American Werewolf in London* (film) includes first four-footed werewolf
1985	Death of Shamdeo; *Teen Wolf* (film)
1988	Monsieur X arrested; McLean Hospital survey published
1990	'Werewolf rapist' jailed; McLean Case 8 full report published
1991	'The Wolfman' escapes from Broadmoor

Notes

1. Barking Mad

1. M. Bénézech, J. De Witte, J.-J. Etchepare, M. Bourgeois, 'A propos d'une observation de lycanthropie avec violences mortelles', *Société Médico-Psychologique* (1988), 464–70.

2. *Op. cit.*, p. 467, author's own translation.

3. E. Dupré, 'La mythomanie: étude psychologique et médico-légale du mensonge et de la fabulation morbides', *Le Bulletin Médical* 23, 25, & 27 (1905), 263–8, 285–90, & 311–15.

4. The term 'lycanthropy' is omitted, for example, by A. Werner, R. J. Campbell, S. H. Frazier, E. M. Stone, & J. Edgerton, *The American Psychiatric Association's Psychiatric Glossary* (Washington DC: American Psychiatric Press, 1984). S. Arieti, *American Handbook of Psychiatry* (New York: Basic Books, 1974), iii, 719–70, refers to the syndrome as extinct.

5. F. G. Surawicz & R. Banta, 'Lycanthropy revisited', *Canadian Psychiatric Association Journal* 20:7 (November 1975), 537–42.

6. H. A. Rosenstock & K. R. Vincent, 'A case of lycanthropy', *American Journal of Psychiatry* 134:10 (October 1977), 1147–9.

7. P. G. Coll, G. O'Sullivan, & P. J. Browne, 'Lycanthropy lives on', *British Journal of Psychiatry* 147 (1985), 201–2.

8. P. E. Keck, H. G. Pope, J. I. Hudson, S. L. McElroy, & A. R. Kulick, 'Lycanthropy: alive and well in the twentieth century', *Psychological Medicine* 18 (1988), 113–20.

9. A. R. Kulick, H. G. Pope, & P. E. Keck, 'Lycanthropy and self-identification', *Journal of Nervous and Mental Disease* 178: 2 (1990), 134–7.

10. B. Bettelheim, *The Empty Fortress: Infantile Autism and the Birth of the Self* (New York: Free Press, 1967), 348–9.

11. P. J. McKenna, J. M. Kane, K. Parrish, 'Psychotic syndromes in epilepsy', *American Journal of Psychiatry* 142 (1985), 895–904, cited by Kulick *et al.* (1990).

2. Animal Magic

1.   If this were the true derivation, then the word should preferably be spelt 'werwolf'. My reasons for not doing so are explained in chapter 5. R. Eisler, *Man into Wolf* (London: Spring Books, 1950), 148, gives a list of Western European variant terms for the werewolf constructed on the basic 'man-wolf' model, including Swedish *varulf*, Danish *vaerulf*, medieval Latin *guerulfus*, twelfth-century Norman *garwalf*, Picard *loup-varous*, Portuguese *lobarraz* (a compressed version of *lobo-barraz*), Calabrian *lupu-minare*, Molfettian *le pomene*, Neapolitan *lupu menare*, Sicilian *lupu-minaru*, Aquileian *lupe-panaru*, and Abruzzan *lope-kummari*.

2.   M. Ruel, 'Were-animals and the Introverted Witch', in *Witchcraft Confessions & Accusations*, ed. Mary Douglas (London: Tavistock Publications, 1970), 333–50.

3.   It used to be thought that the use of tools was a distinctly human attribute: in recent years animal behaviourists have been more ready to question this assumption, pointing to learned tool-use among chimpanzees.

4.   J. Campbell, *The Masks of God: Primitive Mythology* (1959, revised edn 1969), 359.

5.   W. Burkert, *Homo Necans* (Berlin: Walter de Gruyter & Co, 1972; Eng. trans. University of California Press, 1983).

6.   Some scholars argue that the Cain and Abel story was originally the foundation myth of the Kenites, a neighbouring tribe whom the Israelites later assimilated, changing the moral emphasis of their story so that the Kenite culture-hero Cain, who like Romulus killed his brother and founded a city, became the villain of the piece. See Hyam Maccobi, *The Sacred Executioner: Human Sacrifice and the Legacy of Guilt* (London: Thames & Hudson, 1982).

7.   Eisler, *op. cit.*, 167–8.

8.   Campbell, *op. cit.*

9.   L. Frobenius, *Das unbekannte Afrika* (Munich: Oskar Beck, 1923), 34–5.

10.   Campbell, *op. cit.*, 346, citing Comte Bégouën, 'Les modelages d'argile de la caverne de Montespan', *Comptes rendus des séances de l'Académie des Inscriptions et Belles Lettres* (1923), 14 p., 349–50, 401.

11.   Campbell, *op. cit.*, 334–9, citing Kyosuki Kindaiti, *Ainu Life and Legends* (Tokyo: Tourist Library 36, 1941), 50.

12.   See R. B. Onians, *The Origins of European Thought about the Body, the Mind, the Soul, the World, Time, and Fate* (Cambridge University Press, 1951), esp. chapter III.

13.   A. R. Radcliffe-Brown, *The Andaman Islanders* (2nd printing; London: Cambridge University Press, 1933), 129.

14. Paul Barber, *Vampires, Burial, and Death: Folklore and Reality* (New Haven and London: Yale University Press, 1988), 171–4.

15. Barber, *op. cit.*, 94.

16. Told by Mary Phelan to William Beynon, 1947, collected in M. Barbeau, *Totem Poles* (Canadian Department of Resources and Development) 119:1.

17. The actual hunting would probably have been done during daylight. The night was the time for ritual preparation: the day for execution. Solar hunting deities are often visualized as a lion or some other noble beast caught in the act of killing, and, although splendid, lack the mysterious, magical qualities of lunar deities.

18. C. Knight, *Blood Relations* (Yale University Press, 1991).

19. *Gilgamesh* tablet VI, column ii.

20. C. Ginzburg, *Ecstasies: Deciphering the Witches' Sabbath*, Eng. trans. Raymond Rosenthal (London: Hutchinson Radius, 1990), 127.

3. The Bloodline Begins

1. W. Burkert (1983), 120.

2. R. B. Onians, *The Origins of European Thought*, 471–2.

3. Jeffrey B. Russell, *A History of Witchcraft: Sorcerers, Heretics, and Pagans* (London: Thames & Hudson, 1980), 31.

4. The Seeds of Superstition

1. *The Saga of the Völsungs*, trans. George K. Anderson (Newark: University of Delaware Press, 1982), 65–6.

2. E.g. H. R. E. Davidson, 'Shape-changing in the Old Norse Sagas', in *Animals in Folklore*, eds J. R. Porter & W. M. S. Russell (London: D. S. Brewer for the Folklore Society, 1978), 126–42, 258–9, although she regards the time in the forest simply as an apprenticeship in robbery and killing rather than a werewolf-brotherhood initiation.

3. It is not certain that the (probably) Christian author had spotted the analogy. Heroic poetry was for a time regarded as inimical to religious study – 'What has Ingeld to do with Christ?' was Alcuin's famous complaint of 797 to English monks who were showing a dangerous enthusiasm for hearing about the exploits of the former – although it was later to become a commonplace that pagan myths contained teasing half-truths which were only perfectly transmitted in the Christian revelation, and analogies between the myths of each tradition were therefore more frequently made.

4. The period specified in the saga is clearly of magical significance,

although what that significance was intended to be is now rather obscure. 'Every tenth half-day' seems to be a circumlocution for 'every fifth day', as the Old Norse word used, *dægr*, is usually understood to mean a period of twelve hours, rather than the normal twenty-four-hour *dagr*: see Anderson (n.1 above), 141. Ten is the number of Sigmund's brothers, and so may therefore have been appropriate to the wolf-brotherhood, although twelve is a more usual number for such warrior-bands.

5. See Ginzburg (1990), 214 and n. 41, with references.

6. For an illustration of this temple, and others like it, together with a general discussion of Celtic culture, see S. Pigott, *The Druids* (London: Thames & Hudson Ltd, 1968, new edn 1975), 61.

7. Much of it collected in Ginzburg (1990); see especially chapter 4.

8. See Onians, 98 ff.

9. H. R. E. Davidson, *The Viking Road to Byzantium* (1976), 113 ff.

10. H. R. E. Davidson, 'The Significance of the Man in the Horned Helmet', *Antiquity* 39 (1965).

11. H. R. E. Davidson, *Gods and Myths of Northern Europe* (1964, Penguin edn 1979), 147.

12. In chapter 8.

13. Davidson (1978), 126.

14. *Landnámabók*, the book of the settlement of Iceland, written by Ari the Wise in the eleventh century, with later additions.

5. The Wolf in Sheep's Clothing

1. W. Burkert, *Ancient Mystery Cults* (Cambridge, MA & London: Harvard U.P. 1987), 25.

2. *The Confessions of St Augustine*, book 6, chapter 8.

3. M. Eliade, *Occultism, Witchcraft, and Cultural Fashions: Essays in Comparative Religions* (Chicago & London: University of Chicago Press, 1976), 87.

4. The connection is disputed by, among others, Burkert (*op. cit.*, 1987), who sees a crucial incongruity between the raw flesh eaten in the ritual and the cooked flesh of the myth.

5. See Hyam Maccobi, *The Sacred Executioner: Human Sacrifice and the Legacy of Guilt* (London: Thames & Hudson, 1982), chapter nine and *passim*. The idea that Paul constructed Christianity from a mixture of Judaism, Hellenistic mystery cults, and Gnosticism has of course been vigorously contested down the ages; Maccobi gives a list, including Justin Martyr and Tertullian in early times, and Cardinal Newman, C. Colpe, W. D. Davies, W. Meeks, A. Schweitzer, G. H. C. MacGregor,

H. G. Marsh, A. D. Nock, W. Manson, and C. A. A. Scott more recently. Early Christian figures who, like the fifth-century British monk Pelagius, attempted to place more emphasis on Jewish concepts, or, like the second-century controversialist Marcion, sought to revive Gnostic ideas, were simply excommunicated as heretics. The importance of the mystery religions and Gnosticism to Christianity is convincingly maintained by the great biblical scholar Rudolf Bultmann.

6.   John 6: 53–4, Authorized Version.

7.   Maccobi (*op. cit.*, 1982), 155, with references.

8.   Bede, *History of the English Church and People*, book 1, chapter 30 (Eng. trans. Leo Sherley-Price, rev. R. E. Latham, Penguin, 1968).

9.   Ginzburg (1990), 185.

10.   R. S. Gottfried, *The Black Death: Natural and Human Disaster in Medieval Europe* (London: Robert Hale, 1983).

11.   Jacques Le Goff, *Medieval Civilization 400–1500*, Eng. trans. Julia Barrow (Oxford: Basil Blackwell, 1988), 133.

12.   J. Mallinson, *The Shadow of Extinction: Europe's Threatened Wild Animals* (London: Macmillan, 1978), 80, recording that a pack tracked in Alaska travelled 700 miles in six weeks.

13.   K. Thomas, *Man and the Natural World: Changing Attitudes in England 1500–1800* (London: Allen Lane, 1983), 273, with reference.

14.   I Corinthians 5:7.

15.   Quoted by Jacques Le Goff, *Medieval Civilization 400–1500*, Eng. trans. Julia Barrow (Oxford: Basil Blackwell, 1988), 155.

16.   I am grateful to Professor Janet Bately, of Kings College, London, for a discussion of these points. Needless to say, she cannot be held responsible for my conclusions.

17.   Eisler, *op. cit.*, 135.

18.   Eisler, *op. cit.*, 148.

19.   A. de Gubernatis, *Zoological Mythology* (1872), ii, 145.

20.   Jeffrey B. Russell, *A History of Witchcraft: Sorcerers, Heretics, and Pagans* (London: Thames & Hudson, 1981), 53–4.

6. Monsters, Dog-Heads, and Old Irish Tales

1.   Daniel 5:13 (New English Bible).

2.   *Op. cit.* 4:33.

3.   John Block Friedman, *The Monstrous Races in Medieval Art and Thought* (Cambridge, Mass., and London, Harvard University Press, 1981).

4.   Evagrius Scholasticus, *Historiae Ecclesiasticae* 1.7 *PG* 86, 2438, quoted by Friedman.

5.   David Barrett & Michael McCann, 'Discovered: Two-Toed Man', *Sunday Times Magazine* (London), 13 January 1980, 28–31.

6.   Hermann Stadler, ed., *Albertus Magnus de Animalibus Libri XXVI*, in *Beiträge zur Geschichte der Philosophie des Mittelalters* 15 (Münster, 1916), 2.1.4, p. 247, quoted by Friedman.

7.   Some texts have 'Jews' here, but this does not detract from the intended universal scope of the list of nations. Acts 2:5.

8.   Armenian Gospel Book of T'oros Roslin, Baltimore, Walters Art Gallery MS 539, fol. 379r, 1262.

9.   Marginal illustration of Christ with Cynocephali, 'Theodore' Psalter, London, British Library MS Gr. Add. 19352, fol. 23r, eleventh century.

10.   Authorized King James Version. The New English Bible translates the verse: 'The huntsmen are all about me; a band of ruffians rings me round, and they have hacked off my hands and my feet', which removes both the canine and crucifixion allusions. It does, however, have the advantage of being a closer translation of the Hebrew.

11.   E.g. Hugh of St Cher (following Cassiodorus), *Opera Omnia in Universum Vetus et Novum Testamentum* (Venice, 1732), vol. 2, fol. 50v.

12.   E. A. Wallis Budge, tr., *The Contendings of the Apostles* (Oxford, 1935), 173–4.

13.   *Op. cit.*, 72.

14.   J. Fraser, 'The Passion of St Christopher', *Revue Celtique* 34 (1913): 309.

15.   George Herzfeld, ed., *An Old English Martyrology*, EETS:OS 116 (London, 1900), 67.

16.   It would be more accurate to describe the Vézelay tympanum as a depiction of the Mission of the Apostles, although obviously the Pentecost is invoked. There is good evidence of Greek influence on the design of the carving. See Friedman, *op. cit.*, 78 and notes.

17.   A point argued by Glyn S. Burgess, *Marie de France: Text and Context* (Manchester University Press, 1987), 3; 'There *is* no clear distinction between the realistic and the supernatural lays'.

18.   Professor G. L. Kittredge, 'Arthur and Gorlagon', *Studies and Notes in Philology and Literature*, Boston, vol. viii, 1903, 149–275.

19.   Keith Thomas, *Man and the Natural World: Changing Attitudes in England 1500–1800* (London: Allen Lane, 1983), 135.

20.   See Ashley Montagu, *The Elephant Man* (New York: E. P. Dutton, 1979).

21.   Martin Luther & Phillip Melancthon, *Of Two Wonderful Popish Monsters*, trans. John Brooke (London: 1579). For a discussion of this pamphlet, and an analysis of the fears engendered by monstrosity in general, see Arnold I. Davidson 'The Horror of Monsters', in *The*

Boundaries of Humanity: Humans, Animals, Machines, ed. James J. Sheehan & Morton Sosna (University of California Press, 1991).

7. The Werewolf Trials

1. Quoted by Henry Kamen, *European Society 1500–1700* (1984), 37.

2. Lancre, Pierre de, *L'incrédulité et mécréance des sortilèges*, Paris, 1622.

3. Boguet, Henri, *Discours des sorciers*, Eng. trans. E. Allen Ashwin, London 1929.

4. Garnier's crimes in a pamphlet translated by M. Summers, *The Werewolf* (London: Kegan Paul, 1933), 226–8.

5. Anonymous English translation, *A True Discourse Declaring the Damnable Life and Death of One Stubbe Peeter . . . Truly translated out of the high Dutch*, 1590.

6. Barry Holstun Lopez, *Of Wolves and Men* (1978), 206.

7. F. Bavoux, *Boguet, Grand-juge de la terre de St Claude* (Besançon 1956), 12.

8. Figures taken from E. William Monter, *Witchcraft in France and Switzerland* (Ithaca and London: Cornell UP, 1976), 145–51.

9. Bodin, Jean, *Discours . . . et Response aux Paradoxes de M. de Malestroict*, Paris, 1568.

10. *Demonolatry*, book II, chapter 5, English trans. E. A. Ashwin, with an introduction by Montague Summers (London, 1930), 111.

11. Monter, *op. cit.*, citing notes left by Bavoux at the ADD from a talk about werewolves he delivered to the *Société d'Emulation du Doubs*, in 1952.

8. Journey to the Land of the Dead

1. Carlo Ginzburg, *Ecstasies: Deciphering the Witches' Sabbath*, Eng. trans. Raymond Rosenthal, ed. Gregory Elliot (London: Hutchinson Radius, 1990), 153 ff., whence most of the information in this chapter.

2. Hermann Witekind (under the pseudonym 'Augustin Lercheimer'), *Christlich Bedencken und Erinnerung von Zauberey* ['Christian considera-tion and memory on magic'], Heidelberg, 1585.

3. Casper Peucer, *Commentarius de praecipuis generibus divinationum*, expanded edn (Wittenburg 1560). Peucer may have had additional material from Witekind transmitted to him by his father-in-law, Phillip Melancthon. See Ginzburg (1990), 156–7 and *passim*.

4. Carlo Ginzburg, *Night Battles* (London, 1986).

5.   Ginzburg (1990), 155.

6.   R. Kieckhefer, *European Witch Trials: Their Foundations in Popular and Learned Culture, 1300–1500* (London & Henley: Routledge & Kegan Paul, 1976), 71, and references.

7.   Kieckhefer, *op. cit.*, 34.

8.   H. Kramer & J. Sprenger, *Malleus Maleficarum*, Eng. trans. M. Summers (London: John Rodker, 1928), 65.

9.   R. Tannahill, *Flesh and Blood: A History of the Cannibal Complex* (London: Hamish Hamilton, 1975), 111, citing Rémy.

10. P. Barber, *Vampires, Burial, and Death: Folklore and Reality* (Yale University Press, 1988).

11. Ginzburg (1990), 89.

12. Emmanuel Le Roy Ladurie, *Montaillou* (Eng. trans. Scholar Press, 1978).

13. Devlin (1987), 73.

14. R. Tannahill, *op. cit.*, 110, citing K. F. Smith.

15. Robbins, *op. cit.*, 560.

16. Barber, *op. cit.*, 93, citing Trigg.

17. Barber, *op. cit.*, 67, citing Vukanovic.

18. For the *táltos*, see Ginzburg (1990), 161 ff.; for the Romanian *strigoi*, see Mircea Eliade, *Occultism, Witchcraft, and Cultural Fashions: Essays in Comparative Religions* (Chicago and London: University of Chicago Press, 1976), 78 ff.

19. The case was published as 'From the History of an Infantile Neurosis' in 1918.

20. Carlo Ginzburg, 'Freud, the Wolf-Man, and the Werewolves', *Myths, Emblems, Clues* (London: Hutchinson Radius, 1990), 146–155.

9. All Wolves Are Not of the Same Sort

1.   Told by Louis and François Briffault, at Montigny-aux-Amognes, Nièvre, about 1885. Published by A. Millien, *Mélusine* 3 (1886–7), 428–9.

2.   W. Eberhard, 'Studies in Taiwanese Folktales', *Asian Folklore & Social Life Monographs* I (Taipei: The Orient Cultural Service, 1970), 14–17, 27–76, 91–5.

3.   B. Bettelheim, *The Uses of Enchantment: The Meaning and Importance of Fairy Tales* (New York: Alfred A. Knopf, 1976), 166–83.

4.   *Perrault's Complete Fairy Tales*, A. E. Johnson, trans. (Harmondsworth, England: Kestrel Books, 1962), 71–7.

5.   It is not absolutely clear whether the liquid in the Grimm story is hot, although surely it is meant to be – the aroma of sausage would

certainly travel further if it were. Grandmother mentions that she was cooking yesterday, but that would not necessarily mean that the large cauldron of oily water would have cooled down entirely, especially if it had been kept close by the hearth. Very hot liquid would be more efficacious than cold in inducing death, but a peasant storyteller would have regarded it as something of a problem to heat up enough water to kill a wolf at such short notice. Professor Eberhard (*op. cit.*) mentions that storytellers of Grandaunt Tiger occasionally indicated unease that the little girl should ask the tiger to go away and heat up the liquid, on the grounds that this would take too long, and this possible objection would be answered in the Grimm version by the water having already been heated 'yesterday'.

6.   All these theories, together with the relevant texts, are usefully gathered together, with an excellent concluding essay, by Alan Dundes, *Little Red Riding Hood: A Casebook* (Madison, Wisconsin: University of Wisconsin of Press, 1989).

7.   For the background to this scare, see J. Devlin, *The Superstitious Mind: French Peasants and the Supernatural in the Nineteenth Century* (New Haven & London: Yale University Press, 1987), especially 72–80, 198–202.

8.   J. Mallinson, *The Shadow of Extinction: Europe's Threatened Wild Mammals* (London: Macmillan, 1978), 86.

9.   Devlin (1987), 74, citing Tissié, *Les Aliénés Voyageurs* (Bordeaux University, medical thesis, 1887), 31.

10.   Devlin, *op. cit.*, 199.

11.   Reay Tannahill, *Flesh and Blood: A History of the Cannibal Complex* (London: Hamish Hamilton, 1975), 115.

10. Feral Foundlings

1.   Shamdeo's case is summarized from various newspaper reports by Paul Sieveking in the *Fortean Times* 44 (London, 1985), 4–5. The same wolf-boy was known variously as Shamdev, Ramu, Bhaloo, and Pascal. Sieveking cites as chief sources articles by C. Y. Gopinath in the *Sunday* magazine, Calcutta (4 March 1979), and Bruce Chatwin in the *Sunday Times Magazine*, London (30 July 1978), an expanded version of which appeared in the *Chicago Tribune* (22 October 1978).

2.   See chapter 3, *supra*.

3.   Herodotus, *The Histories* I, 108–30. The best-known English translation is that of Aubrey de Sélincourt, available in the Penguin Classics series.

4.   Keith Thomas, *Man and the Natural World: Changing Attitudes in*

England 1500–1800 (London: Allen Lane, 1983), 86.

5.   Charles W. Dunn, *The Foundling and the Werwolf: a literary-historical study of 'Guillaume de Palerne'* (University of Toronto Dept of English, Studies & Texts, no. 8, 1960).

6.   Thomas, *op. cit.*, 36–7.

7.   See Lucien Malson, *Les Enfants Sauvages* (Paris: Union Générale d'Editions, 1964, Eng. trans. 1972), 38 and notes.

8.   (Amsterdam, Rey, 1755.) Eng. trans. R. D. Masters, *Jean Jacques Rousseau: the First and Second Discourses* (New York: Saint Martin, 1964).

9.   Harlan Lane, *The Wild Boy of Aveyron* (London: George Allen & Unwin Ltd, 1977), *passim*.

10.   Lane, *op. cit.*

11.   Charles Maclean, *The Wolf Children* (London, Allen Lane, 1977).

12.   See e.g. Lopez, 54.

13.   Bettelheim's theory was first published as 'Feral Children and Autistic Children', *American Journal of Sociology*, LXIV: 1959, 455–67; and, in expanded form, as 'Persistence of a Myth', Part Three of *The Empty Fortress: Infantile Autism and the Birth of the Self* (New York, The Free Press, 1967), 343–82. I refer to the latter version of his essay.

14.   Bettelheim (1967), 355

15.   Uta Frith, *Autism: Explaining the Enigma* (Oxford: Basil Blackwell Ltd, 1989), 2.

16.   Maclean, *op. cit.*, 294–300.

17.   Rossell Hope Robbins, *The Encyclopedia of Witchcraft and Demonology* (London: Peter Nevill Limited, 1963), 234–5.

11. Doctoring the Myth

1.   T. S. Szasz, *The Manufacture of Madness: A Comparative Study of the Inquisition and the Mental Health Movement* (London: Routledge & Kegan Paul, 1971).

2.   R. S. Gottfried, *The Black Death* (London: Robert Hale, 1983), 109, with references.

3.   J. Weyer, *Witches, Devils, and Doctors in the Renaissance*, gen. ed. G. Mora, ass. ed. B. Kohl, trans. J. Shea (Binghamton, New York: Medieval & Renaissance Texts & Studies, 1991).

4.   Stuart Clark, 'The Scientific Status of Demonology', in *Occult and Scientific Mentalities in the Renaissance*, ed. Brian Vickers (Cambridge University Press, 1984), 351–73.

5.   By Rossell Hope Robbins among others.

6.   See the introductory biographical essay in Weyer (1991), lxxii–

lxxiii. The arguments for Weyer's influence on Freud are those of Peter Swales, author of *Freud, Johann Weier, and the Status of Seduction: The Role of the Witch in the Conception of Fantasy* (privately printed 1982); see his 'A Fascination with Witches', *The Sciences* 22 (1982): 21–5.

7. Gregory Zilboorg, *The Medical Man and the Witch During the Renaissance* (Baltimore: Johns Hopkins Press, 1935).

8. See chapter 7 for Boguet's description of the case.

9. Richard Kieckhefer, *European Witch Trials: Their Foundations in Popular and Learned Culture, 1300–1500* (London: Routledge & Kegan Paul, 1976), 35.

10. Weyer, *op. cit.*, book 6, chapter 4, 516–17.

11. [Della] Porta, Johannes Baptista, *Magiae naturalis sive de miraculis rerum naturalium* (Antwerp, 1560; Frankfurt, 1597; Eng. trans. London, 1658; Fr. trans. Lyon, 1688).

12. Weyer, *op. cit.*, book 3, chapter 17, 226.

13. For a brief list of studies on this subject, see Weyer, *op. cit.*, 734–5.

14. Kieckhefer, *op. cit.*, 41.

15. Quoted by John G. Fuller, *The Day of St Anthony's Fire* (New York: Macmillan, 1968), 115.

16. Fuller, *op. cit.*, 117.

17. R. H. Robbins, *The Encyclopedia of Witchcraft and Demonology* (New York: Crown, 1959), 325.

18. Although early botanical names are notoriously inexact, the plant is probably the *Vitex agnus-castus*, or Chaste Tree, still grown today in ornamental gardens for its fragrant, tubular bluish flowers. As its alternative name suggests, the shrub has an ancient association with chastity: the Greeks used the leaves to induce fertility in women attending the Festival of Demeter Thesmophoria, but, as the women refrained from sexual intercourse during the festival, it became associated with chasteness. This symbolism was heightened in the Christian era by a perceived connection with the Agnus Dei. Branches from the shrub are still used today as a folk-remedy for excessive libido. The use of the leaves at Luc sheds some light on the nature of the men's barking disorder, which was evidently diagnosed as an excess of sexual fervour. The idea that male sexuality is expressed through overtly bestial behaviour is of course relevant to the werewolf legend in general, even if these specific men were not treated as lycanthropes.

19. The story of the outbreak is well told by John G. Fuller, *op. cit.*

20. W. M. S. Russell & C. Russell, letter in *Journal of the Royal Society of Medicine*, vol. 82, June 1989, 379.

21. Fuller, *op. cit.*, 112. Did the afflicted person really ask for a bicycle (*un vélo*), or was it perhaps a knife (*un couteau*) he wanted? Mr Fuller

mentions in the afterword to his book the difficulties he sometimes experienced in transcribing the local accent. If the man really did want a bicycle, it demonstrates how little can be safely read into the ravings of a man suffering ergot poisoning.

22.   Job Fincelius, *Wunderzeichen, warhafftige Beschreibung und gründlich Verzeichnung schrecklicher Wunderzeichen und Geschichten* (Jena, 1556).

23.   C. Ginzburg, *Ecstasies*, 304–5.

24.   The comparison is Fuller's (209).

25.   Eisler, *op. cit.*, 186.

26.   Geoffrey P. West, *Rabies in Animals & Man* (Newton Abbot: David & Charles, 1972), 9.

27.   West, *op. cit.*, 133–4.

28.   L. Illis, 'On Porphyria and the Aetiology of Werwolves', *Proceedings of the Royal Society of Medicine* 57 (1964), 23–6.

29.   See, if you must, the *News of the World* (30 June 1991), 16, brief article entitled 'You say: Wolf Boys are cute'.

30.   J. Rotton & I. W. Kelly, 'Much ado about the full moon: a meta-analysis of lunar-lunacy research', *Psychological Bulletin* 97 (1985) 286–306.

31.   Cyril W. Smith & Simon Best, *Electromagnetic Man: Health and Hazard in the Electrical Environment* (London: J. M. Dent, 1989), 40–1.

12. Howling All the Way to the Bank

1.   A useful anthology of werewolf fiction is Bill Pronzini, ed., *Werewolf: A Chrestomathy of Lycanthropy* (New York: Arbor House, 1979).

13. The Tail of the Wolf

1.   Reported in the *Independent* (3 July 1990), 2.

Index

Names and other references from the notes have been included here only when explicitly discussed in the main body of the text. Foreign words are italicized and their origin given in parentheses.